AF825012

WTO AND IMPLICATIONS FOR SOUTH ASIA

WTO AND IMPLICATIONS FOR SOUTH ASIA

K.C. Reddy
T. Nirmala Devi

SERIALS PUBLICATIONS
NEW DELHI

© K.C. Reddy & T. Nirmala Devi

First Published - 2006

ISBN: 81-8387-048-1

All rights reserved with the Publisher, including the right to translate or reproduce this book or parts there of except for brief quotations in critical articles or reviews.

Published by

SERIALS PUBLICATIONS
4830/24, Prahlad Street, Ansari Road
Darya Ganj, New Delhi-110002 (India)
Phone : 23245225. Fax : 91-11-23272135
E-mail: serials@satyam.net.in

Contents

PART – III
WTO and Singapore Issues–South Asia

PART – IV
Health and Intellectual Property Rights

PART – V
China's Entry into WTO and Other Trade Issues

Preface

The main challenge of the WTO would be internationalization of economic activity. It provides a forum for member countries to discuss issues covered by the WTO Agreement and its components aside from other issues, falling within its mandate. The developing countries will continue to receive the special status in the WTO as in the GATT. However, they have not given any special treatment in the new subjects of the emerging world order. Despite the promise of assistance in various types made by the developed countries, the legal standing is not clear and hence, the developing countries could not reap the benefits. The low-income countries of South Asia have not benefited significantly from the growth of the world economy, largely due to their inward-looking policies of the past. Even after the shift in economic strategies in the early 1990s, the South Asian countries have been affected from the restrictions imposed by the industrial countries in the form of 'new clauses' that are totally outside the ambit of the current trading system. These countries are left with the hope of strengthening their current trade through access to new markets. Increasing politicization of trade, i.e., the linking of market access to political benefits followed by the developed countries is a major bottleneck for the developing South Asian countries. As the major agreements under WTO often change the basic emphasis and in the process fail to articulate the concerns of the developing countries in a desired manner, the South Asian countries have to stick to a common stand and fight for their rights by seeking cooperation from their counterparts elsewhere. In this backdrop, the increasing economic engagement among the developing countries is imperative in order to safeguard their interests at the international markets and also to face the challenges posed by the developed countries with collective, organized and matured negotiations.

The present volume is the outcome of an International Seminar on *WTO and Its Implications for South Asia*, organized by the Centre for SAARC Studies, Andhra University, Visakhapatnam. It was one of the major efforts of the Centre to examine and discuss the problems being faced by the South Asian countries at the multilateral trading system, WTO. The volume provides a broad forum for discussing a wide gamut of issues of trade relations of South Asian countries. It also attempts to examine the emerging trends in the current WTO system. Basing on the broad themes-trade cooperation for development, poverty alleviation, agriculture, Singapore issues, health and IPRs and China's accession into WTO and other relevant issues-the volume covers all the major issues, which have become the hurdles for the trade prospects of South Asia. Nevertheless, the issues included have been comprehensively dealt with. The Seminar was attended by about 25 distinguished participants from India, aside Dr. Ponna Wignaraja, Chairman of SAPNA and former Vice-Chairman of Independent South Asian Commission on Poverty Alleviation, Sri Lanka and Dr. A.R. Bhuyan, Dhaka University, Bangladesh. We would like to convey our sincere thanks particularly to Dr. Nagesh Kumar for his extensive keynote presentation and Dr. Ponna Wignaraja for his comprehensive picture of socially responsible globalization and Dr. A.R. Bhuyan for his perception of LDCs on TRIPS Agreement. We are also thankful to all the contributors for their participation in the seminar and revising the papers on the basis of comments by referees for publication.

K.C. Reddy
T. Nirmala Devi

Contributors

Anita Rao. R & Rajiv Thakur. R: Associate Professors, GITAM Institute of Foreign Trade, Visakhapatnam.

Bhuyan. A.R: Professor of Economics University of Dhaka, Bangladesh.

Chandrasekhar. M & Praseeda. C: Director & Assistant Professor Integrated Institute of Advanced Management, Visakhapatnam.

Hailay Gebretinsae Beyene: Dept. of Economics Andhra University, Visakhapatnam.

Indranath Mukherji: Professor of South Asian Studies Jawaharlal Nehru University, New Delhi.

Krishna Moorthy. D: Associate Professor Sri Venkateswara University PG Centre, Kavali.

Leela. P: Professor, Dept. of Applied Economics Andhra University, Visakhapatnam.

Mahendra P. Lama: Professor of South Asian Studies Jawaharlal Nehru University, New Delhi.

Nagesh Kumar: Director-General Research and Information System for the Developing Countries (RIS), New Delhi.

Nirmala Devi T.: Professor & Director, Centre for SAARC Studies, Andhra University, Visakhapatnam.

Nirmala N.: Associate Professor of Law Andhra University, Visakhapatnam.

Ponna Wignaraja: Chairman, SAPNA & Former Vice-Chairman, Independent South Asian Commission on Poverty Alleviation, Sri Lanka.

Rajesh Mehta, J. George & Pooja Agarwal: Senior Fellow, & Fellows Research and Information System for Developing Countries, New Delhi.

Rajyalakshmi V.: Associate Professor of Law Andhra University, Visakhapatnam.

Reddy. K.C & Yerram Raju. B.: Chairman, A.P State Council of Higher Education, Hyderabad & Former Hon.Directōr, Centre for SAARC Studies, Andhra University Visakhapatnam and : Administrative Staff College, Hyderabad.

Smriti Mukherjee: Professor, Gokhale Institute of Politics & Economics, Pune.

Introduction

K.C. Reddy & T. Nirmala Devi

The need for improving the trade prospects of developing countries under the WTO regime is a matter of significant importance to both the rich and poor countries. The outward-looking policies adopted by most of the developing countries in the wake of globalization and liberalization has further made it critical for these countries. The South Asian countries, particularly India have kept pace with the trend and tried to build appropriate consciousness among the developing countries to take initiatives collectively to move towards this goal. Whenever there is an attempt to escape reduction commitments by the developed countries and divert the attention from agricultural subsidies to market access, special safeguard mechanism, tariffs, quotas etc., India and other Third World countries have been vehemently opposing. However, they were trapped by the discussion around certain issues, which were objected earlier. With several escape clauses at their end, the developed countries successfully dumped their substandard agricultural produce on developing countries, including India. The South Asian countries have suffered from their inability to have adequate monitoring facilities for checking the quality of food imports. In this connection, India with other South Asian countries argued for the elimination of agricultural subsidies in the developed countries as a prerequisite for further negotiations. Many more problems that are being faced by the developing countries pushed India to play a greater attention to increase productivity and create exportable surpluses and making agriculture more competitive. The genuine reforms in the WTO is needed for the South Asian countries for reaping benefits through trade relations. To overcome the prevailing structural weaknesses, India and South Asian countries which are initially agro-based economies need more public investment and policy support in several areas.

The present volume is arranged into five parts: (i) Trade cooperation for development and poverty alleviation; (ii) WTO and South Asian agriculture; (iii) Singapore issues and South Asia; (iv) Health and IPRs and (v) China's accession into WTO and other related issues. These themes are considered highly relevant to the trade prospects of South Asian countries in the multilateral trading system. The volume assumes new significance, as the contributors have tried to focus upon South Asia in the changing global political and economic scenario.

Part I surveys the changing contours of trade development and poverty alleviation. Dr. Ponna Wignaraja analyses comprehensively the issue of de-mystification of the poverty and development policy in South Asia. While analyzing the development challenge in South Asia, he points out the inadequacy of WTO in providing the opportunities to meet the challenges faced by the countries. He observes that the process of poverty eradication in South Asia through conventional development approaches of liberalization and structural adjustment was painfully slow and inadequate. He applies the recommendations of the independent South Asian Commission on poverty alleviation to the present day picture of backwardness in South Asia. He emphasizes the need for people's knowledge, which become people's power, and this in turn, influences participatory development. The underlying premises for poverty eradication in the transition, the critical dimension of the knowledge system and many other relevant issues are focused upon in support of his argument. Lamenting such efforts are lacking in South Asia, he stresses the need to evolve an inspiring vision by making three assertions: the first relates to the need for a new school of thought incorporating fundamentals; the second relates to the need for new social contract between the State and the poor in South Asia; and the third relates to the significance of the new social movements emerging from the ground in every South Asian country in the past 25 years.

Pointing out the growing asymmetries in the world trading system, Dr. Nagesh Kumar presents an in-depth analysis on the significance of the Cancun Meet and its impact on the developing countries in his keynote lecture. He discusses various issues like the promise made by the developed countries for additional market access through agricultural trade, textiles, clothing, movement of natural persons etc. to developing countries, which appear to be not so bright in practice. While explaining the developing country concerns regarding several issues, viz., Singapore issues, agriculture, non-agricultural market access, IPRs etc., apart from various problems being faced by these countries under WTO provisions and specific agreements, he argues a case for reforming the system. As south-south cooperation remains weak owing to the lack of resources, he suggests the development strategy of trilateral cooperation in the form of technical support from the multilateral agency or donor. He also provides an agenda for cooperation among developing countries through exchange of experiences, technical assistance and cooperation, effective coordination of position, vigilance and active participation and proactive agenda, besides promotion of south-south trade.

Part II is devoted to the discussion on the importance of agriculture in South Asian countries and their stand on Agreement on Agriculture (AoA) of WTO. Under the AoA which is meant for encouraging fair trade by removing distortions, agricultural tariffs from developed countries are still substantial, relative to industrial tariffs. This section includes three papers on the relevance of AoA to South Asia. Yerram Raju and K.C. Reddy in their paper argue that the present economic environment is not conducive for radical changes in the industrial countries. Besides, the conflicting nature of WTO trade talks on agriculture is posing problems to the developing countries. The authors call for the policy approaches and strategies to prepare the agriculture sector of India to face the emerging challenges, particularly the AoA. While dealing with the global agriculture trade and the major constraints that face the agriculture sector, they seek policy interventions in the present context. The role of the State is highlighted in their paper for constituting the structural aspects of agriculture markets. The authors also emphasize the critical role of State governments for a common consensus on several policy initiatives and argue for the encouragement of production of exports in some specific sub sectors and for a national perspective for agriculture compatible with market-led growth. They caution that adverse trends in agriculture sector will contribute to decline in several industries like fertilizers and agro-industries, if proper reforms are not implemented. Rajesh Mehta Jacob George and Pooja Agarwal undertake a broad survey of agriculture market access modalities, which have gone through remarkable changes and their implications for South Asian countries under alternate scenarios. Discussing this through Harbinson's revised draft modalities and estimate of average tariff reduction, stipulated minimum reduction in tariff orders etc, sees the distortion in the delicate overall balance of package. They conduct the simulation on the basis of Harbinson's formula and brought out the fact that the present bound average of India would get reduced. The authors observe that higher reductions at higher levels of tariff are deceptive, given the tariff profile. They emphasize that the bargaining strength of India in particular and of South Asia in general lies in steadfastly holding on to the removal of the 'import sensitive' phrase from the "Derbez Draft". They also make out that the much-acclaimed value-added agricultural product export models to start with are not feasible in the post-millennium round, if the present trend continues in the OECD. Leela outlines the hardships experienced by the developing countries in exporting to industrial markets, due to the turning out of environmental standards into environmental non-tariff barriers, in addition to the compliance costs and huge investments. She observes that if the developing countries are to reap the benefits, the subsidization given to the farm sector in developed countries is to be removed. While discussing the necessity of extending government support and the technical assistance to the developing countries, which should also make efforts to produce organic agricultural products to obtain greater gains, she emphasizes higher public investment in agriculture in order to improve the efficiency and productivity of developing countries' agricultural exports.

Part III includes two important aspects of Singapore issues, viz., competition policy and core labour standards in relation to South Asian countries. Smriti Mukherjee, while dealing the competition policy in India and South Asia, assess the various issues in general and in the SAARC region in particular by providing the comparative picture of Sri Lanka and India. She argues that the benefits accruing to the two policy changes, i.e., globalization and liquidation of government monopolies will not be lost on account of new barriers to trade and the free entry of multinational corporations (MNCs). The unity of developing countries is emphasized in her paper for attaining the future benefits. Nirmala explains that the inclusion of core labour standards in the agenda of WTO is supported by developed countries while the developing countries vehemently oppose to the linkage on the ground that it will effect their comparative advantage. She emphasizes that in the backdrop of declining the labour standards throughout the world, linkages of core labour standards to WTO is not a solution, but undertaking of effective regulation of globalization policies and extension of productive labour legislation to the unorganized sectors would be helpful.

Part IV analyses the health and intellectual property rights in the backdrop of South Asian countries. Indranath Mukherjee recalls the earlier ministerial conferences and their relevance to South Asian countries. He argues that the lack of adequate safeguards for developing countries for fully taking advantage of the flexibilities in the WTO agreements in TRIPS prompted to urge WTO to enact enabling waivers to its provisions. He emphasizes that Doha Declaration is a landmark decision, which has provided both opportunities and challenges for South Asian countries. He sees the influence of powerful pharmaceutical companies in the industrial countries, which is responsible for the lessening of gains of the developing countries. He undertakes the opinion that the South Asian countries should combine with other developing countries and to maintain a common stand to make necessary amendments to the WTO text. Bhuyan's paper is an attempt to look at the position of least developed countries in the TRIPS Council negotiations. He outlined the challenges of these countries, viz., the major challenge in the area of patent protection which makes rent transfer from these countries to developed countries in agriculture, textiles, agriculture chemicals and medicines; the adverse affect in respect of technology transfer, use of seeds by farmers and the availability of essential drugs; the undesirable affects of uncontrolled diffusion of IPRs; absence of reverse engineering which develops indigenous technology; and the importance of the issue of patenting of plants and animals to these countries. He concludes that the least developed countries have to comply with patents for pharmaceutical products; attract investments to the same sector; need for foreign investment and transfer of advanced technology; protection of IPRs for providing incentives. Rajyalakshmi in her paper, argues that trade-related

IPRs has thrown considerable challenges to the public health. While explaining the reaction of the developing countries to this, which led to the adoption of Doha Declaration, she sees that TRIPS and Doha contain flexibilities, which could be utilized by countries to safeguard their public health. She identifies these flexibilities in TRIPS and further examines how India has responded. The New Patent (Amendment) Act, 2005 is focused in her paper to assess the extent to which the TRIPS space has been used, in order to safeguard its public health. Chandrasekhar and Praseeda in their paper, raised the issues of sustainable development, emerging trends in disease and health care in general and in India in particular and implication of Cancun Meet, while dealing with the IPRs with the issue of health. They provide a number of suggestions for improvement, including international level negotiations to protect the rights of the developing countries, R&D, policy support and bio-diversity legislation etc. which require a harmony of government, local bodies, NGOs and private sector. Anita Rao and Rajiv Thakur in their joint paper on pharmaceutical industry undertake the comparison between 1970 and 2002 and explain options available for Indian pharma industry, viz., competition with the MNCs by producing their own inventions; producing under license and making up drugs which are free from patents. They outline the measures such as the strategic approach to global markets; strong R & D for the enhancement of skills; diversification of research options; good infrastructure facilities; and high competitive workforce for the successful implementation of the above.

Part V includes important topics, though divergent but relevant to South Asian countries, i.e., China's entry into WTO, Nepal and WTO; challenges and opportunities of trade of India under the WTO and the SAFTA and the impact of WTO on South Asia. Nirmala Devi, analysing the past experience of growth and trading pattern in the South Asian countries in the 1980s and 1990s, observes that China's robust growth rate and trade performance is in no way comparable with the South Asian countries. Discussing the shifts in the economic strategies of India and other South Asian countries on the one hand and China on the other, she identifies increasing partnership in trade, particularly between India and China in the recent years. She discusses both - positive and negative – sides of China's accession into WTO and its impact on South Asia and opines that the exact impact of the accession of China depends upon the future balancing of these two affects. She emphasizes the de- politicization of global trading system, in order to offset the developed countries' linkage of market access to political benefits and also the dire need of south-south cooperation, particularly the economic engagement of China and India to protect the cause of their fellow developing countries. Mahendra Lama's paper on the challenges and opportunities of Nepal under the WTO focuses on the vital importance of WTO membership for the country. He analyses the bilateral trade agreements of Nepal and other trade issues, aimed at improving the system. By outlining the major challenges of Nepal in the arena of primary commodities, anti-dumping, social clause, movement of natural persons, reforms and IPRs, agricultural subsidies, MFA phasing out, competition policy etc., and the restructuring of the existing institutions of Nepal need to be comprehended very thoroughly before Nepal really implements them. The author concludes that enhancing capacity to develop opportunities; encouraging high quality research; development of institutional and human capabilities; and increasing awareness about trade related impact would help the country's negotiations with the rest of the world. Another serious exercise in exploring the challenges and opportunities of India under the WTO is undertaken by Krishna Moorthy. His paper deals with the implications of WTO Agreements for India and the existence of regionalism, particularly South Asian Free Trade Area (SAFTA). He analyses the intra-SAARC trade and India's export and import relations with the regional members while estimating the trade intensity indices the role of India in regional investments is also highlighted, besides its natural leadership in the region. He focuses on the need for improving economic relations between India and Pakistan, the addressing of the economic insecurity of the smaller countries, and the importance of improving the infrastructure of India to facilitate the connectivity with the neighbouring countries and points out the removal of political differences for the development of the SAARC region. Hailay Gebretinsae Beyene's paper on the impact of WTO on South Asia is an attempt to study the trade related issues of the region, in view of their future prospects. He argues that the shift of exports to processed industrial goods is responsible for maintenance of high tariff peaks by the developed countries, which in turn became detrimental to the South Asian countries. He suggests that the South Asian countries need to build their competitive advantage through conscious strategic interactions such as grading the technology profile of their textile and clothing and other exports; increasing the value addition in the traditional commodities, preparation of sound marketing, strengthening of cooperation and coordination of South Asian countries in WTO negotiations to tackle the intense competition.

PART - I

Trade Cooperation for Development and Poverty Eradication

1

Linking Socially Responsible Globalization with National Governance, Decentralization Reforms and Poverty Eradication: The Challenge for WTO

De-mystification of the Poverty and Development Policy for South Asia

Ponna Wignaraja

Section 1: The Development Challenge in South Asia

The development challenge facing South Asia is reflected in the address of President of India in the event of Republic Day in 2000. He stated:

> "Fifty years into the life of our Republic we find that Justice–social, economic and political–remains an unrealized dream for millions of our fellow citizens. The benefits of our economic growth are yet to reach them. We have one of the world's largest reservoirs of technical personnel, but also the world's largest number of illiterates, the world's largest middle class, but also the largest number of people below the poverty line, and the largest number of children suffering from malnutrition. Our giant factories rise out of squalor, our satellites shoot up from the midst of the hovels of the poor. Not surprisingly, there is sullen resentment among the masses against their condition erupting often in violent forms in several parts of the country. Tragically, the growth in our economy has not been uniform. It has been accompanied by great regional and social inequalities. Many a

social upheaval can be traced to the neglect of the lowest of society, whose discontent moves towards the path of violence".

This stark warning signal, linking the inadequacy of mainstream development thinking and action in South Asia in the past fifty years with poverty, violence and governance issues was also stated twelve years earlier in the unanimous Report of the Independent South Asian Commission on Poverty Alleviation, established by the Heads of State/Governments of South Asia (SAARC Secretariat 1992). In 1992, fifteen South Asians looking at the South Asian reality, unambiguously stated that:

> "Poverty in the South Asian Region, based on conventional "poverty line" estimates is of the order of 440 million and is likely to increase."
>
> "The magnitude and complexity of this problem in South Asia is staggering. When coupled with the multifaceted crises currently facing South Asian countries, the problem is becoming unmanageable, not only putting democracy at risk but also posing a threat to the fabric of South Asian societies."

In 2002, the SAARC Secretariat established a second Poverty Commission and their Report stated "the current status of dollar-a-day poverty incidence in South Asia is around 37 percent (given increased population from the previous decade absolute numbers are high). The report continued "Inequalities are not only restricted to incomes, but also in economic assets and social conditions. Rising inequalities have fuelled social conflict."

Two recent World Bank Reports admitted that the challenge is formidable. The Reports have accepted that the private sector alone cannot respond to the challenge of poverty. They go together. "Too often service delivery fail poor people–in access, in quantify and quality. Merely innovating with service delivery arrangements will not be enough. It involves changing not only public sector institutions but also the foreign aid is transferred. These warning signals and challenges relating to 40 percent of the people living in poverty were not taken seriously. Before advocating policy options it is essential to probe the 'why' of the inadequacy of the WTO and related paradigmatic response and the 'how' of meeting the challenge, both globally and nationally–at the macro policy level as well as at the micro level.

Section 2: Re-evaluating the Inadequacy

The inadequacy of the mainstream development paradigm based as it was on narrow economics and technocratic approaches, has been partially recognized in various previous critiques since Independence and de-colonisation in South Asia from the late 1940s.

However, these critiques were at the periphery of the discourse. These critiques were also fragmented and addressed only parts of the challenge. The initial addition of "social" to "economic" development by reformists to and the more recent substitution of "human" development is hardly sufficient. The critiques did not lead to a coherent alternative vision and to coherent time bound strategies and actions. They failed to address the fundamental contradictions that had emerged and were continuing to deepen in the South Asian reality. There was also no in-depth realization that despite, political decolonisation there was a major new unfinished agenda on sustainable development and forms of democratic decision making, which had to be addressed with greater clarity.

The dominant mainstream development thinking was inspired by external intellectual forces and a global agenda, over which South Asia had little control. It still is Continuity and imitation, rather than the need for social transformation dominated the discourse, as well as, the political decision making processes. This point needs elaboration with some of the stands in the discourse.

At independence, nearly all South Asian countries got caught up in a false debate. Historically there was this tremendous resurgence, a social foment social movement that brought independence to most South Asian countries. It took the immediate form of a political movement, but had a content, which transcended the political agenda. It included several fundamentals in a holistic approach to the life of the people. It was expected to lead not just to political independence, but also to a good life and dignity for all. Mahatma Gandhi was, among others, at the center of the movement for social transformation. But the debate at that time, put simply, revolved around capitalism vs. socialism or modernism vs. tradition. The result was an electric mix of strategies and policies. The elites and professionals took charge and exercised the power of managing the transition. The fundamentals in the paradigm they adopted were not rooted either in the culture or the people.

The focus was not on how to probe the reality and take Gandhianism and the complex independence movement as a point of departure, and go on to our own brand of culturally rooted South Asian modernity. Gandhi never said "do not go to modernity". He did not say–go back to a romanticized tradition. He provided a very forward-looking kind of alternative modernity starting at the base of our societies and in terms of fundamental cultural values. He said, "The world has enough for everyone's need, but not for everyone's greed" and "break the barriers between mental and manual labour through constructive work". These were based on culturally rooted values and perspectives. He was a symbol and set a personal example, but died before the initial holistic vision matured in practice.

Looking back, another phase of the old debate went on between Neo-Classicism and Marxism, as if these were the only two options that were available to us in our development strategy and polity. There was a vacillation between a kind of "top down" bureaucratic planning and leaving major decisions to the market. There was insufficient questioning of the underlying ideological orientations in terms of the cultural values and people. The centralized decision making processes in both systems were imitated – the centralized state and the boardrooms. South Asia opted for centralized representative democracy and other centralized political processes. It was thought that the poor could be tranquillized with safety nets, welfare and charity. In the process the potential for participatory development and participatory democracy was missed. The eclecticism of policies and strategies excluded them.

The lessons of this inadequacy have yet to be learned. The challenges in South Asia at the beginning of the millennium have to be confronted not only by reviewing our past actions, but also by learning how to re-vision development thinking. A major social transformation has to be envisioned, taking into consideration of objective forces of history and potential for human action. This involves levels of consciousness of the people and releasing their creativity, wise use of natural resources and managing the knowledge system. Now social science methodologies are required to facilitate this paradigm shift to a more holistic one. This holistism was there in South Asia's earlier spiritual heritage, in teachings of people like Sultan Bahu and more recently in Vivekananda and Tagore. The realization that South Asians should have an opportunity collectively to think on South Asian problems holistically uncluttered by ideologies and strategies from far distant places, no matter how rational they may appear to be, dawned on some within the SAPNA Network nearly a quarter of a century ago in the mid 1970s.

Even at this late date, it is necessary to get a collective consensus on the holistic vision. There seem to be many visions. Some visions appear to be progressive on the surface, but are really only marginally reformist. The so-called decision to mainstreaming is in reality still tinkering with externally inspired paradigms and fragmented frameworks of thinking and action.

SAPNA started this process of collective creativity in South Asian dissenting from the mainstream intellectual paradigm and the eclectic mix. What is more innovative about SAPNA is that right from its inception in mid 1970s, SAPNA did not confine itself to a critique of the system as it worked. SAPNA investigated the South Asian reality from a South Asian perspective and began on the basis of lessons from the ground to identify undogmatic critical elements, which could be a basis for an alternative paradigm for a culturally rooted pattern of development and democracy in South Asia. In this process the eradication of the worst forms of poverty in South Asia, in a given time frame, became the "entry point". The methodology was holistic, involving interdisciplinary action research, collective reflection and social praxis to manage a social transition.

A fundamental difference in the SAPNA approach to poverty eradication and approaches in the current transition was that SAPNA did not consider the poor as the problem, but considered them as part of the solution. The second element in the difference is that SAPNA strategy for poverty eradication is based on a pro poor growth strategy based on the efficiency of the poor and their participation as subjects and not on a redistributive strategy of welfare, safety nets and charity, which at best can only be residual.

Section 3: Constructive Dissent to Mainstream Thinking and Actions: Report of the Independent South Asian Commission on Poverty Alleviation

It was not until 1991 that SAPNA's constructive dissent could be brought squarely into the mainstream debate/dialogue on development. In 1991, the Heads of States of SAARC had themselves begun to sense the sharpening contradictions and polarization between rich and poor in South Asia and the link between poverty and violence. By then the multifaceted crisis was increasingly visible–demographic pressures, extensive erosion of the natural resource base, growing foreign debt burden and reverse flow of resources from South Asia to industrialized countries, large scale unemployment of educated youth and youth alienation, low growth, increasing lack of credibility of the state and ethnic and gender conflicts. By then these Heads of State also began to better understand the inadequacy and disarray in conventional development thinking and action. This led to their establishment of the 1992 Independent South Asian Commission on Poverty Alleviation to sort out the confusion and provide practical solutions, which they could implement in a given time frame. The inclusion of several SAPNA Network Members in the Commission and in its advisory group provided SAPNA with the ability to make a coherent intellectual contribution to reinforce the debate/dialogue and practice of decentralized participatory democracy and development in general and to macro micro policy options and institution building for sustainable eradication of the worst forms of poverty. The establishment of the Poverty Commission permitted the constructive dissent and the coherent ideas in an alternative paradigm that were emerging even in a rudimentary fashion to be mainstreamed.

The Independent South Asian Commission on Poverty Alleviation (ISACPA) was an innovative collaboration between SAARC Governments and an Independent Group of South Asians. They formed an inter-disciplinary team and carried out their in-depth inquiry over an eight-month period. Extensive consultations were also held with other experts, organizations of the poor and high-level policy-makers, including the SAARC Heads of State themselves. The terms of reference required the Commission to clearly diagnose what went wrong with past at poverty alleviation, draw positive lessons from the ground, where the poor have been mobilized successfully to contribute to growth and human development and, finally, to identify the critical elements in a coherent but practical overall strategy of poverty alleviation in South Asia. These terms of reference also reflected on underlying realization that without poverty eradication, liberalization and the one-billion-strong mass market in South Asia could not come into its own.

The Report that emerged was a unanimous one. Achieving this unanimity by a diverse group of South Asians in relations to such a complex problem area is worthy of note as it reflected collective creativity. The collective analysis was not based not on a priory theorizing or on borrowed ideologies as in mainstream development thinking. It was based on an understanding of the South Asian economic, social, cultural and political reality, as well as, on the hard lessons on the ground of nearly half a century of development experience. This was the first time that South Asian Heads of State had themselves sought independent advice from a group of South Asians and provided them with an opportunity to collectively look critically at the post independence South Asian development experience and the polity and draw the lessons. The Report that resulted was not merely a report on poverty in a narrow sense. It conveyed some sharp political messages, an overall development perspective and practical recommendations to the SAARC Heads of State on a coherent transitional development framework and agenda for the eradication of the worst forms of poverty, in a given time frame. This transitional strategy was based on the factor in surplus in South Asia i.e., the creativity and efficiency of the poor who could be an asset and not on capital, the scarce factor, as in conventional development theory. The Report took the form of three coherent messages and one composite strategic recommendation.

Message No. 1

The number of people living in poverty in the region, in 1991, based on the conventional 'poverty line' estimates would be between 330 to 440 million. The reality is more likely to be in the higher range. The structural adjustment policies, which accompany the open-economy industrialization strategy currently being adopted by most SAARC countries, are likely to put further strains on the poor, particularly in the shorter term. The conclusion was inescapable that the magnitude and complexity of the problem of poverty in South Asian countries, not only put democracy at risk, but also poses a threat to the very fabric of South Asian societies.

Message No. 2

The conventional development interventions with its faith in "trickle down" and administrative redistribution to the poor, over the past 50 years, inadequate. These interventions also assumed a conflict free social framework for change. Technocratic solutions, policies and projects were designed to get to pre-determined objectives, which had little relation to the reality on the felt needs of the majority of people. Even in its own terms, the resulting growth rate also was too low to have a significant impact on the levels of living of the large number of poor. In a few exceptional cases, where the low growth was redistributed to produce a high human development index, it could not be sustained. The role of the State had to change from that of a highly centralized doer to that of an enabler land supporter of numerous partners.

Message No. 3

The eradication of poverty in South Asia would required a major political rather than a technocratic approach in which social mobilization and empowerment of the poor play a critical role. In the past 10 to 15 years a sufficient body of new experience has matured at the micro level in the South Asian countries, which demonstrates that the poor are efficient. Where the poor participate as subjects and not as objects of the development process, it is possible for them also to generate additional growth. In this pattern of growth human development and greater equity, are not mutually exclusive trade-offs, but are complementary elements in the same process.

Recommendation

There should be a Pro Poor development approach, which is unambiguously reflected a coherent plan for the poor. This should constitute the strategic thrust within the overall national development plan. The new premise for action is an overall pattern of development, which in a transitional time frame moves on two fronts: (i) A cautious open-economy industrialization front with pro poor reforms; and (ii) The pro-poor poverty eradication front with rigorous social mobilization and participation.

These two parallel strategic thrusts having long and short-term time frames can be harmonized as the two processes evolve. The recommendation elaborated how the pro- poor Plan can generate pro-poor growth with a lower capital output ratio. Growth in the formal public land private sectors, will be complemented by that generated by organizations of the poor to reach a growth rate of approximately 9 percent through the three sectors.

At the Seventh SAARC Summit in Dhaka, in April 1993, the Heads of State unanimously endorsed the Poverty Commission recommendations and reiterated their commitment with the Dhaka Consensus to continue to accord the highest priority to the eradication of the worst forms of poverty, within a ten-year period. This commitment as repeated in the SAARC Summits of 1995 and 1997. In other words, the SAARC Heads of State accepted ownership of the strategic thrust. It was also decided to have policy dialogues with the International Development Community in reinforcing the development co-operation partnership and ensuring vigorous implementation of the recommendations in the Report.

This Consensus of the Heads of State of SAARC constituted at that time a major coherent response to a critical element in the multifaceted crisis in South Asia and reflected the strong compulsions to bring poverty to the center stage of national and international concern with innovative action. It also opened up nee political space in South Asia for a political approach to poverty eradication through social mobilization and participation of the poor in development. What is also interesting is that the Heads of State, in their statements, underscored the critical link between the success of national and regional efforts aimed at poverty eradication and the external factors affecting growth and development. They urged all major actors in the world economic scene, particularly the industrialized countries and the multilateral and regional financial institutions and non-governmental organizations to create an enabling international atmosphere that is supportive of poverty eradication programmes in South Asia. They felt this would require a new dialogue with donors.

The first dialogue was organized with the World Bank in 1993. The members of the SAARC Standing Committee officially approved the World Bank's invitation to discuss the Poverty Commission Report at a high level Workshop on Poverty Reduction in South Asia, with the participation of the Secretary-General SAARC and members of the Poverty Commission. Representatives of the World Bank, International Monetary Fund, Asian Development Bank, UNDP, IFAD and UNICEF participated. The process was repeated in a second dialogue with the Government of the Federal Republic of Germany, in 1995, which is now a leading advocate of the global Copenhagen Plus Five Declaration on poverty reduction by 50% by 2015. Both dialogues sought to identify several areas of consensus in the diverse experiences, approaches and perceptions among the different groups of participants to the problem of poverty and its solutions. There were a number of unique features to these dialogues. First, they helped the donor organizations to understand the innovative approach to pro poor growth, human development and equity that was presented by the Independent South Asian Commission. Second, it helped to generate a dialogue between the various donor organizations that wished to harmonize their approaches and the advice they were to give South Asian governments. Third, the dialogue brought together diverse strands of thought within these organizations to focus on the deepening crisis in the South Asian region and question why aid was not reaching the poor. Finally, the dialogue also helped to highlight the need for conceptual clarity and better co-ordination between these donor organizations and give greater coherence to their aid and non-aid policies towards South Asia.

In both dialogues there was consensus that the process of poverty eradication in South Asia through conventional development approaches of liberalization and structural adjustment was painfully slow and inadequate. The time horizon for the open economy and simplistic structural adjustment policies to have a positive impact on the poor lat best was much longer than originally estimated. On the contrary, it was more likely to have adverse effects on the poor in the short term. It was also agreed that participation by the poor as subjects in the process and rigorous social mobilization is a key component of a comprehensive poverty eradication strategy. The dialogue helped move the discussion towards the emerging paradigm shift.

In retrospect, this initial movement of a coherent set of ideas and the paradigm shift from dissent to mainstream was short-lived. Having originally taken ownership, neither South Asian States nor the international development community fully internalized or embraced fully the coherent set of ideas for transition, as a point of departure for further thinking and action.

Section 4: Underlying Premises for Poverty Eradication in Managing the Next Transition

At the beginning of the new Millennium, given the deepening crisis of development and continued increase in poverty in South Asia and ten years after the 1993 Dhaka Consensus on poverty eradication, it is time that we revisited the fundamentals for poverty eradication in the coherent transitional strategy enunciated in the Report of the South Asian Poverty Commission, which could help reverse some of the contradictions and imbalances resulting from the mainstream development paradigm, shift has unfolded over the past 50 years.

The critical fundamentals are: (i) The long revolution and social transformation. (ii) Perspectives and Values (iii) Countervailing Power: A Political Approach (iv) Growth, Human Development and Equity: No Trade Offs (v) Refocusing Praxis and Participation.

Though the premises underlying these fundamentals are stated separately, they are not only interrelated but essential pre-requisites in moving forward.

The Long Revolution and Social Transformation

The first premise that needs to be internalized is that eradicating poverty of such a magnitude in South Asia requires a major social transformation and structural changes, not marginal tinkering and ad hoc reformist damage limitation palliatives. It has to go beyond the past the simplistic growth and redistribution and human face models. Structural change was more than mere financial and budgetary discipline and ad hoc redistributive justice.

This social transformation has to be conceived as a long revolution implying a complex chain of long and short time frames–not a one-shot 'big bang' revolution. The ten year plans that were formulated and carried out using factors in short supply, like capital and imported technology ignored the real factor endowments of South Asian societies, which lay in the basic' values and creativity of its people, in its natural resources base and knowledge systems.

It is time to make the assertion that in the past half century since Independence South Asia has not made a major social transformation through the kind of rational structural changes that were called for. Structural changes when attempted were equated to one-dimensional land reform processes or merely to achieving budgetary and financial discipline or fragmented trained development or weak decentralization reforms. Even here we embraced received wisdom from outside instead of moving in a series of transitions building on what we had.

A structural change that is transformative had to be rooted in the people and encompass the whole society, without exclusion. Creativity, innovativeness and a problem solving approach to life has always been a characteristic of South Asian societies. This creativity was also underpinned by a co-operative spirit, no predatory relations with nature an a simple way of life which included satisfaction of basic needs o fall, as well as, a concept of inner spirituality, constructive work and leisure. Cultural scientific pursuits, and appropriate technology were integral to the way of life of the people. What was to be excluded was mindless consumerism, 'dog eat dog' competitiveness and waste of four natural resource base and knowledge.

A second fundamental transormative issue that eluded us was the issue of self-reliance. South Asia had too long depended on external inspiration and hegemonies. Rural South Asia where 70 percent of the people lived was dominated too long by the city. The rural poor were subservient to the rural rich. South Asia could not develop unless this dominance dependence syndrome was creatively mediated. To break out of this, required a major social mobilization effort and a wise use of all local resources–natural, financial, knowledge and most of all the creativity of all the people, not just a few. It laws in this way that the necessary psychological and institutional staying power, if or sustainability of the transformative process could be built up. In retrospect is it not evident that we ended up with 'soft' societies, where the majority of people including the poor and young persons become alienated?

Thus, the binding constraint for development became the inhibition of the fullest expression of the people's creativity, their lack of identity with work in which there was fulfillment, and their inability to relate harmoniously with nature. De-alienation of people is an important dimension in the process of building self-reliance. The right to participate by everyone not a few in decisions that affect their lives is another fundamental premise. This is what participatory democracy means. It goes with the co-operative spirit and a rising of consciousness in the social mobilization process. It is anti-ethical to the domination and dictatorship of an elite. Participatory democracy can be more fully practiced with effective decentralization and devolution of power to the people.

Finally, the rhetoric of "One World" and international development cooperation with aid mesmerized us into thinking that there was a short cut. This also was a part of the South Asian elitist vision, which has created "soft" and unequal societies. Now, it is more of the same with rapacious pursuit of globalization, without learning the lessons of history and throwing caution to the winds. The inescapable conclusion is that if a long revolution is a meaningful pathway to social transformation through series of transitions which is rooted in people, holistic and sustainable, then fragmented and eclectic conceptions of complex social processes are irrelevant both to understand and intervene in the complex crises that face most countries of South Asia today. The narrow ideological theorizing of the past and attempts to force complex reality to fit simplistic mish mash of theory have in most countries prevented the flowering of concepts and ideas relevant to a more systematic transformative evolution of either participatory democracy or development rooted in the culture and the people.

Perspective and Values

The structural changes at the macro and micro levels outlined above has to start with a clear perspective and be value-led. This is fundamental for correct action. Before action is taken, the underlying values need to be made explicit. It is then that praxis, the action-reflection-action process, becomes an instrument for initiating and reinforcing the positive macro or micro structural changes desired or underway. Sultan Bahu, a 17th century Sufi poet whose universal message of a human society was a positive influence on fundamental South Asian values, stated: "That which consciousness reaches far is always a step ahead of the actual. When one possibility is actualized, a new possibility is born."

The perspective from which the search for the underlying paradigm begins is that participatory democracy and development are two sides of the same holistic vision that has inspired human endeavour in different South Asian socio-cultural settings over the past 2,000 years and more of recorded history. The values that have emanated from this deeper interpretation of the vision, even though somewhat diffused in practice, have been implicitly incorporated, in one way or another, in these two fundamental cornerstones. Several fundamental values, which existed in traditional South Asian societies, must be identified and re-examined in this connection. Some critical values relate to looking at life in its totality and all its richness, participation of the people in decisions that affected their lives; sharing and caring for the community, co-operative activities beyond individual self-interest; trust, innocence, simplicity, thrift; a work ethic with a fine-tuned balance between work and leisure; harmony with nature and a rational use of both natural and financial resources; communal ownership of the commons; and complementarity between men and women, as well as, gender equity. The Report of the Independent South Asian Commission on Poverty alleviation translated some of these values into rights and gave high priority to sharing and caring, the right to food, the right to work and right to information in the transition.

To elaborate further, historically in all South Asian cultures there were built-in methods of consensus making. One example is the republican tradition of the Lichchavis in ancient South Asia, elaborated in classical Buddhist texts. Another is the Krishna-Arjuna dialogue in the Mahabharata, which also illustrates correct decision-making at a higher level of consciousness. This provides the intellectual underpinnings for a 'just' war against a repressive and undemocratic regime (Rajagopalachari 1968). Poet Kambar in describing Ram Rajya (a good society) in his translation of the Ramayana into Tamil (pre-historic) says". There was no one who did not have enough, there was no one who had more than enough."

A recent study of the Hindu Veda reveals that women in Hindu society asserted their rights throughout history against male domination. It also shows, through the concept of Ardhinarishwara, the complementarity of men and women in Hindu society (Gourie Ponnaiah 1989) The literature is full of instances of people's participation and democratic practice at the base of the system alongside wise and compassionate leadership at the top. Democratic consensus making was very much a part of the Asian tribal mode of governance. Peer pressure was a major deterrent to corrupt practices. This also extended to every day activities such as the taking of loans and credits, where peer pressure ensured repayment. There was an open information system at the level of the community, which further reinforced the principle of equity and checks and balances and accountability. Democracy in labour relations, exchange labour, common ownership of land and other productive assets further reinforced cooperative values, mutual aid and equity. The knowledge system that evolved in these cultures and from this valuational framework, by intuition, as well as, by trial and error, propelled the process with its own rationality and mediated various tensions in the process. It hears repetition that this knowledge system was scientific in any terms (Wignaraja 1989). The technology that resulted provided the material basis for sustainable, essential needs-oriented development and for predominantly self-reliant societies aware of their reality. The knowledge system also helped to resolve some of the sharper contradictions whenever they arose, providing a wide range of technological choices in keeping with the fundamental human values, and cultural norms. Having said this, intellectuals and activists alike have a long way to go in clarifying some of the fundamental features of the culturally rooted historical paradigm processes, instrumentalists and organizational forms. The task is made very complex because of both the historical contradictions that have existed in these societies and distortions in the modes of production, community spirit and consensus-making that set in as colonialism, modernization, industrialization, westernization and other dependency creating external interventions and penetrations occurred. A distinction has to be made between what are fundamental contradictions and those that are marginal and therefore simpler to resolve.

In the new social movements and experiments in South Asia, one sees glimpses of an older civilization rhythm in their relationships of people to people and people to nature and people to their knowledge system. The Chipko Movement with the poor women hugging the forest trees not only illustrates the understanding of the need for harmony with nature, but also demonstrates the ability of organized poor women to prevent destruction of nature with all its adverse consequences and bio-diversity, the eco-system and their survival resource base. The attempts to reverse past processes and regenerate the natural resource base. Some such movements and experiments as they now exist are fragile, while in other cases they still remain only at the levels of an experiment or of the desirable. Whatever their degree of manifestation in reality, these relationships needs to be further reinforced as part of an ongoing process of social transformation towards real democracy and sustainable development (Wignaraja 1993).

Understanding these peoples' responses is not an easy task. The objective of the exercise is not to go back to the past, viewed with romanticism, but to understand the contradictions, then to observe the seeds of change, learn the lessons that reflect some of the democratic and wider development values. The hard lessons from the g round can be learned through social praxis in moving towards a more humane and qualitatively better society for larger numbers, building on the sustainable processes already initiated in the new social movements. A new reading of indigenous value systems and traditions, both from written and unwritten sources, is also essential for a deeper understanding of the nature of democracy and the human development and accumulation process in the South Asian context. Some of this recorded history is not only confined to printed history books. It is also increasingly available in manuscripts, written on ola leaves or inscribed in stone, which even predate recorded Greek and Roman history. They complement the oral transmission of history, intuitively recognized, time tested and communicated through mythological stories and anecdotally handed down over a long period of time. In addition, cognitive knowledge was itself part of the knowledge system in most Southern Asian countries. It gave depth to the understanding of the Southern Asian cultures and civilizations they were interpreting. Much of this cognitive knowledge can be subjected to scientific validation. This is a challenge for research, research methodology and scientific validation of history.

Countervailing Power: A Political Economy Approach

Another fundamental in rethinking past paradigms of development and democracy relate to the question of participatory democracy. In this regard, devolution of power and empowerment of the poor and vulnerable groups, as opposed to representative democracy and highly centralized elite power requires clarification. There is little need to criticize the dangers of centralized power, representative state structures and absolute power that corrupts. What needs to be elaborated is the concept of participatory democracy and the building of countervailing power, initially within the political spaces that are already available.

Conventional thinking on both development and democracy was based on a harmony model. This needs to be demystified. The assumption of harmonious communities in a conflict-free social framework for change has no basis in reality, whether at local, national levels in South Asia or at global levels. This is another myth.

At the local level, for instance, rural communities in South Asia in today's historical conditions are not homogeneous entities. Sometimes, where land reform has occurred or in a tribal society in which land is communally owned and traditional social values continue to exist, the situation may be comparatively harmonious. But even there, the degree of harmony will have been reduced by colonial penetration and other forms of external intervention. These interventions themselves have generated further local, national and global contradictions. They have also contributed to the erosion of traditional communal bonds and values and disrupted the traditional system that assured a more equitable access to resources by the poor and vulnerable groups. In the South Asian villages, deep-seated contradictions exist between different groups with conflicts of interests. There are sharp relationships of dominance and dependence. These relationships give power to the dominant (the landlord, the trader, the moneylender, the bureaucrat; et.al), bringing about a crisis of immediate survival for the poor. Serious divisions exist among the poor themselves, based on case, religion, gender, age, etc. These divisions, the people's passivity, the resultant reluctance to take economic, social and political initiatives collectively to improve their lives, and their inability to change their lives individually, further compound their difficulties. It also increases the possibilities of leakages in resources meant for the poor. These factors also prevent the poor from benefiting from technocratically evolved development packages. The same conflict syndrome, between those who have power and those who do not, can be identified in the actual working of the national and global systems. Therefore, the rhetoric of harmony and interdependence at all levels cannot be a point of departure from which to rethink the question of transition to participatory democracy and devolved power. Sometimes, class differentiations are blurred by caste or tribal loyalties. This makes analysis in conventional social categories irrelevant.

Any meaningful approach to social change that will not benefit the rich at the expense of the poor, or the powerful at the expense of the powerless, must be both political and transformative. It should not be a purely technocratic, fragmented, as purely sectoral.

The project approach with "tool kits" is inadequate. A political process has to be initiated. The political space for a political approach exists already in some countries, while in others it needed to be created. A great deal of social mobilization is required. This involves remoulding of elites as well as mobilizing, raising consciousness of the poor and help them to build their own organizations is required. The poor need to investigate and understand their reality and reflect on how they can move out of poverty to dignity through their own efforts. This process may not happen spontaneously and may have to be facilitated by committed catalysts.

Participation is of central concern in any discussion of development in wider human terms. It is sheer pretension to think that the multifaceted crisis of South Asian countries can easily be overcome or that the reshaping and development of these societies in a more balanced and sustainable way can be undertaken without the participation of the poor as subjects in that process. If participation means democracy, representative democracy as now practiced is a singularly limited form. People participate in elections. But such formal participation is a mere token, unless power is shared, particularly at local level. It is not a matter merely of decentralization, but of devolution. Participation also means trusting the people and commitment to a more egalitarian society., that would ensure equal access to resources, not only to land but also to education, food and health. Where formal power is in the hands of a few and power is not shared but grossly misused, participation in the first instance results in building countervailing forms of power, leading ultimately to a healthier democracy.

Furthermore, if development results from releasing the creative energies of the people, particularly the poor and the vulnerable, then they must be the final arbiters of their lives. Participation and self-reliance are thus interrelated. This form of development goes beyond merely meeting the material needs of the people and beyond considerations of redistributive justice alone. To participate people need to form their own organizations. The poor need, through their own organizations, to counter the socio-economic reality around them and the forces that keep them in poverty. Such participation then opens up possibilities for people to bring about changes in their conditions through their own reflections, collective actions and assertions of the right to resources to which they are entitled. This results from a learning process, a process of further consciousness-raising and self-transformation. In this sense participation is also a basic human need. The extent of participation will depend initially on the political space that is available for the participatory process to start, particularly at the local level, and on the opportunities for an intervention in the existing socio-economic system by those who have a higher consciousness and commitment.

The very nature of participatory, self-reliant development activities is such that they will eventually attract the attention of the power structure, still working within the confines of the failed centralized paradigm. Some of these new participatory activities will be co-opted by the system, others exterminated. While some are repressed, many still survive. Those, which survive, existing in isolation, do not add up to much in terms of social transformation. But if they are properly linked and multiply themselves through the processes of mobilization, conscientisation and organization, they can become a countervailing power in the social context and help to widen the political space for change even further. Countervailing power is necessary to retain the vitality of the poor. It is a living, collective consciousness of the poor and a vigilance of the poor against the abuse of formal power. It is the capability to resist such abuse and to assert the will and rights of the large numbers of poor whenever formal power deviates at the macro, as well as the micro-level. It is critical for ensuring accountability by those who wield power. They must be held accountable for its proper use to the poor, and not merely for its abuse. Thus, building of countervailing power at all levels becomes a fundamental component in a participatory democratic and sustainable development process and constitutes a critical point of departure for rethinking development and democracy. Countervailing power does not preclude new partnerships with sensitive institutions, state or others in the support system like Government Entities, Banks, NGO's or Donors.

Growth, Human Development and Equity: No Trade-Offs

As this multifaceted crisis deepened, the accumulation process set in motion either by means of private capitalism or of state capitalism, a process that was basic to the old concept of economic developments land its reformist option, turned out to be insufficient, and the pressures mounted for an alternative accumulation process. It was not a matter of growth first and equity afterwards. Redistributive justice and 'trickle-down' were simply not the issues.

Most of South Asian countries were predominantly rural, peasant societies, with traditional knowledge system and non-predatory relations with nature. And yet, nearly four decades ago, when these countries began to emerge as politically independent nations from centuries of colonial rule, they adopted a development model that was indifferent if not inimical to the large numbers who live in rural areas. Support for this model, which essentially permitted the continuation of existing international economic relationships, came from two external sources: the industrialized countries of the west and the industrialized, centrally planned countries of the Eastern bloc. The framework that has influenced this development process in the past half-century assumed that there were 'developed' countries and 'developing countries and that if the experience of the former, along with some capital and technology was transferred to the latter the gap would be narrowed. The objectives and processes were viewed in economic terms and great reliance was placed on economic factors and centralized decision-making to achieve results. This framework assumed that rapid economic growth could take place if there was central planning and control of the economy (by the state or the private sector) as a 'top-down' process with emphasis on industrialization, modernization and urbanization. Capital, the factor in short supply in the so-called developing countries was seen as the main input into the process. Internal capital accumulation, it was assumed, would be assisted by free and massive inflows of foreign capital and technology. The cumulative benefits of growth in the modern sector–public or private–were expected eventually either to 'trickle down' automatically or at best to be handed down in an administrative fashion ' delivered' to the poor. Material accumulation either in public or private forms were expected to solve other human problems.

The widening gap between the industrialized and South Asian countries, the results of the so-called green revolution which initially helped the rich farmer get richer and made the poor poorer within these countries, the massive transfer of resources from poor countries to rich, illustrated both the danger and the limited relevance of this framework to the majority of people in South Asia. They confirmed the limitations of the narrow, techno-economic model of development, even in its own terms.

The realities of the quantity and quality of foreign aid, of transfers of technology, and of the weak internal mobilization efforts ensured that the prevailing assumptions regarding the possibilities for rapid growth were of little operational value. Neither the quantity of aid nor its quality nor the kinds of technology transferred were sufficient or appropriate to transform these societies, let alone to lift them out of the poverty trap into modernization and industrialization. Even as there is general apathy towards aid and capital flows to South Asia in most industrialized countries today, there is also a growing body of opinion which supports the view that the earlier methods of aid giving and technology transfer are things of the past. They have created impoverished rural areas and increased the dependence of South Asian countries within an inequitable global order. Furthermore, the transnational corporations that control the stock of modern technology, and are still the main instruments for its transfer, extract high prices for their know-how and equipment. The highly capital intensive and import-substituting technology that continues to be implanted into South Asia with little social control or social conscience bears insufficient relation either to real factor endowment, particularly of labour, or to the existing knowledge system, or to the wide range of technological choices available. The entire process has been wasteful and the contradictions too sharp and numerous for any orderly form of management of the process as a whole for the real benefit of poor countries.

Throughout the 1960s and early 1970s some token attempts were made to modify the narrow techno-economic notions of development and to affect some reforms. The reformists argued that a modified framework of economic development could still be made to work 'efficiently' if (a) redistribution or social justice were built into the objectives; (b) elements of popular participation (mainly some consultation with the people or manipulation of the people) in an essentially top-down planning process were allowed; (c) a continuous process of transfer of a proportion of the income and technology from industrialized to South Asian countries could be ensured, particularly through the UN system and its specialized agencies such as the World Bank, the International Monetary Fund and the regional banks. More recently, a 'human face' has been added to the reformist option.

But the reformist position continues to be based on conventional development thinking and practice. Even with greater social justice and safety nets built into it and with greater human capital formation, the development process is still considered mainly as an economic exercise, subject to allocation of scarce resources by governments and big private sector corporations. Furthermore, a conflict-free social framework for change is assumed. The vision of 'one world' continues to pervade the international rhetoric, along with the assumption that these changes –brought about under existing conditions and within unchanged structures–will result in an orderly and continuous transfer of resources from industrialized countries to South Asia. Underlying all this are further assumptions; that the problem of development is still mainly in the poor countries; and that a consistent set of policy packages based on technocratic considerations can be evolved and carried out from the top, both internationally and within individual countries. The basic assumption continues to be that the modernization/industrialization process, with some consultation with the people and the goodwill and assistance of 'developed' countries and the international community, will bring about positive social change. The poor are still considered to be objects and the targets of the process and at best to be provided with safety nets, while adjusting to an inequitable global system and a national system devoid of vision or capacity.

What then, is the alternative development pathway for South Asia? As mentioned earlier a sustainable development strategy for the present needs to search for alternative driving forces for a self-sustaining accumulation process. With the inadequacy of mainstream development action being established, the accumulation process on which it was based is also being questioned. The compulsion for seeking alternative-driving forces for accumulation, even in its narrower conception is therefore mounting. This is not a matter of giving credit to the poor. It is a matter of embarking on a new pattern of growth with the poor where growth, human development and equity are not trade-offs, but part of the same complementary process. It also seems necessary for South Asian countries to adopt a more complex development strategy that combines human development, growth, equity and technological change with a wiser and more creative use of local resources and knowledge. In such a strategy, the people's creativity, locally available resources and, local knowledge systems, savings become critical instruments. Imported capital and technology, the factors in short supply, can be supplementary.

The new strategy, moreover, does not have to be reflected in a single, replicable model each country has its own socio-cultural specificity and will have to chart its own social transition. In this transition all countries, however, will need to pursue internally a basically two-pronged strategy that will permit them to maintain the gains from past attempts at modernization and industrialization with appropriate damage limitation and to make a direct attack on poverty in all its manifestations, an attack in which the poor themselves are the subjects and not the objects of the process. Initially two prongs of the strategy may have different time horizons and some contradictions, but over time they can be harmonized. South Asian regional cooperation can reinforce national efforts. This kind of regional cooperation will also permit South Asian countries to adjust to the global system on more favourable terms.

Recent studies by South Asian scholars confirm that human development, growth and equity need not be trade-offs in the South Asian social-cultural setting. Studies by international commissions of enquiry such as the South Commission have endorsed the concepts of people-centred development, wise resource use and building technological capability in a step-by-step manner by widening the availability of technological choices. The 1990 United Nations Development Programme report on the concept of human development demonstrates that it is possible to achieve a high level of human development and quality of life even at initially low levels of income. Even the World Bank in its 1990 report on Poverty drew attention to the importance of participation by the poor in poverty alleviation and their contribution to development. It also drew attention to several successful micro-level people's movements and experiments in South Asia that, from small beginnings, have grown larger, increasing people's creativity, local resources and local knowledge. LUN Conferences and the new ecological movements have increased awareness of the need for a wiser and more equitable use of natural resources. No longer can 20% of the world's people use 80% of the world's resources and also erode the resource base needed to sustain further generations.

Refocusing Praxis and Participation

Another fundamental that requires further elaboration is the methodology of praxis. Some systematic efforts are now being made to break out of conventional social science methodologies into participatory action research by groups of South Asian scholars and activists working together. Beginning in the 1970s some new thinking was initiated. Social praxis and participatory action research, which goes with, it takes off from the cultural and historical experiences in South Asia. It criticizes predetermined universalism and stresses pluralism, including geo-cultural specificity. As has been stated in the past, social sciences have evolved through the study of Western societies. Hypotheses and value judgments have emerged from that historical cultural world and continue to influence a major part of the academic community and through it the educational, technical and administrative systems. Some social scientists have begun to break out of the mould.

In the 1970s in their book Towards a Theory of Rural Development, Wahidual Haque, Niranjan Mehta, Anisur Rahman and Ponna Wignaraja elaborated a basic premise in this line of research. Development they indicated, is simultaneously a 'top down' and 'botton-up'process (De Silva 1988). There are the national macro perspectives and the constitution micro grassroots contradictions. Successful development is viewed as a process of human development, a process of social transformation in which the people are both the subject and the object. In such a process the people participate at all levels of decision-making in matters affecting the totality of their lives and through this process of empowerment a more democratic process is initiated. Self-reliance is both a means and an end in this process. It is a process that releases the creative energy of people, assures equal access to resources for all, tends to eliminate the different between mental and manual labour, and uses technology appropriate to these social goals. This research though giving some space to micro-macro linkages was primarily concerned with the grassroots micro problematic. It saw the issues of people's participation, conscientisation, and the building of countervailing power as part of an ongoing social process, the long revolution towards social and structural change.

This analysis demonstrated the possibilities of incorporating social justice and participation into a process of accumulation and economic growth that would involve and benefit the poor and the vulnerable in the all-around development of their lives. The methodology was praxis. In particular, there was increasing evidence that such processes were sustainable at the micro level. Two critical instrumentalities that are at the core of the methodology are now apparent. One is the knowledge system inherent in the culture, which must inform the whole process. The other is the role of the facilitators/animators without whom the process cannot multiply and go to scale during a given time frame. These facilitators/animators are different from the conventional Marxist vanguard.

Praxis and Participatory Action Research (PAR) were located outside this knowledge system. Therefore, it was necessary to demystify both the nature of this knowledge and the premises and method of this knowledge transfer, before proceeding to the concept of cognitive knowledge and to the many stocks of knowledge and technology that can be drawn on for praxis, PAR and sustainable development. The framework then can be elaborated in relation to the relationship between knowledge, action and power on which PAR is premised. This then helps to bridge the gap between real knowledge and wisdom, and development action and social change. Praxis and PAR must be premised on the wider alternative knowledge system that is available, in which the knowledge system provides the power to bring about a change in the condition of the knower and generates the new social process. It also gives a wider range of technological choices.

The second issue relates to the role of the facilitator or animator. In order to initiate praxis and enable the people to bring out their creativity with a spirit of self-reliance and self-involvement, and also to assert their right to participate in development as subjects in the process, an appropriate stimulation is required. Sometimes an independence struggle or a violent protest movement against oppression, exploitation and repression can spontaneously conscientise and help organize a people, as happened in India in 1947 or Bangladesh in 1972. But the point here is how this creativity may be released and sustained under less dramatic conditions and prevailing socio-political circumstances. The creative spirit exists in all human beings and does not always manifest itself spontaneously. The challenge is to bring out this quality and the strength and the dignity of the people that goes with it. A growing body of experience shows how a facilitator/animator can initiate and catalyze this process. It also deals with dialogue as a mode of promoting participation; the training of committed facilitators and animators through participatory methodology and identifies steps for initiating Participatory Action Research (PAR). Finally, the question of the progressive redundancy of the external facilitator/animator as the sustainable and self-reliant base and process gets underway must be further analyzed.

Sectioin 5: The Knowledge System: A Critical Dimension

To move in this transition from the dominant macro-framework of development and democracy towards a new paradigm based on the interrelated fundamental premises and the micro-level development praxis it is important to be probe deeper and be unambiguous about what knowledge and whose knowledge is to be involved and how culturally relevant knowledge is to be used in catalyzing the transition to rigorous social transformation, sustainable development and eradication of the worst forms of poverty, in a given time frame.

An attempt is being made here to simplify, without being "simplistic", the concept of knowledge as an instrumentality in relation to power and development action. In the South Asian cultural context this is not an easy task, because the metaphysical perennial philosophies, which provided the valuational framework, integrity and the intellectual underpinnings for the culture and knowledge system, are deep and complex. There are neither simplistic dogmas nor dialectics alone. It cannot be done in the Cartesian mould. Yet the need for relevant development action rooted in the culture compels an enunciation of several relationships, relating to knowledge, power and action. Three propositions are made in the form of simple assertions. They are: (a) The crisis of the modern knowledge system confirms the need for devising new methods of scientific inquiry for the next transition. (b) The availability of many stocks of knowledge also means a greater choice of technology for sustainable development and poverty eradication. (c) The traditional knowledge system of the poor now assumes greater validity and relevance in relation to sustainable development.

The Crisis of Modern Knowledge

The modern knowledge system, incorporated into mainstream development thinking and action was deeply wedded initially to economies and single discipline analysis, with most of its unrelated to wider to human needs. The concept and practice of modern economic development has now been questioned. Politically, it is inconsistent with its claims of equality and justice by disrupting local communities and polarizing society into those with access to resources and power, and those without. Knowledge and Technology laws a critical element in this process. Knowledge and choice of technology also becomes a critical element in reversing this process. Knowledge is power. The relationship between knowledge, the development action that flows from it and power then becomes the critical issue.

The model of economic development (with or without the reformist human face as an additive), which has been critiqued, placed reliance on the modern Western knowledge system and the technology that went with it to initiate the process. Along with capital, a f actor in short supply in South Asia. The claim of modern knowledge was that the kind of development it generates can be extended to cover all situations and the entire g lobe. This has not happened. The cultural dislocations that have been created along side economic development have confirmed that culture and development are intertwined. This was highlighted as early as the 1950s, when the major "economic development" intervention and the aid relationship was initiated (Wignaraja 1953). "While considerable thought has been expended in recent years in attempting solutions to the numerous immediate problems confronting developing countries, very little attention has been placed on the reality that development takes places within an established cultural pattern. The process of culture change that is set in motion during economic development tens for most part to be ignored. When it is recognized, it is merely hoped that time will bring about the necessary adjustments." Modern Western knowledge is part of a particular cultural system with a particular relationship to power. Though projected as above and beyond culture and politics, and being scientific and rational, modern knowledge has an in-built mission. It has become the most effective legitimizer for the homogenization of the world and the erosion of its cultural and ecological diversity and richness. Modern Western knowledge in posing as the universal and as inherently superior to the local and diverse becomes exclusive and undemocratic. The ruling elites in industrial countries and the emergent elites in South Asia who adopted this paradigm of economic also took over the limited perspective on choice of technology (Wignaraja 1989). That there was a larger knowledge system and greater choice of technology rooted in the people was by and large ignored.

Further, the modern Cartesian knowledge system being inherently fragmenting and having in-built obsolescence, create an alienation of wisdom from technology and dispenses with the wisdom, in its pre-occupation with quantitative analysis it further distorts reality and disregards aesthetic and human dimensions, experiential learning and intuitive insights. As a consequence, to put it, both simply and sharply, in wider human terms modern Western knowledge used by itself by its application to South Asian development not only distorted the entire valuational framework buy also the priorities of the majority of people who are poor. When in addition it excluded them and created in its wake the process of moving them further from marginalisation to dispensability, this inadequate process became irrational and unacceptable–economically, politically and culturally (Vandana Shiva 1989). A positivist orientation cannot provide cognitive validation (let alone connative or total validation) to all people in all situations. The scope of the problems in South Asia is too vast and complex. Further to disregard the knowledge people have, derived from the aesthetic, experiential and intuitive insights is to disregard the essential links between knowledge, culture and development. This linkage does not permit the intellectual process to be divorced from values and will under the guise of objectivity and only results in a narrow technocratic approach. In South Asia social scientists of different disciplines, are trying collectively to locate this knowledge that is responsive to their socio-cultural realities (Gourie Ponnaiah). This re-discovery of indigenous scientific traditions also helps to build the alternative paradigms.

A holistic approach is essential to understanding reality. This means that single discipline analysis, which flows from the Western knowledge system, is insufficient. A few factors singled lout from a rich social reality become very abstract. The separation of the researcher and the researched cannot also product a meaningful understanding of reality. There is little justification for carrying forward the myth of scientific objectivity, particularly when the objective is to bring about a change in reality. The oppressed become truly oppressed only when they become repressed in the mind, i.e., when they do not have access to the sources of the knowledge from which they drew strength and sustenance and which was also destroyed in the colonial period. To break out of this crisis of the modern Western knowledge system which penetrated South Asian value norms, a major "de-colonization of the minds" of scholars and practitioners alike is required.

The Premise of Many Stocks of Knowledge and Choice of Technology

To move from the economic development model to a framework of development in holistic human terms that is participatory and sustainable, it is not sufficient to merely critique the old model and the knowledge system on which it was based in general macro or philosophical terms. Before homogenization can be replaced by pluralism, globalism by localism, economism by humanism, unlimited progress by notions of self-control, restraint and simplicity, there are some specific elements, which need to be de-mystified. It was assumed that the world had only a single s tock of knowledge and technology. The knowledge systems and technological choices available to South Asia and its people including the poor are in reality much wider. The premise of one stock of knowledge and technology, i.e., modern Western technology, locate di-industrialized countries, led to other false assumptions. Technology was used as objective criteria to judge the intrinsic level of development of human beings and society. Those societies that can sustain a higher level of technology w ere judged to be inherently superior. This gave a further moral bas is for social subjugation and neo-colonialism.

The technical assistance progarammes of the post World War II period and the extension, worker concept are both part of this approach. There is sufficient evidence even from U.N., World Bank and other studies on Appropriate Technology to confirm that, by any standards, even in its own terms the kind of knowledge and technology transferred from industrialized to South Asian countries is neither sufficient nor appropriate. Even as there is general apathy towards transfer of capital from most industrialized countries today, there is also a growing body of opinion which confirms the view that the earlier kind of technology transfer may not be entirely desirable, for it may have helped to displace the people from their own s tock of knowledge; it may have create d "soft" societies, eroded the resource base, impoverished poor countries further and increased their dependence on rich countries (Wignaraja).

This is not an argument against the selective transfer of modern technology or international development co-operation as such, but it questions the fundamental assumptions land the way things have worked. Further, the transnational corporations, which control the stock of "modern" technology and which are still the main instruments for its transfer, continue to extract high prices for their know-how and equipment the "borrowed", highly capital-intensive technology which is continuing to be implanted in the South Asian countries has little relation either to real factor endowment, particularly labour, or to the existing technological stock born of the people's knowledge system. The entire process of transferring technology in this manner is wasteful and the contradictions numerous. In any event, after fifty years, even in its own terms, the technological capability to sustain a modern economic growth process in South Asia has not been built up, except possibly to some extent in India. Even here life for three hundred million Indians may be good, but there are another five hundred million.

The transfer of the modern stock of technology from industrialized countries to the poorer countries, mainly through "market" processes along with finance, created islands of modernization, but a s has been repeatedly mentioned, left large numbers of people uninvolved and without benefit. In fact the overall process resulted in a dual society, land a further impoverishment of rural areas where the majority of people live through both a destruction of the environment and transfer of resources first from rural to urban areas and then back into the industrialized countries. The massive reverse flow of resource s is only now being clearly identified as these countries themselves move into the debt crisis. These consequences do not mean that this modern stock of knowledge cannot be used s electively with appropriate adaptation. What it means is that the massive intervention with so-called "experts" and transfer of technology, needs to be questioned and evaluated, in the light of the greater technological choice now available.

Given the intrinsic interconnectedness of knowledge and power in each culture, it is necessary to examine the social basis of different knowledge systems that are available. People in South Asia have a great deal of scientific knowledge, which can be applied to their daily lives and problems. This knowledge has been acquired intuitively or by trial and error. It is not mere traditional romanticism or religious mysticism. Much of the available traditional knowledge and technology can be used as it is. Some of this traditional knowledge is half-forgotten and would need to be revived. Revival of this traditional knowledge can only be undertaken through a participatory process within the culture. Some traditional technology would need to be upgraded in its own environment, and not in research institutes abroad where the adaptation process itself is biased by different values. Further, when repatriated its use in the country of origin becomes very costly. Appropriate R and D systems, which do not now exist or exist in a very fragile form, are also required for upgrading this knowledge and giving it further scientific validation. As this knowledge is upgraded it also has to be returned to the people in the same cost effective participatory process and in an idiom they could understand.

It is also now possible to assert that a new process is emerging and is observable in the South Asian reality. As a result of a two-way interaction between committed South Asian "experts" and the people during participatory action research, a new technology is gradually being created in these countries which does not exist in the categories referred to earlier, i.e., modern intermediate and traditional. The experience here differs from the concept of "experts go learn from the people" (which was implicit in the Chinese cultural revolution) or "experts go tell the people" (which is what the transfer of technology and the extension service instrumentality is about). The new technology results from another variant of the new and still fragile R and D system, gradually being built up by committed experts and the people in South Asian countries living and working together over time to evolve a more humane society, using initially locally available resources and knowledge. This process also reflects the interception of different perceptions of life land knowledge between these two groups. It results from the committed expert or de-professionalised intellectuals identifying with the people and committing themselves to bringing sustainable development and social change (Wignaraja). These are the new kind of facilitators of the people's praxis whose role will be analyzed later, along with that of the animator.

Likewise, in industrial countries themselves, as a result of alternative life styles experiments and ecological movements, the energy crisis, ecological concerns, youth alienation and the search for human values, individuals and groups are experimenting with new technologies. These technologies are related to new values, and not to those, which emanate from the market. In the process they themselves are creating a new knowledge base on renewable resources, food habits and health. Sometimes, this represents reviving traditional knowledge in those cultures. Sometimes it represents taking knowledge from South Asian (and other poor) countries and adapting it. This technology may in the long run be more relevant for development in South Asia, than the un-adapted transfers from the modern sector in those countries. The fundamental argument here synoptically presented is that for sustainable development and poverty eradication there is a plurality of "stocks" of knowledge and a greater choice of technology than was available in the old framework of development. Without a participatory process this knowledge will not however surface. It also implies a possibility of a different and two-way knowledge transfer between rich and poor countries as structural and valuational changes in industrial themselves take place and a new International Order in a positive sum game shapes up.

Knowledge Management: Traditional Knowledge of the Poor as the Point of Departure

The third proposition thus relates to the legitimacy of the people's knowledge system. This is also equally the knowledge system of the poor. This knowledge and traditional technology can no longer be dismissed as romantic and unscientific. It can le a critical element in sustainable cost-effective development and poverty eradication. Given the intrinsic interconnectedness of knowledge and power in each culture, it is necessary first to examine the social basis of people's knowledge systems in South Asia.

Given the onslaught of modernity over the last three hundred years–what remains of different traditions is a fractured and sometimes on the surface a distorted notion of what was. In pursuing this line of reasoning it is necessary to acknowledge that traditional systems of knowing and validation too were not without their limitations. The social organizations that sustained them had their own contradictions. Antagonistic and non-antagonistic contradictions had to be sorted out. Traditional value systems themselves sometimes lost their validity as historical processes unfolded and the problems of sustainable development became more complex. The conventional approach to economic development also had the devastating effect of suppressing local knowledge and technology. It equated economic poverty and lack of things with people's mental ignorance. A whole knowledge system, which often provided more sophisticated and subtle solutions to peoples survival and the totality of their lives were ignored. There was a great deal of rational decision making implicit in what South Asian poor actually did, which was part of the cultural heritage. This was in its own terms scientific validation. What is more is that much of this can be subjected to even modern scientific validation.

People had an intimate knowledge of their environment and natural resource base. This was often far superior to those brought in by many foreign development "experts". They often knew what to eat, when to eat certain foods, what time of day and sequence in which certain foods should be eaten to get maximum biological and nutritional results. What is more, they knew how to grow the traditional foods, cost effectively and with the least risk through time tested methods. South Asian farmers knew that thin topsoil rapidly loses its fertility when improperly cultivated without a particular pattern of crop rotation which; renewed the soil. If circumstance permitted, they practiced either shifting cultivation or an intensive pattern of crop rotation, both of which permitted the soil to regenerate itself. There were systems of water storage and management that were both scientific and efficient. The seeds issue has brought to the fore the variety of plant life and their uses in peasant societies, which was part of the knowledge system. Since the forests were their lifeblood, poor people knew how to use forests for food, fodder and medicinal herbs and permit nature to regenerate itself. They knew that extensive lumbering and felling of forests for the modern industrial sector and distant consumerism also would affect climate and rainfall (Vandana Shiva). This half forgotten body of knowledge is being revived in people's movements and struggles.

Similarly, the people had developed many cost effective preventive health systems, on the assumption that prevention was better than cure. Their holistic approach to life required them to be healthy; as sickness prevented them from producing and generating the income to meet their basic needs and those of their families. They knew how to balance work and leisure time, so that there was a continuous renewal of their creative energy. The Vedic knowledge system and the Yoga techniques that went with it for instance, reinforced this and helped to bring out human potential and capability that lay dormant in people (Iyenger 1966). Here too a great deal of modern scientific validation has been given to this cost effective health care practice. The impact of Yoga exercises and meditation techniques, using sound waves, which release stress and increase a person's creativity can be tested with the use of an encephalograph machine and the benefits analyzed by means of quantum physics and the vacuum state theory. These techniques are now bring widely disseminated in industrial countries and even being incorporated into the technology for survival in outer space, apart from its relevance for human development. Ayur-Veda, the six thousand year old Science of Life, practiced in India, is another such example. While not romanticizing the traditional knowledge system of the poor the argument here is essentially that this traditional knowledge was a process in which many people share. It is neither elitist nor eclectic. There is an element of experiential learning which became systematized, scientifically validated and was shared communally for sustainable development. The conclusion is inescapable that the sequence for reversing the adverse consequences of past development processes, would be to start with the traditional knowledge people have and build on it, drawing upon the wide range of technological choices available.

During the 1970s and 1980s in South Asia a number of institutions have emerged which are involved in participatory action research (PAR) for poverty eradication. The focus of their work was precisely to see how people's creativity and their knowledge system could be a basis of building countervailing power and to exert vigilance and correction over processes pertaining to the all round development of their lives and that of the communities in which they lived. This in turn related to the internal and external transformation and social change necessary for their survival and sustainable development. PAR combines scientific research, informal education and political action. It also implies creation of reliable knowledge for use in the process of transformation by committed action researchers and the vulnerable people themselves. The objective is to enable the poor and other vulnerable groups to bring about the social transformation at the micro level, primarily by their own actions. In the process they would first investigate and elaborate on their own perceptions of reality. Through collective interaction and learning from each other they sharpen their perceptions and understanding of their problems. Then they establish their priorities and find the solutions with their total knowledge and awareness.

There are four lessons from experience on how the people knowledge system can reinforce praxis and poverty eradication. First, the knowledge which people have can be retrieved. Some of this knowledge is in continuous usage, some of its is half forgotten, while some of it may be diffused, distorted and romanticized. This retrieval process itself has to evolve through an interaction between committed intellectuals and the people. Through analyzing people's experience, a collection of relative facts and factors, which are relevant and useful for overcoming the crisis of immediate survival or sustainable development, emerges. This then is systematized. Sometimes more sophisticated scientific validation and adaptation to emerging conditions may be required. This process illustrates that forms and relations of knowledge production have as much value as the forms and relations of material production. There are several aspects of this collective effort; at knowledge retrieval (Oriando Fals-Borda 1984) There is the collective effort of learning about ones reality. Information is pooled in-group dialogues. New data may also be obtained in the process. There is also a critical recovery of historical data. These are facts from history, which can reinforce the systematization of the knowledge base as it is today. Once this knowledge has been retrieved through collective investigation of the current reality, as well as, a critical recovery of history, it has to be systematized and given scientific validity through interaction between the de-professionalised experts and the people and through the new R and D systems that are emerging, whether at the local level or in umbrella institutions which are catalyzing and/or supporting the process.

Secondly after the knowledge is retrieved, systematized and validated in its own cultural setting, it has to be disseminated to those from whom the knowledge was retrieved often as part of one participatory process. This has to be done not only through the written world and in local languages, but also through the oral tradition of communication and other cultural practices such as street plays, poetry and other forms of culturally relevant expression related to human sentiment and imagination. Retrieval, systematization and dissemination has to be seen as a part of a continuum. Today, audiovisual forms with modern technology could also be selectively used to reach wider audiences as part of the conscientisation ands awareness building process. These stages are not seen as separate from research. Poor people investigate their reality and there is a continuous feed back and built in evaluation, which then feeds into the subsequent action. The totality represents PAR. This is another element in the process from which further lessons can be learnt. The discussion will then move from investigation, action research, and the critical recovery of the knowledge system to the question of organization for further collective reflection and action and the role of the external and internal animator in the process.

Though Praxis and the methodology of PAR releases the creative energy of people, brings out the knowledge system and sets in motion an ecologically sound socio-political dynamics within each culture, which can lead to a new kind of transitional pathway to sustainable development. It could also be the precursor to building a new kind of State structure, which should be participatory, pluralist, truly democratic. This support system also helps in the further multiplication of the process in a non-alienating manner. These do not follow the conventional socialist or capitalist state formations nor the traditions of institutions of the "representative" parliamentary democracy or bureaucratic type. It promotes a new kind of committed leadership both external and internal; and an open state system based on freely communicated knowledge with the micro-level organizations providing a countervailing force. In other words, PAR looks to a better sharing of power, a better balance between the state and peoples organizations and of course between people and nature.

These socio-political tasks, which are intended, both the reverse past processes and moves through a transition to sustainable development cannot be planned through conventional top down planning methodologies, which are too prescriptive. In dealing with an open social system, which is complex and unpredictable, a great deal of flexibility is required. There are targets, but not fixed in a rigid project oriented manner; there is a continuum of self-corrective activities with internal evaluation. The process of mobilization, conscientisation and organization is a continuous one. Progress is not in a liner fashion, there is forward momentum and setbacks and conflicts. Ecological factors and natural resources may provide positive or negative influences. However, the people persist in an action reflection action process based on their values and the total knowledge system until the goals are achieved. This is how people's knowledge becomes people's power, and this in turn influences participatory development.

Section 6: Knitting Together

In concluding and knitting together the fundamentals of poverty eradication in South Asia, three assertions are made for consideration by those committed to meeting this challenge.

The first relates to the need of or a New School of Thought, incorporating the fundamentals. The path to this lies by synthesizing the commonalities in the vast number of lessons of experience from the ground and their implications for a transitional strategy for eradicating the worst forms of poverty in South Asia in a given time frame, leaving only a residual numbers to be carried by welfare, safety nets and charity. The distinguishing characteristics of this New School of Thought will be its cultural relevance and rootedness in the values of the poor. It will be pluralistic and inclusive of all communities and groups in a universal at sense. It will have a coherence resulting from a common methodology and a rigorous approach towards mobilization, conscientisation and organization of the poor as subjects in the process of development. The political approach and transformative momentum would help secure the process from becoming soft, technocratic and eclectic.

The second assertion relates to the need for a New School Contract between the State and the Poor in South Asia. The failures of the past and disarray in development thinking and action require a major new inspirational drive and dynamic which can create a basis for bringing diverse social forces and communities into new partnership. The Social Contract is the only instrument, which can help regenerate the trust, which has been eroded. This Social Contract is premised on going beyond the old social contract between Management and Labour, the Keynesian Consensus, which led to the Welfare State and the current discussion on a SAARC Social Charter. The Dhaka Consensus on Eradication of Poverty by the Year 2002 taken at the Dhaka SAARC Summit of 1993 and repeated at the SAARC Summits of 1995 and 1997 was not an end in itself. It was the first step in the New Social Contract between the State and the Poor in South Asia. It was envisaged that this Social Contract should incorporate culturally relevant values such as 'sharing and caring' and also the Right to Food and the Right to Work. Such a Social Contract would enable the States of South Asia to replace the welfare state concept with a more inspiring concept which could also help to mitigate the violence and multifaceted crises in the Region and within individual SAARC countries.

The third assertion relates to the significance of the New Social Movements emerging from the ground in every South Asian country in the past twenty-five years. The new social movements can provide the material bases for both the New School of Thought and the New Social Contract. These New Social Movements differ from the old social movements, which were engaged in anti colonial struggles, the trade union action and party politics. These new movements represent a new group of actors interested not in State power, as such, but in creating people's power where a participatory democratic society is the persistent quest. Larger and larger members of people are no longer willing to accept fatalistic, exploitative, alienating or repressive regimes and state structures, or a development paradigm a form of countervailing power. In these new movements they are also demonstrating ways to humanize the larger macro processes and asserting that the terms of incorporation into the mainstream can be changed at all levels.

It is sufficient to say that both the social movements and experiments are mobilizing, conscientising and organizing people for social transformation in one form or another at particular levels. The people's responses and experiments, even if they may not always achieve the proportions of a movement, have a varied mix of activities, ideologies, operational methodologies and scales. They also have things in common in that they attempt to empower the poor and vulnerable in one-way or another. Some start with protests against the system and others start with small development activities with differing entry points and then assume movement proportions.

Several positive lessons may be drawn from the wide variety of new social movements and micro-level grassroots experiments. The movements are the result of broader-based people's responses to ecological, ethnic or gender conflicts. The micro-level experiments are not homogeneous and differ in their origins. Some are the result of romantic and idealistic approaches taken by charitable institutions, religious organizations, the "small is beautiful" advocates etc., which have tried to teach the people to do 'good' things, often treating the village as a harmonious entity or 'community'. These groups then may link together to form a movement or to reinforce a protest action. Some of the people's movements have been sustained over time; others are eruptions and die down after a while. Some experiments represent real seeds of change; others are mere ephemeral bubbles.

In recent times, the new democracy movements and people's struggles in evidence in all South Asian countries, have been dramatic countervailing responses to repressive regimes and military dictatorships. Ecological movements such as Chipko to the Narmada Andolen in India and people's movements against the commercial destruction of rain forests, and other kinds of economic development that are predatory on nature help build countervailing power. The women's movements in nearly all South Asian countries and their impact on gender and equity issues are equally significant. Smaller development experiments that demonstrate how people cope simultaneously with the multiple crises in their lives locally survive and move on, through their own efforts, to dignity and improve their quality of life, are also increasingly evident. Social movements and experiments may arise spontaneously or be initiated and multiplied by sensitive external facilitators and local change agents. Sometimes they have a charismatic leader. They may be protest and/or damage-limiting responses, or they may be positive development actions. In some instances, these two types of activity link to build new coalitions. Macro-level democracy movements need to be reinforced with micro-level development actions and deeply rooted in people's lives. Some movements evolve in a zigzag fashion. But the fact is that these social movements and experiments, as a new socio-political phenomenon and a new socio-political force, have come to stay and can no longer be ignored.

The question then is, can they achieve greater coherence and sustainability? This question not only brings us back to the other two assertions, i.e., the need for a more coherent New School of Thought to provide the intellectual underpinnings and the New Social Contract which can provide the political space to initiate a more orderly an manageable transition in South Asia.

References

Development Dialogue (1977:2), and the Follow-up Study Published in *Development Dialogue*, 1979:2, under the title Bhoomi Sen–A Struggle for People's Power", These were Later Published in De Silva et.al. *Towards a Theory of Rural Development*, Progressive Publishers, Pakistan 1988.

Gourie Ponnaiah (1989), "Ideology and the Status" of Hindu Women in the Challenge in South Asia: Development, Ponna Wignaraja, Akmal Hussain (eds.), *Democracy and Regional Co-operation*, Sage Publications, India.

Gourie Ponnaiah (1989), "Ideology and the Status of Women in Hindu Society" in Ponna Wignaraja and Akmal Hussain (ed.), *The Challenge in South Asia: Development, Democracy and Regional Co-operation, Sage Publications*, New Delhi/Newbury Park/London.

Iyengar, B.K.S. (1966), *Light on Yoga*, George Allen and Unwin Ltd., London.

Oriando Fals-Pordo (1984), "How to Learn, Participatory Action Research", *Development4*, No. 2, Rome, p. 18.

Rajagopalachari, C. (1968), *Mahabharata*, Bharatiya Vidya Bhavan, Bombay: 'The Mahabharata Further States: The Knowledge, that is Merely so much Indigested Information Crammed into the mind, cannot Instill Virtue', p. 1221.

SAARC Secretariat (1992), *Report of the Independent South Asian Commission on Poverty Alleviation: Meeting the Challenge*, Kathmandu, Nepal, November.

SAPNA (South Asian Perspectives Network Association), means Dream/Vision/Perspective in all South Asian languages. SAPNA is an Association, which permits South Asians to think collectively on South Asian problems. See SAPNA progress.

Shiva, Vandana (1989), "Two Kinds of Rationality", *Staying Alive,* New Delhi: Zed Books, p. 29.

Shiva Vandana (1989), "Women in the Forest", *Staying Alive*, Zed Books, New Delhi, p. 55.

Wigńaraja, P. (1953), "The Conflict Between Economic Rationality and Cultural Values", Brussels, Civilizations, Vol. 3, No. 1, p. 53.

Ibid.

Ibid.(1989), "The Knowledge System", and D.L. Sheth, "Catalyzing Alternative Development Values, The Knowledge System, Power", in *The Challenge in South Asia.*

Ibid. (1989), "Towards a new Praxis for Sustainable Development in South Asia" in Ponna Wignaraja and Akmal Hussain (ed.), *The Challenge in South Asia: Development, Democracy and Regional Co-operation*, India: Sage Publications.

Ibid., p. 61.

Ibid., (1993).

2

Beyond Cancun: Some Proposals for Reform of the World Trading System

Nagesh Kumar

Section 1: Significance of Cancun

The completion of the Uruguay Round of multilateral trade negotiations with the setting up of WTO to succeed GATT in 1995 marked an important turning point for the world economy. What started as a process of trade liberalization under GATT has come to embrace broader parameters of policy hitherto subject to decision-making at the national levels. The Ministerial Conferences of WTO generate a lot of interest among the policy makers and the civil society, given the importance of decisions taken for the development prospects and people's lives in the member countries. The collapse of the Cancun Ministerial Conferences of WTO in September 2003 generated a lot of heat as had its preparatory process. It is not for the first time that a Ministerial Meeting in GATT/WTO failed to reach an agreement. However, there was a crucial difference. This time, it has collapsed because of a sharp polarization on the North-South lines. Three subsequent meetings of the General Council have not been able to break the impasse and bring the process back on the track. Some observers term this collapse as a catastrophe for the world economy while others think that this outcome is better than a bad deal. So the judgment depends on which side of the development spectrum one is. Cancun has helped served a good purpose of highlighting the emerging asymmetries in the world trading system and in the process of decision-making that further perpetuate these. At last, developing countries managed to build their effective coalitions and hold together till the end despite heavy pressure exerted by the world's biggest economic and political powers and stopped them from pushing their agenda. Therefore, Cancun heralds a new beginning for the multilateral trade negotiations.

Section 2: Growing Asymmetries in the World Trading System

The following is the summary of some the asymmetries that have cropped up in the world trading system.

The purpose and objective of the multilateral trade negotiations (MTNs) is to liberalize trade so that efficiency gains become available to the world economy at large. However, it has been recognized that there are unequal players in the game and developing countries are limited in their financial and physical capacities to undertake equal commitments. They need flexibilities to pursue their development policy objectives that have been available to developed countries in the early stages of their development. Hence, the concept of special and differential treatment (S&DT) to developing countries on a non-reciprocal basis was built into the process.

The Uruguay Round placed substantial obligations on developing countries with respect to the liberalization of trade. Developing countries undertook commitments to expand tariff bindings to cover 61 per cent of their imports compared to 13 per cent earlier and have offered $ 15 billion worth of concessions by way of reducing their trade-weighted average bound tariff on imports from industrialized countries by 28 per cent. They were also made to accept commitments to liberalize their policy regimes with respect to intellectual property rights, investments, and trade in services.

Developing countries were lured into accepting these substantial commitments by the promise of additional market access to them by developed countries through liberalization of agricultural trade, textiles and clothing and movement of natural persons. The gains from the UR proposals of liberalization in these areas were estimated to the tune of US$ 213 to US$ 510 billion-a-year rise in world income with developing countries benefiting to the tune of $86 to $122 billion. Contrary to these claims, it has now been empirically shown that much deeper commitments have been undertaken by developing countries in the UR and the mercantilist balance resulting from trade liberalization has been in favour of developed countries. The UR Agreements, such as TRIPS and TRIMS, are leading to significant income transfers from developing countries besides reducing the policy space for development. The S&DT provisions have been considerably diluted and reduced to just longer transitions for implementation.

The developed countries while preaching the virtues of free trade to developing countries have been resistant to bringing down peak tariffs, high specific duties, and tariff escalation that affect imports from developing countries. A startling example is the fact that tariffs collected by the US on $2 billion worth of imports from Bangladesh are higher than those imposed on imports worth $30 billion from France.

The market access commitments in textiles and clothing have been backloaded and only about 20 per cent of imports under specific quota restrictions have been liberalized in the seven years of implementation till 2002. The agriculture trade liberalization in developed countries has been undermined by dirty tariffication. The average applied tariff rates applicable to agricultural products compared to those in industrial goods have been higher by 641 per cent in Japan, by 353 per cent in the EU, and by 100 per cent in the US.

Despite the promise of improved market access in the services of interest to developing countries, very few commitments have been made by developed countries in Mode 4. Furthermore, almost all these commitments are subject to limitations, such as economic needs test that usually render them ineffective. New barriers to movement of natural persons are being evolved in different parts of the world, such as legislations outlawing business process outsourcing. Studies have found staggering welfare losses for the world economy from the protected markets for labour. Even a limited liberalization of labour markets covering just 3 per cent of work force has the potential to generate welfare gains of US$ 156 billion per year, according to recent studies.

There has been continued resort to quotas and other NTBs. As many as 30 per cent tariff lines in basic metal industries in the US, for instance, are subject to core NTBs. There has been a proliferation of NTBs in the form of environmental and food safety standards much higher than the internationally agreed norms. There has been increased resort to contingent protection against developing countries. There is a proliferation of regional and bilateral free trade arrangements in the developed world that are diverting trade and investments away from developing countries.

There seems to be a protectionist backlash in the developed countries inspired from the strategic trade policy aiming to strengthen the competitiveness of their national champions at the cost of sustainable and equitable growth of world trade. While heavy subsidization of developed country agriculture has become well known from the ongoing debates in the context of WTO's Agreement on Agriculture, the continued and rising subsidization of industrial sector remains virtually unnoticed. Not only have developed countries exploited the gray areas available in the multilateral rules, they have included exceptions for the kind of policies and practices that they wish to make use of such as R&D subsidies. The US has been giving US$ 4 billion in subsidies to the exporting enterprises under the Foreign Sales Corporations (FSC). These subsidies have been deemed illegal by the WTO's Panel on a complaint brought by the EU. These are now being replaced by even bigger tax cuts worth US$ 120 billion over the ten years for companies having manufacturing bases in the US.

The agricultural subsidies too are growing despite the promises of reduction made in the Uruguay Round and the Doha Declaration. The US has announced the most generous farm subsidy package in history in its Farm Bill 2002. Arguments like multi-functionality are made to justify ever increasing agricultural subsidies. Even export subsidies (called export credits in the US) are not reduced.

While trade related performance requirements such as local content regulations have been phased out under TRIMS Agreement, developed countries extensively resort to policies like screw driver regulations, rules of origin, buy local regulations that are akin to local content regulations.

The process is not leading to growth of world trade either. Quantitative studies do not find the process of GATT/WTO to be leading to either trade liberalization or growth of trade. The developing countries, with the exception of China, have not been able to increase their share in world trade. The terms of trade of developing countries have deteriorated. As a result of these trends, the growth rates in a large number of countries in 1990s has been lower than in the 1980s and inequalities have risen in a large number of developing and transition economies.

This situation is in sharp contrast to the avowed goals of the WTO as set out in the preamble to the Marrakesh Agreement recognizing the 'need for positive efforts designed to ensure that developing countries...secure a share in the growth in international trade commensurate with the needs of their economic development... mutually advantageous arrangement directed to the substantial reduction of tariffs and other barriers to trade and to the discriminating treatment in international trade.'

Section 3: Asymmetric Process of Decision-Making

The Doha Ministerial Conference attempted to restore the emphasis on development in the WTO. The Doha Declaration called for positive efforts to ensure developing countries benefiting from enhanced market access and balanced rules. In substantive terms, the highlights of the Doha Agenda included a commitment in the area of agriculture to substantially improve market access, progress towards phasing-out of all forms of export subsidies and substantial reduction of trade distorting domestic support. It also accepted the primacy of public health concerns and offered to provide flexibility to poorer countries from the provisions of TRIPS Agreement to import cheaper generic medicines. In the area of market access for industrial products, commitments were made to eliminate or reduce peak tariffs, high tariffs, tariff escalation and NTBs, in particular, on products of export interest to developing countries. Commitments were also made to review the S&DT provisions for developing countries to make them more precise, effective and operational.

However, the progress since the Doha Ministerial has been far from satisfactory. Almost all the deadlines proposed, that were important from the point of view of developing countries, were missed. The draft modalities for market access in agricultural as well non-agricultural goods that were proposed by developed countries suggested that the principle of less-than-full-reciprocity as enshrined in the Doha Mandate had been undermined. On the other hand, developing countries were being pushed to agree to give the negotiating mandate on the Singapore Issues at the Cancun Ministerial.

The highhanded attitude of developed countries prompted developing countries to form issue-based coalitions to protect their interests at the Cancun Ministerial Conference held to advance the Doha Agenda. On the Singapore Issues, for instance, a Group of 16 countries led by Malaysia with the support of 30 least developed countries in a submission to the Conference firmly opposed a negotiating mandate. The group of 74 African, Caribbean and Pacific (ACP) countries also registered a negotiating mandate on these issues. In utter disregard to these submissions backed by nearly 80 developing countries, the revised draft Ministerial Text issued on 13th September (Derbez Text), proposed to give negotiating mandate on all of these issues except for Competition. Competition was dropped because of unwillingness of one of the quad countries to negotiate it. It was clear who were calling the shots. From a development point of view, the Draft Ministerial Text proposed the worst possible combination namely to have binding international rules on investment but not on competition. Expectedly, developing countries heavily criticized the draft Ministerial Text.

Similarly on agriculture, developing countries led by Brazil had formed a coalition of 17 countries that had submitted a counter proposal in Geneva to the US-EU proposal, which eventually grew to 20 countries (G-20). The Derbez text on agriculture too tended to follow the US-EU proposals in most part and completely ignoring the alternative proposals put on the table by G-20. In addition, a group of four West and Central African countries was seeking elimination of extensive subsidies given in the US to cotton farmers that was leading to starvation of cotton farmers in these countries. This group was also received support from a number of countries including India. However, Derbez Text was silent on these demands.

It is clear, therefore, that the process of preparation of the draft Ministerial Texts or the decision-making is highly asymmetric. It systematically takes on board only the proposals and views articulated by the quad countries (viz., the US, EU, Canada and Japan) and neglecting the widely shared views of developing countries. Therefore, a reform of the world trading system and the process of decision-making is necessary if the system is not to further perpetuate the growing asymmetries and erode its long-term sustainability itself.

Section 4: Some Issues for Reform of World Trade Architecture

The continuing stalemate in the trade talks gives an opportunity to the international community to pause and undertake a thorough reform of the world trading system. A list a few suggestions for reform of the world trading system of broader nature before addressing select sectoral issues is given below.

An Independent Commission to Make a Development Review of the Multilateral Trading System

The developing countries should call for appointment of an Independent Commission to review the developmental consequences of Uruguay and Doha Rounds before moving forward. This Commission should identify asymmetries that have crept into the system and recommend directions of reform of the priorities, procedures and rules to giving a real meaning to development on the trade agenda. This should be a high powered Independent Commission appointed by the WTO Members comprising respected eminent experts from different parts of the world to have credibility, influence and authority for action and suggesting a thorough reform of the system.

Reform of Decision-making Process

The decision-making process in WTO clearly needs a reform for its long-term sustainability. The general perception is that the decision-making process in WTO is non-transparent, and not inclusive. The will of a handful of powerful countries viz., Quad countries, is imposed on the entire membership in the name of 'Consensus'. In an organization whose membership comprises of countries at varying levels of development, their concerns and interests are expected to be different. Obviously these differences limit the possibilities of arriving at a consensus. In order to arrive at the 'consensus' sometimes-powerful members push relatively poorer members to accept their position by several means including diplomacy and even arm-twisting.

Members have also complained of the lack of participation in decision-making process where informal consultations between few powerful players have far greater influence on WTO decision-making than the formal processes. A more democratic system of decision-making baaed on secret voting and decision based on majority would serve the organization better and make it more participatory. All negotiating texts and drafts should be introduced in open-ended meetings and late night meetings and marathon sessions should be avoided. No decisions should be imposed on members without wide consultations and discussions. Chairpersons drafts should be representative of all the interventions. The Ministers may consider changing the statute to bring about this profound change in the decision-making process in the interest of its long-term survival.

Broad based and Representative Secretariat

Given the large stakes of different players in the multilateral trading system, vested interests begin to operate. In this context the role of the Secretariat becomes critical. It has some times been observed that Secretariat is not discharging it role with the kind of objectivity that it should be. As of now the WTO Secretariat is highly dominated by the developed countries. More than 80 per cent of the staff members of the Secretariat came from the OECD countries with over 61 per cent coming from just six developed countries, viz., France, the UK, the US, and Canada, Spain and Switzerland. There is hardly any representation from a large number of developing counties. It is important that the WTO Secretariat has a proportionate representation of developed and developing countries. A more representative Secretariat will be able to discharge its mandate much more objectively.

A WTO Watch Dog of Developing Countries

Developing countries, individually, lack the capacity–physical, analytical and financial–to identify and pursue the cases of non-implementation or unilateral policy decisions concerning trade policy on the part of developed countries and s eek their reddresal under the existing framework. The recent case of the trade distorting export subsidy valued at $4 billion under Foreign Sales Corporations (FSC) by the US government which was successfully brought by the EU to the DSB is a case in point. Needless to mention that no developing country possesses the capability to do the same. There is a need for setting up a WTO Watchdog by developing countries. In the interest of building a fair and just world trading system, developed countries should create a trust fund for maintaining the WTO Watchdog. This body should be equipped with the necessary professional, analytical, legal and financial expertise to scrutinize the implementation of commitments by developed countries and where appropriate to bring them to DSB on behalf of developing countries.

Strengthening the Provision of Technical Assistance

Developing country implementation of their commitments often implies major changes in their legal and institutional framework and involves substantial technical and financial resources that may be beyond the capability of many countries. In this regard it is often being felt that the WTO should provide major technical and financial assistance not only to least-developed countries but also to the developing countries for implementation of their commitments in an effective manner. So far the experience with technical assistance has not been satisfactory. Generally the technical assistance provisions included in the Agreements are treated only as the best endeavour clauses. The funds committed by developed countries to the WTO's Trust Fund for Technical Assistance and the Joint Integrated Technical Assistance Programme (JITAP) to be modest. These funds need to be augmented. The provisions of technical assistance should be made more effective by linking the implementation of standards.

It is often being observed that developing countries are often better placed to help and cooperate with fellow developing countries than any other countries from the developed pat of the world. However, owing to lack of resources the potential for South-South cooperation has remained untapped. In this regard, adopting a different strategy of trilateral cooperation may help to a great extent. In this a multilateral agency or a donor agency from North may step into support technical assistance among developing countries.

Section 5: Select Sectoral Issues

The developing country concerns regarding select major sectoral issues on the WTO agenda is furnished below

Singapore Issues

The effort of developed countries in WTO has been towards expansion of negotiating agenda since its inception. At the first ever Ministerial Conference of WTO, held in Singapore in 1996, itself they demanded the negotiating mandate of WTO be broadened to include trade and investment, trade and competition policy, government procurement, trade facilitation, labour standards and environmental standards. Having undertaken heavy commitments in the just concluded Uruguay Round, developing countries resisted these demands. As a part of the compromise arrived, Working Groups were set up at the WTO on investment, competition policy, and transparency in government procurement to conduct study processes without any negotiating mandate. The Council for Trade in Goods was also directed by the Ministerial Conference to undertake exploratory and analytical work on the simplification of trade procedures in order to assess the scope for WTO rules in this area. Developing countries managed to put labour standards and environment off the WTO agenda for the time being.

These so-called Singapore issues, viz., investment, competition policy, government procurement, and trade facilitation, were the most contentious ones at the Doha Ministerial. Even though the Working Groups set up on these issues by WTO at the Singapore Ministerial have not completed their work, the developed countries wanted to launch negotiations right away. Developing countries resisted a negotiating mandate and wanted the Working Groups to complete their assigned work prior to negotiations. After many deliberations, developing countries succeeded in postponing the decision on the launch of negotiations on these issues subject to an 'explicit consensus' on the modalities of negotiations.

Although the four issues are unrelated and raise different types of concerns, they are being bundled together. However, there are similarities in the sense that the North-South divide is quite apparent in each case. Secondly, in most cases there is a wide divergence of views even among the developed countries themselves. Debates at the Working Groups on the subject over the past six-seven years have failed to produce a consensus and establish conclusively the need for binding rules.

Investment has been one of the most contentious area among the Singapore issues. Here developed countries seek to write trade type multilateral framework for treatment of foreign investments including national treatment, MFN and transparency, among other provisions. There is a conceptual basis for trade liberalization on the principle of comparative advantage where countries with different comparative advantages benefit from trading mutually.

On the other hand, FDI flows emerge because of differences in the levels of development and bundles of created assets of national enterprises. From the start, therefore, MNE entrants enjoy an edge over local enterprises. There is hardly any conceptual basis for national treatment given to foreign enterprises. FDI, like domestic investment, is a development and industrialization issue rather than a trade issue. That WTO lacks competence to deal with the investment and development is clear from the fact that the Working Group on Trade and Investment set up as per the Singapore Meeting in 1996 has not been able to complete its work so far.

Countries at different levels of development receive different types of FDI, for instance, an underdeveloped country will attract resource-seeking or labour-seeking inward FDI and investments in capital and intermediate goods industries in subsequent stages. The one-size-fits-all approach to FDI evolved through MFI in WTO cannot serve the best interests of countries at different levels of development. Studies find a critical role of host governments' interventions such as selective policies and performance requirements in determining the developmental impact of FDI or the quality of FDI flows. Evidence on extensive use of such policies by developed countries in different stages of development has also been documented. Developed countries themselves were not willing to agree to unhindered national treatment to foreign investments under the OECD's proposed Multilateral Agreement on Investment as is clear from a list of over 700 exceptions appended to the draft treaty. A multilateral regime will take away the ability of the hosts governments' to direct FDI in accordance with their development policy objectives and thus will affect the overall 'quality' of FDI follows.

Proponents of a WTO rules on investment argue that such a framework would help developing countries to increase their attractiveness to foreign investors. However, as numerous empirical studies have shown, FDI inflows are largely driven by the gravity factors such as market size, income levels, the extent of urbanization, geographical and cultural proximity with the major source countries of FDI, and the quality of infrastructure. The policy factors or investment treaties play a relatively minor role if at all. The US is the most important source of FDI in China and Brazil even though they do not have even a bilateral investment treaty with the US.

A general impression that is created by the protagonists is that an adequate framework for protection of investment and dispute settlement does not exist. There exists an elaborate framework for investment protection and dispute settlement at the bilateral as well as multilateral levels. Besides an extensive network of about 2100 bilateral investment promotion and protection agreements or treaties (BIPAs or BITs), multilateral instruments for protection and guarantee of international investments do exist viz., the Multilateral Investment Guarantee Agency (MIGA), the International Convention of Settlement of Investment Disputes (ICSID), the UN Committee on International Trade Law (UNCITRAL), and the International Chamber of Commerce (ICC).

Proponents of MFI are seeking to protect only the rights of investors or corporations and nothing is being proposed in terms of their obligations or any other provisions for protection of host country interests. While the ability of the host governments to impose performance obligations is sought to be curbed, that of corporations to impose restrictive clauses on their subsidiaries that are often trade distorting, is not regulated. An ideal accord would have to have symmetry between rights and obligations of host as well as home governments and investors. However, the proposals made by six developing countries including India, China, Pakistan among others, seeking investors/and home country interests to balance the framework attracted a sharp reaction from developed countries.

Given the little experience that developing countries have in dealing with competition policy even at the national level, it is premature to consider a multilateral framework. There is also divergence of views even among developed countries on the subject especially with some countries seeking only a non-binding voluntary framework for cooperation among competition authorities. Developing countries also have genuine development concerns in implementing competition policies.

Transparency in government procurement seems to be an intermediate step in evolving a framework providing national treatment. Binding rules on the subject may thus take away valuable development policy space from governments. Similarly, there is hardly any rationale for binding rules in the case of trade facilitation either. Technical assistance and autonomous policy decisions should be preferred over binding rules which will put heavy burden of compliance on developing countries.

Therefore, there is very little rationale to support a negotiating mandate on any of the Singapore issues at the WTO. There does not seem to be an emerging consensus even among the developed countries. For instance, the US does not favour a negotiating mandate on competition. In the post-Cancun discussions in Geneva, a number of developing countries such as Mexico and Indonesia have argued for completely dropping the Singapore Issues off the WTO agenda. This seems to be the best course of action as of now for developing countries at large. In the face of growing resistance from developing countries on these issues at Cancun, the main proponent of these issues at WTO was willing to drop 'two or even three of the four' issues leaving only trade facilitation. EU should stand by its position in future negotiations.

Agriculture

The basic concern on agriculture has been the attempt of developed countries to secure market access in developing countries for their agricultural exports while resisting to phase-out of the domestic support and export subsidies that they give to their farmers. The agricultural subsidies in the OECD countries have grown and now add up to nearly 31 per cent of the value of agricultural output. While developed countries are so much concerned for protecting only 3 to 5 per cent of their population that is dependent upon agriculture with highly distorting subsidies, they went developing countries to drastically bring down the tariff barriers that developing countries use to protect their small and marginal farmers dependent on agriculture for their livelihood. In 50 developing countries more than half of the population is critically dependent on agriculture for livelihood. Countries with such high dependence on agriculture for livelihood should get a special dispensation under S&DT provisions in agriculture. Unless the distortions caused by domestic support and export subsidies given by developed countries cannot be removed, developing countries cannot afford to put the livelihood of their poor masses at risk. Hence, an ambitious approach to phase-out of subsidies in developed countries hold the key for agricultural trade liberalization. Developed countries, on the other hand, are trying to get away with much lower ambition on subsidy reduction while having much higher level of ambition in respect of tariff reduction, as was clear from the US-EU proposals, which found their way in the Derbez Text.

Non-Agricultural Market Access

A major concern of developing countries with the process of trade liberalization for non-agricultural products in the Uruguay Round has been the persistence of high and peak tariffs, specific duties, tariff escalation and non-tariff barriers in developed countries on goods their export interest. It has also been shown that process of trade liberalization has been asymmetric with developing countries taking deeper commitments compared to developed countries. The Doha Ministerial Conference sought to address this asymmetry by proposing negotiations on the market access for non-agricultural goods on the basis of the modalities to be agreed by May 2003 to eliminate barriers to market access in particular on products of export interest to developing countries. Subsequently, a Negotiating Group on Market Access (NGMA) has been set up at the WTO and different countries have presented proposals on modalities for trade liberalization. Following these proposals, the Chairman of NGMA had proposed draft modalities in May 2003 and on 19 August 2003. Broadly the approach to modalities proposed by developed countries was to undermine the concept of less-than-full-reciprocity and seeking sharper reduction in tariff rates in developing countries using non-linear formulae. As endorsed in the Doha mandate, the principle of "less-than-full-reciprocity" needs to be respected in any future negotiations on the modalities of tariff reduction.

Intellectual Property Rights

The international environment with respect to intellectual property has changed considerably with the conclusion of the TRIPs Agreement in the Uruguay Round. The TRIPs Agreement accommodates the demands of the industrialized countries for higher international standards of protection by mandating the extension of patent ability to virtually all fields of technology recognized in developed country patent systems, by prolonging the patent protection for a uniform term of twenty years, and by providing legal recognition of the patentee's exclusive rights to import the patented products.

Besides its wide-ranging adverse effects on the technological capability, balance of payments and economic growth of developing countries, the implementation of TRIPs has created an anomalous situation where the knowledge created from traditional and communities innovation systems is left free for commercial exploitation without any compensation as against intellectual property resulting from formal innovation systems being protected from unauthorized commercial exploitation. This resulted in private enterprises obtaining patents on the traditional knowledge of particular communities/countries without the prior informed consent of the owners of knowledge. Developing countries, which happen to be rich in genetic resources and traditional knowledge, have been seeking a redressal of this asymmetry. In recognition of this concern the Doha Ministerial instructed the Council for TRIPs to examine 'the relationship between the TRIPs Agreement and the convention on Biological Diversity, the protection of traditional knowledge and folklore'. The TRIPs Agreement needs to be amended to provide a framework for prior informed consent of the holders of traditional knowledge or biological resources and a system of benefit sharing.

Section 6: Conclusion

An Agenda for Cooperation among Developing Countries is provided in the following:

> The emerging WTO regime has important implications for the national development, trade, investment and technology policies of member countries. The ongoing round of negotiations will have an important bearing on the developmental process of the developing countries. Therefore, the developing countries need to deliberate over the mandate given by the Ministerial Meetings and prepare themselves to take part in the ensuing negotiations effectively to safeguard their interests. Issues of preparedness on their part would also include taking advantage of the emerging multilateral regime rather than passively implementing their commitments. This calls for strategic thinking and concerted action at different levels.

Not only do developing countries lack strong analytical capabilities in fully comprehending the developmental implications of the commitments implicit in the negotiations, the situation is further complicated by the mis-information that is promoted by developed countries to achieve their strategic objectives. Very often the training courses offered by international organizations in the name of technical assistance are also influenced by the viewpoint of the donors, viz., the developed countries and fail to highlight the concerns of developing countries. A list a few areas for mutual cooperation among the developing countries in general and South Asian countries in particular is presented below.

Exchange of Experiences

Exchange of experiences and professional expertise among developing countries may facilitate full exploitation of the policy spaces that may be available in the WTO Agreements. An example in this regard is the TRIPs Agreement where several flexibilities are available to be exploited to moderate the potential adverse effect of the Agreement such as provisions for compulsory licensing, research exception, Bolar provisions, gray market imports, anti-trust regulations, breeders exceptions, among others.

Technical Assistance and Cooperation in Implementation or Compliance of Commitments

Compliance with emerging high SPS/TBT standards for instance is becoming an important factor in export competitiveness. The compliance with these standards entails huge technical and financial costs. Cooperation among developing countries may be in sharing the services of experts, setting up the common testing and verification laboratories, translations of standards, etc.

Effective Coordination of Positions

Cancun has demonstrated the crucial importance of coordination of positions by developing countries. After all the WTO negotiations are power games. Any coordination between developing countries at the issue level or regional levels would be more effective than individual country positions. Developing countries should establish communications among their respective trade ministries and their missions at WTO to facilitate such coordination.

Vigilance and Active Participation in the Proceedings

Given the high stakes involved, developing countries need to participate in the negotiations effectively and with extreme vigilance. They need to back up their preparations with adequate legal and analytical expertise. Introduction of small phrases, which may appear innocuous, may eventually lead to some burdensome commitment, as is clear from the example how a reference to counterfeit goods in the Punta del Este Declaration snowballed into the TRIPs Agreement.

Proactive Agenda

Developing countries generally confine themselves to defensive and reactive strategy. They should have their own positive and proactive agenda. They should identify and articulate their concerns with the asymmetries creeping into the multilateral trading system and seek their redressal with effective coalition building. Some of the proactive measures that they can seek, for instance, include framework agreements on movement of natural persons, on transfer of technology and on special and differential treatment.

Promotion of South-South Trade

Developing countries could also evolve their own approaches for promoting mutual trade at multilateral, regional, sub-regional or bilateral levels to exploit their synergies for mutual benefit. Developing countries in different part of the world have evolved regional economic integration schemes. In South Asia now two schemes of regional trade liberalization have been signed viz., SAFTA and the BIMSTEC FTA recently besides a number of bilateral deals. These are certainly desirable. In addition must be paid to revitalization of the Global System of Trade Preferences (GSTP) for promoting South-South trade.

PART - II
WTO and South Asian Agriculture

3

The WTO and South Asian Agriculture: Key Issues and Policy Interventions

B. Yerram Raju & K.C. Reddy

Section 1: Introduction

The implementation of the WTO rule-based multilateral trade is proving to be much more difficult than was anticipated in December 1993 when the Uruguay Round of trade negotiations ended. The failure of the Fifth Ministerial held at Cancun, Mexico in September 2003 to carry forward the agenda of the Doha Development Round of trade talks launched in November 2001, highlighted the deep divisions among the 148 member countries from across the world.

The present economic environment is also not conducive to any radical change in the position of major trading countries on key issues. The growth of the global economy has been slowing down since 2001, with countries like USA, Germany and Japan either in different stages of a recession or still on the threshold of a weak recovery. World trade grew at only 2.5 per cent in 2002 and is expected to remain below 3 per cent in 2003-04, as the prospects for a robust global economic recovery are not very bright by present indicators.

The WTO's Agreement on Agriculture (AoA) is at the center of most of the conflicts in the WTO trade talks as agriculture is the core issue for most of the member countries, three-fourths of whom are developing countries. The future of the agricultural trade talks will have a direct impact on the livelihoods of over two billion people, dependent on the agricultural sector throughout the world.

South Asian Agriculture has peculiar politico-economic dimensions and ethnic and cultural issues accompanying them. Unfortunately, many of them did not receive due consideration from the beginning of the Uruguay dialogue. In India, several State governments whose understanding was crucial for certain commitments that followed negotiations were kept in the dark. This paper looks at some of the policy approaches and issues involved in preparing the agricultural sector of India to face the emerging challenges of trade liberalization in the context of WTO and AoA. Section 2 gives an overview of global agricultural trade in the context of WTO and AoA. Section 3 turns to the key issues and constraints facing the agricultural sector. Section 4 outlines policy interventions to reshape the agricultural sector in the context of the emerging economic environment and the WTO's international trade regime and conclusion is provided in section 5.

Section 2. Key Issues in World Agricultural Trade[1]

The Agreement on Agriculture

The WTO's AoA was aimed at removing some of the present distortions in agricultural production and trade by restricting market-distorting government interventions by member-countries in these two areas. These objectives of the AoA are to be achieved through reductions in domestic support and export subsidies by developed and developing countries at specified levels over specified time periods; and increasing market access through phased tariff reductions on agricultural commodities. These measures are to be implemented over a six to ten-year period by both groups of countries and completed by 2005. The implementation of these policies by all member countries–cuts in domestic support, export subsidies and tariffs-are expected to result in freer markets for agricultural commodities and the end of market- distorting surpluses and falling prices.

According to the World Bank, successful trade liberalization could result in income gains of $280-520 billion for all trading countries. It could also lift an estimated 144 million people out of poverty by 2015. The experience so far has been that none of these optimistic forecasts have been reached. Some of the reasons relate to the pattern of world agricultural trade and the dominance of the key players in world trade. This has resulted in a wide gap between the aims of trade liberalization under WTO and the actual outcomes.

Problems in Global Agricultural Trade

The US is the world's largest trading country, followed by the EU and Japan and these three players together account for over two-thirds of world trade. The share of developing countries in world trade is less than 30 per cent, with India's share at 0.8 per cent.

Global trade in agricultural products constitutes about 10 per cent of total world trade, which stands at around US$6 trillion. World agricultural exports are projected to reach $640 billion in value by 2012. The US and other industrialized countries are dominant importers in the 1990s, as these countries imported 70 per cent of the total value of food items in world trade.

Implementation Problems

The failure by many of the developed countries to fully implement the AoA's provisions forms a major obstacle in achieving consensus in the trade talks as far as the developing country perspective is concerned. There are several flaws in the approach of the AoA, which were not adequately addressed at the time of the Uruguay Round. The AoA links several countries with diverse economic structures and different stages of agricultural development within a single framework with weak concessions for developing countries under the Special & Differential provisions.

A major reason for the ineffectiveness of the Domestic Support reduction is the existence of the Blue and Green Box. The exemptions possible under the Green Box and Blue Box-a huge $311bn subsidies annually in the OECD countries–on the grounds that they are minimally distorting to production have diluted the reduction commitment under the AoA. Similarly, the Market Access commitment has been made less effective by the extremely high bound rates, which were fixed prior to the mid-1980s by many of the developed countries, and these became the basis for negotiating tariff reductions in the Uruguay Round. Tariff peaks have not been significantly affected by the stipulated 20 per cent tariff reduction requirement for developed countries and this level of reduction is insufficient to achieve any significant degree of market access for many of the developing countries' exports.

Domestic Support to Agriculture

Though exact comparisons of agricultural subsidies across countries may not be possible or precise due to differences in Producer Support Estimates (PSE) calculated by OECD countries and subsidies computed in India, the available data reveals a huge gap between India and some of the developed countries, particularly Japan, which pays out the largest subsidy per hectare in the world to its farmers. As a result of this policy that directly influences production, enormous surpluses have emerged in major agricultural commodities in these countries resulting in downward pressure on international prices for agricultural commodities with adverse impact on the livelihoods of resource-poor farmers in developing countries.

Prices of major agricultural commodities have been declining by 20 to 30 per cent and there has been no evidence of effective subsidy reduction by the EU and US. The US has, in fact, brought in new farm legislation in May 2002 that provides for continued domestic support to its farmers to the extent of $180 billion annually over the next decade of which 70 per cent are direct support payments to producers. The bulk of this farm subsidy–more than 80 per cent–is paid out to 1,50,000 farmers across the US. The EU–with its expanded membership of 25 member countries over the next few years-does not propose any structural reform in the subsidy package to its farmers until 2013. It is, therefore, difficult to expect any substantial change in the subsidy regime of the major players in the near future. As a result, the favorable outcomes for developing countries are unlikely to emerge in the medium-term. The EU and the US are broadly together on the track of urgency to tackle the disguised subsidies. The joint EU-US position paper of August 13,2003 gives leverage to the EU to apply the Swiss formula (1976) only to a certain number of commodities (to be negotiated) and for the rest, Uruguay Round kind of formula of an average of 36 per cent cut over the next five years. Government support to several crops is in the range of 50-60 per cent of the farmers' income from them.

Non-Trade Barriers

The use of non-trade issues such as environmental norms and labour standards as Non-Tariff Barriers to trade have also contributed to limiting exports from developing countries to some of the developed country markets. New forms of protectionism are emerging as countries attempt to protect their markets through NTBs. There has been a growing demand for environmentally friendly products in the developed country markets in the last decade or so, leading to the emergence of "Green Trade". (Ojha 2001). It is not yet clear whether and to what extent the trade regime requirements under WTO conflict with environmental protection measures adopted by national governments. Market restrictions in areas like the EU, in fact, are so strange that, under something called Headnote 7, for instance the EU charges a lower import duty for expensive imports and a higher one for cheaper imports, effectively blocking out cheaper imports. These measures distance the developing countries perpetually.

TRIPS and its Implications

Intellectual property rights were brought within the scope of the GATT/WTO framework for the first time through the Agreement on Trade Related Aspects of Intellectual Property Rights (TRIPS). As a result, there were stipulations on the nature of patents (process and product) and their duration (20 years) to bring them more in line with the practice prevailing in advanced industrialized countries like the USA, with some degree of flexibility on certain aspects to be decided by member countries. Tighter protection was granted to patent holders under TRIPS in a manner that would favour those with a competitive advantage in knowledge-based industries that generate intellectual property. Such industries include emerging frontier technologies such as information, computer software, biotechnologies, etc. and also chemicals and pharmaceuticals. Given the huge gap in intellectual property generation between industrialized countries and developing countries, apart from the costs of monitoring/implementing an IPR regime, it is unlikely to promote healthy competition and technology transfer. On the other hand, the patent system under TRIPS when it becomes fully operational after 2005, is expected to lead to a marked increase in prices of drugs and pharmaceuticals. In December 2003, the Government of India introduced the Patents (Amendment) Bill, 2003 in Parliament. The Bill provides for introduction of product patent protection in all fields of technology as per the TRIPS Agreement.

The implications for agriculture of a new patent regime are mainly with regard to availability and price of seed for farmers. The new seed policy enables self-certification by the private manufacturers, cooperatives and NGOs. There are about 100 national seed laboratories and 20 State seed certification agencies in the country. The Andhra Pradesh State Seed Certification Agency was not able to meet the growing demand for certified seed and there were numerous complaints from the farmers that the seed certified by such organization did not germinate in large number of cases. The compensations for failure also endangered the interests, as they were not related to the input costs till the stage failure was noticed. In testing of new varieties and hybrids prior to commercial production, several violations to scientific norms were also noticed. (Janaiah 2004) In other words, regulatory mechanism to enforce standards is in the nascent stages not only in India but in several other developing nations.

Regional Trade Agreements (RTAs)

An issue that has gained importance in terms of its impact on the pattern of trade flows is the growing number of Regional Trade Agreements (RTAs) between member countries in various groupings. The EU, for example, has a system of concessions with the African/Caribbean/Pacific (ACP) countries while USA has the Caribbean Basin Initiative with certain countries in that region. The number of RTAs has been steadily increasing in recent years and about 60 per cent of world trade is carried on within their ambit. In May 2003, there were over 265 RTAs notified to the WTO. About 90 per cent of these RTAs were in the form of Free Trade Agreements (FTAs) and only 10 per cent were customs unions. (RBI 2002-03). Bilateral agreements are also permissible within the WTO framework, raising questions about the concept of Most Favoured Nation (MFN), a core principle of the multilateral trade regime by which a concession offered to one country/trading partner has to be offered to all.

The growth of RTAs is expected to continue side by side with the growth of multilateral trade, as there are several advantages in such agreements among smaller groups of countries. The future trend will be one of increased regionalism in trade coexisting with the wider multilateral framework with more and more countries pursuing both trade strategies – a scenario that may be termed as

WTO-plus (Debroy 2004). An Agreement on a South Asian Free Trade Area (SAFTA) was signed at the 12th SAARC summit held in Islamabad in January 2004. This would subsume the on-going trade liberalization process under South Asian Preferential Trade Area (SAPTA) by 2006. A whole set of trade facilitation measures are being put into place within the framework of regional cooperation. These measures include: Harmonization of standards, reciprocal recognition of tests/accreditation of testing laboratories/ certification of products, simplification of customs clearance procedures, harmonization of national customs classification based on HS coding system, simplification of banking procedures for import financing and transit facilities for efficient intra-SAARC trade. India has recently reduced import duty on a wide range of items–from textiles and glassware to marble and machinery parts–originating from SAARC countries.

India is looking beyond SAARC towards increasing trade relations with more countries in the Asian and South East Asian region and is a signatory to several bilateral trade agreements, the latest being with Thailand. FTAs/PTAs are already in place or being negotiated with Sri Lanka, Bangladesh, Afghanistan and Singapore and ASEAN. An FTA for IBSA (India, Brazil and South Africa) is on the cards with negotiations slated for early 2005. Trade relations between India and Pakistan are also expected to improve once Pakistan accords MFN status to India (India had accorded such status to Pakistan in 1996). The trade potential for both countries through closer cooperation is estimated at as high a figure as $15billion. India and Pakistan account for over 40 per cent of the world's production of cotton, with China the share goes up to 60 per cent. Closer cooperation to face world markets could favour exports from these countries.

Section 3: Challenges Facing India's Agricultural Sector

The impact of WTO on the country's agricultural sector has two aspects: (i) the possibility of increased agricultural imports as a result of reduced tariff barriers and (ii) the possibility of increased export opportunities as a result of increased market access through trade liberalization.

The WTO trade negotiation framework offers each member country an opportunity to strike a balance between these two aspects through reciprocal arrangements with its trading partners on the issues of market access and tariff reductions. To do this, each country would have to have a clear policy perspective regarding its short-term priorities and long-term economic interests.

There are several factors that will influence the impact of WTO on Indian agriculture in the next few years. Some of the factors are:

- The pace of recovery in the global economy which is dependent on the revival of the $11 trillion US economy.
- Agricultural policy reform in the countries that are key players in world agricultural trade.
- Fluctuations in international prices for major agricultural commodities that India produces and exports governed sometimes by non-market considerations.
- Dynamics of demand and supply in commodity-specific global markets.
- The pace of India's second generation reforms and the broad thrust of economic policy in the next few years.

Policy interventions will have to strengthen the capacity of the agricultural sector to withstand shocks and pressures from global market forces as well as increase the agricultural sector's flexibility to respond to market signals through crop shifts. Given the ground realities of world trade as outlined in Section 2, how is Indian agriculture positioned to face the challenges of opening to global markets? If the Doha agenda is completed on schedule (and the AoA re-negotiated by 2004 end) and if the EU and USA reduce their agricultural subsidies–unlikely prospects in the present scenario-will Indian agriculture in its present state be able to respond adequately to more liberalized global trade that will result?

India's agricultural sector is one of the largest in the world with 650 million persons dependent on it for livelihood security and the second largest population in agriculture after China. From the freezing to high and medium temperate zones that produce a wide variety of crops and fruits that are grown any where else in the world, from the perennial rivers to the severe drought round the year, from the black cotton to sandy loams and deserts, India represents the world agriculture. The sylviculture, horticulture and aquaculture similarly represent the universe.

In terms of land resources, the country is favorably placed with the second largest share of arable land in the world after USA. India also has the largest livestock population in the world and is a leading producer of milk and eggs, fruits and vegetables and cereals. Thirty-five crops are grown across the country, with two-thirds grown on more than one million hectares each. India aims to increase its share in world agricultural trade by promoting diversification with shift to high value crops, and increased value addition. However, the priority for agricultural policy before producing for export markets has to be to ensure domestic food security. It has all the potential to dominate the world agricultural production and trade, once the policy environment and support systems are built with consensus among the States. The developed countries are aware of this threat and hence the problems in the negotiations in WTO.

Areas of Concern

The dry land areas of the country constituting two-thirds of the cultivated area account for a large share of output of coarse cereals, pulses and oilseeds. This is also where the majority of small and marginal farmers have their holdings. The impact of more liberalized trade through tariff cuts is expected to have an impact on the oilseed sector. At present, while production of oilseeds such as rapeseed-mustard and soyabean is fairly competitive, oil processing is highly uncompetitive (Chand, et.al 2004). This has led to India becoming the world's largest importer of edible oils with more than 40 per cent of domestic demand met through imports. This level is unsustainable and there is an urgent need for the oilseed and oil processing sectors to be made more efficient. After 2004, with further tariff reductions under AoA, the protection from high bound rates of 300 per cent on palm oil and 100 per cent on vegetable oils may be significantly reduced.

The future policy thrust for Indian agriculture involves three objectives in the present context: (i) ensuring food security to a huge and growing population (estimated to cross 1.3 billion by 2020); (ii) ensuring livelihood security for millions of resource-poor farmers and tenant farmers particularly in dry land areas who face threats from two sources: the on-going crisis in the agricultural sector begging to be tackled adequately and the global market forces; and (iii) promoting export oriented agriculture (with emphasis on specific crops and regions) to capture the advantages of trade liberalization.

These objectives require focused strategies in agricultural sub-sectors. The need to ensure food security involves emphasis on food grain production, which despite record production levels, faces declining productivity growth rates in the States with major shares in food grain output. The second objective requires a focus on dry land areas that have a major share in the output of coarse cereals, pulses and oilseeds. The third objective may require a new look at high value, high-tech agriculture keeping in view the pattern of demand in domestic and international markets. For any policy to work in reshaping Indian agriculture, development of rural infrastructure is of paramount importance. Marketing of agricultural commodities is one of the vital links in the chain of value addition from farm to retail outlet.

Several studies have shown that India is competitive in several commodities such as rice, certain fruits and vegetables, spices and condiments, and marine products. However, competitiveness is a dynamic phenomenon and can change quickly over time. Intense competition is likely to emerge among developing countries producing similar agricultural products for the same developed country markets. Cost competitiveness, high quality standards, and effective marketing strategies will become critical in such a scenario. The stipulations of the Agreement on Sanitary and Phyto-Sanitary Measures and the standards set for food products by international bodies such as Codex Alimentarius Commission (CAC) need to be adhered to. Concerns relating to food safety, environmental protection and bio-technological interventions in agriculture are growing among global consumers and these concerns need to be reflected in research and new technologies to be used by agricultural producers.

Section 4: Areas for Policy Intervention

This section looks at some of the policy interventions in the WTO context.

Some thing internal

Agriculture is a concurrent subject in the body politic and the recent rhetoric on agriculture on the eve of elections to the Parliament of India should not be easily glossed over. The government that was silent for almost five years announced a high powered Committee to frame a National Policy for agriculture with a two-year time frame, constituted a working group to look into the issues plaguing the flow of credit for agriculture; ordered a slash in the interest rate for direct agriculture to 9 per cent (this is itself higher by 1.5 per cent than the interest charged on mortgage loans by several commercial banks in the country) set up a Rs.50,000 crore fund to ensure credit related infrastructure etc. It is worth watching whether these intentions and announcements would fetch the votes from the 200mn farmer population. When a sleeping giant wakes up suddenly, it requires a big shake up. Reforms in agriculture are given a script at long last.

Even at the Central government level, there are at least ten Ministries concerned with agricultural sector: Ministry of Agriculture; Ministry of Environment and Forests, Ministry of Rural Development dealing with the waste land development and watershed management; Ministry of Food Supplies; Ministry of Food Processing; Ministry of Irrigation; Ministry of Cooperation, Ministry of Finance dealing with issues relating to credit; Ministry of Science and Technology dealing with issues relating to biotechnology; Ministry of Commerce dealing with trade-related issues. Each Ministry has its own empire to protect and resources to spend. Ministries of Power and Non-conventional energy and Ministry of Law and Justice have their own role to play. Given the accommodation that the Prime Minister has to make in providing berths in the Ministry based on caste, creed, region and the religion, it will be difficult to expect any sensible consolidation of these Ministries. The State governments have similar corresponding arrangements and accommodation to make. Building consensus on issues that cut across the domestic markets would itself be a stupendous task. If consensus eludes, appoint a Committee and this was precisely the attempt of the government that is sure of coming to power before the end of May 2004.

Role of the State

The State continues to play a very important role in the structural aspects of Agricultural Markets. They broadly relate to (a) development and regulation of primary markets and (b) regulation of market conduct through a series of legal instruments.

The provisions under the legal instruments, most being consumer protection measures are used to regulate the activities of traders and processors pertaining to trading, stocking maintenance of quality, grading, packing, processing, blending and movements. The government also regulates the future trading in agricultural commodities. (Acharya 1998).

Indian regulated market laws over-specified conduct. It is highly ideological law stipulating that one contractual form is efficient. "The law needs to be reformed so as to state what is unacceptable conduct, thereby freeing a larger legitimate contractual space". (Harriss-White 1996).

Enforcement has to be standardized and powerful and at the same time should have positive incentives for compliance. This would facilitate farmers converting their farmsteads into viable enterprises eligible for financing on their own merit. The Draft Model State Agricultural Produce Marketing (Development & Marketing) Act, 2003 circulated to the States still fall short of the WTO compatibility and therefore requires wider debate before implementation.

Section 5: Conclusion

Agriculture is a concurrent subject and therefore, the State governments should be persuaded for a consensus on several policy initiatives required to be taken to ensure WTO compatibility. Reshaping and modernizing Indian agriculture to face the pressures of the next few decades is a huge and complex task and requires a wide range of policy interventions. There is a need to raise India's competitive advantage in specific agricultural products through increases in productivity and use of cost-effective farm practices. Crop diversification and regional specialization in crop production can yield better results. Low cost technologies, which raise yields, will need wider adoption by our farmers along with bio-technological interventions that are environment-friendly and sustainable. Certification of quality seeds and their wider availability to farmers needs to be ensured.

Production for export has to be encouraged in specific sub-sectors such as fruits and vegetables, spices and condiments, medicinal herbs, floriculture, aquaculture, and other sectors that are emerging with export potential in response to demand in global markets require (i) resource mapping for more region-specific and crop-specific interventions; and (ii) analysis of conditions influencing supply and demand of agricultural commodities in major trading countries so as to anticipate changes in global markets. Monitoring of domestic and international prices for agricultural commodities would also help in crop planning and reduce instabilities resulting from unanticipated price changes.

A national perspective for agriculture compatible with market-led growth, its implications for regional comparative advantages and preferred opportunities; a time frame and a clear set of priorities for investment and creating infrastructure, has to be created. (Rao and Jeromi 2000).

An economy bereft of reforms in the agricultural sector saw the decline in fertilizer industry, agro-industries, etc. The emerging biotechnology industries would require longer lead-time for agricultural applications. The regulator in government should have the vision and the financial sector should provide for appropriate gestation for new projects and acquire the much-needed capabilities to assess risk objectively and hedge it, properly. When agriculture becomes a performing asset and farmer is respected in the country, the economy would surpass the existing 7-8 per cent growth level. It is appropriate to recall what Richard H.Tawney, an English economist, wrote in his work *Religion and the Rise of Capitalism.* (Tawney 1952) "If economic ambitions are good servants, they are bad masters." Eager economists and populist politicians should have a common agenda of taking the substantial slice of our economy, viz., and agriculture on a sustainable growth path and this should be thc rockbed of negotiations on the WTO table for India.

The crucial agriculture negotiations are scheduled to resume in March 2004. India will insist on inclusion of special provisions for developing countries in the framework of negotiations. The government's clear stand is that its assent on modalities would be conditional to the provisions addressing the sensitivities of developing countries. India is also trying to push for a separate negotiating body at WTO for issues related to the Special and Differential (S & D) treatment for developing countries. Identifying the currently non-binding provisions under WTO and making them mandatory are the immediate tasks before the Trade and Development Committee. It remains to be seen how the alignments crafted at the Fifth Ministerial in Cancun succeed in achieving advances on the key issues of interest to India and other developing countries. The WTO framework has to ensure that "trade and economic growth benefit those who need it most." (Panitchpakdi and Clifford 2001).

References

Acharya, S.S. (1998), *Indian Journal of Agricultural Economics*, Vol. 53 (3), pp. 311-313.

Chand, Ramesh, Jha, Dayanatha and Mittal, Surabhi (2004), "WTO and Oilseeds Sector: Challenges of Trade Liberalisation", *Economic and Political Weekly*, February 7.

Debroy, Bibek (2004), "What's Happening on IBSA"? *The Economic Times*, February 10.

Harriss-White, B. (1996), *A Political Economy of Agricultural Markets in South India*, New Delhi: Sage Publications, pp. 300-337.

Janaiah, A. (2004), *Indian Journal of Agricultural Marketing*, cited in Shortfall in Seed Production, *Business Line*, February 20.

Ojha,Vijay Prakash (2001), "Trade and Environment: A Developing Countries' Perspective", *RGICS Working Paper Series, No. 28*, Rajiv Gandhi Institute for Contemporary Studies, New Delhi.

Panitchpakdi, Supachai and Clifford, Mark L. (2001), *China and the WTO: Changing China, Changing World Trade*, John Wiley & Sons.

Rao, V.M. and Jeromi, P.D. (2000), Modernising Indian Agriculture: Priority Tasks and Critical Policies, *Development Research Group, Study No. 21*, Department of Economic Analysis and Policy, Reserve Bank of India, Mumbai.

Tawney, R.H. (1948), *Religion and the Rise of Capitalism*, Penguin, London.

Government of India, Department of Agriculture & Cooperation, Ministry of Agriculture (2003), *The State Agricultural Produce Marketing (Development & Regulation) Act, 2003* (Draft Model Act)

Reserve Bank of India (2002-03), *Report on Currency and Finance*, Mumbai.

4

Agriculture Market Access Modalities

Implication for South Asian Countries under Alternate Scenarios

Rajesh Mehta, Jacob George & Pooja Agarwal

Section 1: Introduction

The Cancun Ministerial Conference in mid-September 2003 did show that the South Asian countries in particular and the developing countries in general could partake in negotiations with informed discussion. The engagement between the developing and developed countries therefore was indeed a serious business. The coalition of developing countries could appreciate the negotiating positions of alliance members as well as identify various implications in quick real time that served their own countries' interest. Agricultural negotiations in this context are a case in point.

The point being raised after the Cancun setback is whether or not India (and other south Asian countries) should have agreed to reduce her agricultural average final bound tariff by 37.5 per cent as per Harbinson's formula or get constricted into a tight bargaining terrain. The coordinates of this later terrain, dictated by the EC-US joint text proposal, expected an unjustifiable reduction in the range of 45-83 per cent in the most likely case scenario of India's average bound tariff in agricultural products.

However what was agreed upon at the Doha Ministerial is not the direct premise for this paper. As the negotiations would be resumed soon, some queries need to be raised in order to prepare for these discussions. Notably, the market access pillar in the agriculture negotiations plays a crucial role and the bargaining terrain has become extremely tight for developing countries. Therefore, issues that arise, for example, what are the coordinates of this tight bargaining terrain for India and other south Asian countries in WTO; will it be possible to get into serious engagement with other states towards an amicable outcome; what options and range of market access choices are available to the developing countries in the current negotiations, etc. need consideration. These questions among others have acquired a mystical air after the December 2003 General Council decision to use the "Derbez Draft" text as the premise to carry forward the agriculture negotiations.

The Doha Ministerial Declaration, however, in November 2001, gave 31 March 2003 as the deadline (that was missed) along with a host of other tasks. Consequently, the Harbinson Draft modalities paved the way during mid-August 2003 for a series of "framework papers" leading to the General Council Chair, Mr. Carlos Perez del Castillo [Castillo Draft] suggestion of a draft Cancun Ministerial Text on 24 August 2003. Harbinson's revised modalities, it may be recalled, did not result in agreement amongst members regarding formula-based commitments to the three pillars of AoA, namely, domestic support, market access and export competition. The inherent balance between these pillars, especially in terms of the expected ambitious reduction commitments from developing country members *vis-à-vis* the industrialized developed country members has been at the center of the discussion.

The multilateral trading framework of the WTO has come to characterize the market access and dispute redress mechanisms that may not be effective in some of the alternate frameworks. In this paper, therefore, we are concentrating our attention on the market access reduction commitments. We plan to concentrate on the most contentious issue of market access, namely, reduction to tariff levels. In this respect, we would like to trace the expected scenario from the south Asian countries' perspective in the journey starting from the draft 'modalities' of Harbinson to the Cancun Conference Chair, Mr. Luis Ernesto Derbez's draft text on agriculture tabled on 13 September 2003 in Cancun. This topic is going to remain significant because the members have to continue with their engagements in pursuit perhaps of reaching some conclusions. In the absence of a clear understanding about the implications of the suggested framework in the Derbez Draft, a proactive agenda unfortunately cannot be framed. We hasten to add that the remaining two market access issues, namely, special safeguards (SSG) and tariff rate quotas (TRQs), though important requires independent treatment and will be taken up separately.

The market access modalities as proposed in Harbinson's draft are examined in Section II with respect to some select developing (including South Asia) and developed country cases. This is followed in Section III by a scrutiny of the framework paper submitted jointly by EC-US on 13 August 2003 during a meeting of the heads of delegations (HODs) in Geneva. We generate a simulated scenario in Section IV since the EC-US framework paper does not specify any numbers for working out commitment levels by the member countries. Section IV also brings in the market access parameters of the "Derbez Draft." The concluding observations and policy recommendations are contained in Section V.

Section 2: Market Access Modalities

The multilateral trade negotiations are primarily aimed at ensuring market access to all members and at putting in place an effective dispute settlement mechanism. The market access pillar in this context for agricultural products has special significance because many countries did not have an appropriate tariff schedule. After the Uruguay Round this was attempted. This was expressed as commitments by different member countries under the Agreement on Agriculture (AoA). Since 2000 these AoA commitments are under review.

Following Paras 13 & 14 of the Doha Ministerial Declaration (DMD), the Special (negotiating) Session of the WTO Committee on Agriculture submitted the first "modalities for the further Commitments" on 12 February 2003. The revised version of the *First Draft of Modalities for further Commitments'* with respect to tariffs has proposed a core modality of differing sets of reduction in tariffs based on a linear reduction formula along with bands/slabs, one for the developed countries and the other for the developing countries. This has come to be referred as Harbinson's Revised Draft Modalities.

Harbinson's Revised Draft Modalities

The major stipulations with respect to type of tariffs, base period and time frame can be summarized as follows:

- tariffs, except in-quota tariffs, to be reduced by a simple average for all agricultural products subject to a minimum reduction per tariff line;
- base for the reductions to be the final bound tariffs as specified in the schedules of Members;
- time period for tariff reduction, except for the preferential schemes to be implemented in equal annual installments over a period of five years for the developed countries and ten years for the developing countries.

The core modality formula for the developed countries stated in the revised First Draft of Modalities (box 1) can be mathematically denoted in the following way:

$$T_1 = T_0 * (1\text{-}A/100), \qquad \text{..........(1)}$$

Where,

T_0 and T_1 = Uruguay and simulated post-Millennium final bound tariffs

A = tariff reduction (linear) percentage in slabs

$A = 60$, if $T_0 > 90$

$A = 50$, if $15 < T_0 \leq 90$

$A = 40$, if $T_0 \leq 15$

A clear indication is also provided for processed products. The rate of tariff reduction for the processed products is expected to be equivalent to that for the relevant product in its primary form multiplied at a minimum by a factor of 1.3. The scope for raising this factor, we suppose, could be available, as we shall see below in the "Castillo Draft". The proposal by the Chairman, Mr. Stuart Harbinson, however, is silent on it.

Box 1

Harbinson Revised Market Access Modalities–March 2003

Developed Countries

(i) tariffs greater than 90% *ad valorem*–a simple average reduction rate [60] per cent subject to a minimum cut of [45] per cent per tariff line.

(ii) tariffs lower or equal to 90% *ad valorem* and greater than 15 per cent *ad valorem*–a simple average reduction rate [50] per cent subject to a minimum cut of [35] per cent per tariff line.

(iii) tariffs lower than or equal to 15% *ad valorem*–simple average reduction [40] per cent subject to a minimum cut of [25] per cent per tariff line.

(iv) where the rate of tariff reduction for the processed product shall be equivalent to that for the product in its primary form multiplied at a minimum by a factor of [1.3].

Developing Countries

(i) tariffs greater than [120% ad valorem]–simple average reduction rate [40] per cent subject to a minimum cut of [30] per cent per tariff line.

(ii) tariffs lower than or equal to [120% ad valorem] and greater than [60 per cent ad valorem]–simple average reduction rate [35] per cent subject to a minimum cut of [25] per cent per tariff line.

(iii) tariffs lower than or equal to [60% ad valorem] and greater than [20% ad valorem]–simple average reduction rate–[30%] subject to a minimum cut of [20] per cent per tariff line.

(iv) tariffs lower than or equal to [20% ad valorem]–simple average reduction rate–[25%] subject to a minimum cut of [15] per cent per tariff line.

(v) for all Special Products (SP) products simple average reduction [10%] subject to a minimum cut of [5%] per tariff line.

Similarly, Para 12 of the revised First Draft of Modalities elaborates on the formula for reduction commitments by the developing countries, except 'SP' products i.e. special products with respect to food security, rural development and/or livelihood security concerns, which is mathematically presented below:

$$T_1 = T_0 * (1\text{-}A/100), \qquad \ldots\ldots\ldots(2)$$

Where, $A = 40$ if $T_o > 120$

$A = 35$ if $60 < T_o \pounds\ 120$

$A = 30$ if $20 < T_o \pounds\ 60$

$A = 25$ if $T_o \pounds\ 20$

Thus, it can be noticed that against the provision of three slabs for developed countries, four slabs have been provided for in the case of developing countries. Remarkably, three slabs for developed north and four slabs for the developing south was purported to address all the pointed submissions by member countries. Besides, for all SP products a simple average reduction of 10 per cent subject to a minimum cut of 5 per cent per tariff line has also been envisaged.

A close look at these slabs along with an examination of the minutes of the Special Session of the Committee on Agriculture becomes necessary so as to understand why such a formula was recommended. The examination reveals that the issue at stake is whether or not the primary premise of the core method, namely, "the higher the tariff the greater the required average reduction rate" serves the greater interests of the developing member countries (WTO 2003a). There have been repeated articulations in these meetings of occurrences of developed country overexploition of the inherent market access clause in the special and differential treatment especially with respect to lower tariff reduction targets and a longer implementation period.

One of the important queries about the revised formula would be regarding its strong reservations. This will arise as a natural corollary. We have attempted to examine this query after applying the minimum simple average reduction stipulated in different slab specific averages to a few select countries that represent both the developed and developing countries. It is made clear in the following section that explains finer points in methodology of the tariff reduction calculation based on the suggested modality. The select countries are Bangladesh, Brazil, India, Pakistan, Sri Lanka, South Korea, Australia and the USA.

These countries have been selected for the ease in their data availability and handling since what we attempted to do is a test case. Besides, these countries do represent different agricultural growing landscapes as well as country alliances. In this regard it is worth mentioning that due to non availability of the bound *ad valorem* equivalents of the developed countries our exercise became all the more difficult. Such non-transparency in the relevant information domain by the developed countries is indeed unfortunate, despite the clear instructions of the WTO Secretariat. Also, since the base year is not very clear in the draft modalities we faced many problems while converting specific duties into their ad valorem equivalents.

For illustration, in table 1 below we present a picture of simple average tariffs and the range of final bound rates for select countries. Two things are worth noticing in this table. First, that developed countries like Australia and US record a low final bound average in comparison to the south Asian and select developing countries. Such low bound tariff levels in the US have not been attained in a short span but over longer periods through a combination of factors. The historical bearings of highly protective tariffs interestingly need to be recalled in the contemporary discourse (Edward & Ryley 1994). The evolutionary benefits of these kinds surely can be experienced by developing countries and opportunities should be provided.

Secondly, the US has a very wide range of tariff bindings in comparison to other countries like Australia, Bangladesh, India, Pakistan, Sri Lanka and Brazil. The dispersion being so huge in the case of the US, subsequent reduction commitments in the bound rates have to be worked out carefully for a meaningful outcome.

Table 1
Simple Average and Range of UR Final Bound Rates for Select Countries

Country	*Final Bound Average (%)*	*Range of Bindings (%)*
U.S.A	9.5	0-822.9
Australia	3.8	0-29
Brazil	36.6	0-55
Korea	63.8	0-887.4
Bangladesh	197.1	50-200
India	114.5	0-300
Pakistan	100.1	30-200
Sri Lanka	50	50

Source: Computed by authors from www.amad.org.

An Estimate of Average Tariff Reduction

Calculations of the reduction in final bound averages are based on the formula stated in the draft of modalities, "TN/AG/W/1/Rev.1". The data on bound rates for the selected countries has been taken from www.amad.org. For USA the bound rates, which were stated in the form of specific duties, were converted into their *ad valorem* equivalents using the following formula:

Final bound *Ad valorem* equivalence = (*Ad valorem* equivalence of1999/ Specific duty of 1999) * Final specific duty.

For developed countries like USA and Australia, the simple bound average has been estimated for all commodities. Alongside, calculations based on the three slabs as indicated in equation (1) above have been carried out separately with respect to agricultural tariffs as follows:

(i) greater than 90 per cent *ad valorem;*

(ii) lower than or equal to 90 per cent *ad valorem* and greater than 15 per cent *ad valorem;* and

(iii) lower than or equal to 15 per cent *ad valorem.*

This was done after excluding in-quota tariffs. Then we arrived at three averages for these slabs, which were subject to reduction by 60 per cent, 50 per cent and 40 per cent respectively, which gave us three post millennium average values for the developed countries.

Similarly for developing countries, the simple bound average for agricultural tariffs is calculated separately for all commodities and for four slabs in the following four categories:

(i) greater than 120 per cent *ad valorem;*

(ii) lower than or equal to 120 per cent *ad valorem* and greater than 60 per cent *ad valorem;*

(iii) lower than or equal to 60 per cent *ad valorem* and greater than 20 per cent *ad valorem;* and

(iv) lower or equal to 20 per cent *ad valorem.*

Then, four averages are arrived for these slabs that were subject to reduction by 40 per cent, 35 per cent, 30 per cent and 25 per cent, respectively, which gave us four simulated post-millennium average values in the case of developing countries.

Later it is found out the weighted average of these averages, i.e., three averages in case of developed countries and four averages in case of developing countries, by multiplying the average values with the number of commodities falling in that slab. This weighted average is simulated final bound average for the post-millennium round negotiations of all agricultural commodities. This value is used to find out the per centage point decline in the final bound averages depicted in fig. 1.

It is now apparent that the developing country negotiators were able to crack the "mathematical wizardry" of the modality (i.e. formula) and see through the game plan for agricultural products.

For example, in our limited test case of five developing countries. With the exception of Bangladesh, because no reduction commitments are required by least developed countries (LDCs), the highest (42.9) percentage point decline in average bound rates from the base year is expected to be made by India in the post-millennium round. Pakistan would be next in the row with 35-percentage point reduction in its bound average. The Republic of Korea, Sri Lanka and Brazil follow in that order with about a 23, 15 and 11-percentage point declines, respectively.

That USA with a token 5 percentage point while Australia's meager 1.6 percentage point decline from the base year in the respective agricultural commodities average bound rates in the post-millennium round stands in stark comparison. The irony of the lopsided implication of these modalities is highlighted when we consider the myriad agricultural landscapes prevailing in the developing countries and compare these with the precision farming system of the developed north. Notwithstanding the low base year tariff values in countries with high merchandise trade, another elaboration of a "bad deal" for the developing countries in the revised modalities framework can be provided by looking at the estimated percentage decline in the average bound rates during pre and post-millennium rounds. This is borne out by a number of empirical studies that support the view that developing countries have been disprotecting their agriculture (Rao 2001). The averages of the tariff lines, in fact, are indeed deceptive.

Table 2 presents the case to illustrate that the averages of decline, though more in the case of developed countries (USA and Australia) as compared to south Asia and select developing countries (Brazil, India, Pakistan, Sri Lanka and S. Korea) is in fact an easy ploy to camouflage reductions across tariff lines. The picture becomes clearer if we recall from table 1 that the final bound average in USA was at 9.5 per cent with a wide range.

India in particular and the South Asian countries in general with a relatively high bound average and narrow range would be required to make deeper cuts in the tariff that is depicted in fig. 1. This means that the formula is more advantageous to the developed countries as it underplays very high tariffs.

Despite a greater more number of bands/slabs for the developing countries, the flexibility and comfort levels of the developing countries appear to be diminishing under this formula.

We will examine this in greater detail in Section IV. However, it needs to be recalled that a group of developing countries, including India in their joint submission did point this out very clearly (WTO 2000).

Fig. 1: Percentage point Decline in average Agriculture Bound Rates (from base year) in post Doha Ministerial Negotiations

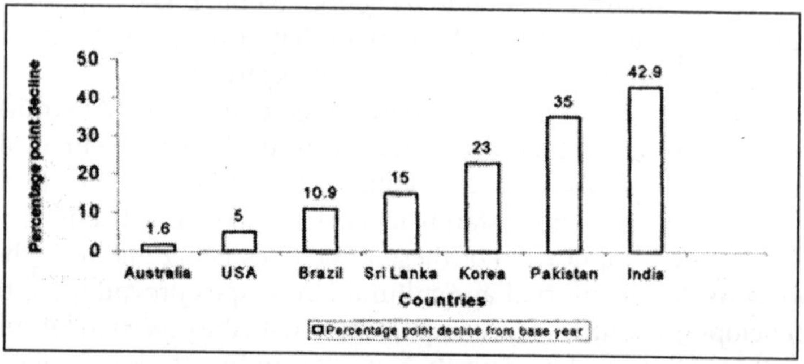

Table 2
Percentage decline in Pre-and Post-Multilateral negotiations based on Harbinson's formula: Bound Averages in Agriculture Products

Countries	*No. of TL*	*% Decline*
USA	1611	52.3
Australia	780	42.1
Brazil	1423	29.8
Korea	1307	36.1
India	666	37.5
Pakistan	685	35
Sri Lanka	658	30

Source: *Calculated by authors based on binding rate data from www.amad.org.*

This is yet another instance that highlights the "unfairness" of a global trading system that gives only a few members better access at the cost of excluding a large number of developing countries. The overall balance in terms of international trade gets disturbed for many first time players in the world market for agriculture products. In the case of sensitive food products for which tariffs are higher than average, the destabilizing instruments of the domestic markets do not lend themselves to easy address.

The message that needs to be highlighted here is that tariffs undoubtedly play a much wider and more significant role in the developing countries and therefore the significance of the bound rates is heightened in the absence of other horizontal as well as vertical trade instruments, including institutional arrangements.

Stipulated Minimum Reduction in Tariff Rates Across Different Slabs

The application of formula to developed countries when plotted with relevant pre-millennium and post-millennium round rates in fig. 2 with the minimum stipulated cuts in tariff show a notable pattern. Indeed, this is a cause of serious concern to the developing countries since many other important issues of tariff rates quota, domestic support and export subsidy get woven around this reduction commitment. While, the three slabs are prominently captured, the concentration of tariff lines in the second slab especially, is expected to occupy a wide range of tariff, say 13-60 per cent in case the Draft modalities come into operation in the near future.

The point to note here is that against the backdrop of experience gained during the implementation period, the new round is not expected to show a marked decline in the minimum cuts for the developed countries in general and is clearly depicted in fig. 2. This in fact reinforces the practices of OECD countries whereby during the pre-millennium round high tariffs on products which they produced were reduced by a smaller percentage on the one hand and reduced low tariffs were reduced by a larger percentage on the other hand. Such mathematical jugglery with tariff lines and percentage cuts gets compounded when non-*ad valorem* tariff forms are frequently used. The net result that could be expected under

Fig. 2: Application of Harbinson's Formula on Developed Country Bound Rates

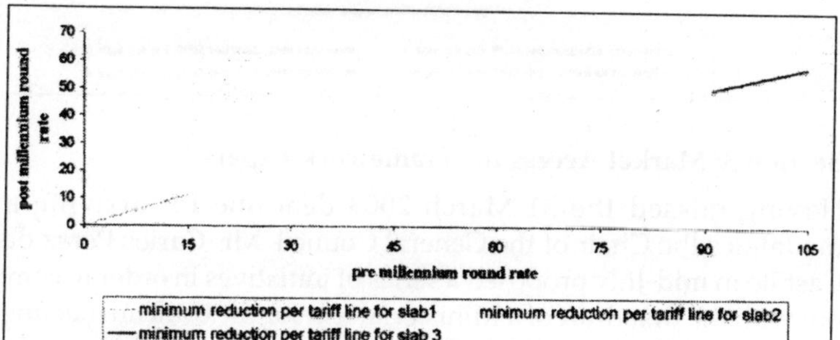

this scenario that of an extremely limited market access to the developing countries agricultural exports.

For the developing countries (and hence south Asian countries), the middle two slabs (fig. 3) could be expected to have a minimum cut in the new round that would range between 20-40 and 40-85 per cent, respectively. This is tantamount to the developing countries loosing the flexibility of the bound rates available during the pre-millennium round. As developing countries are small players in the international trade in agricultural products they do require special safeguards as regards market access before they get fully integrated into the world market machinations. Therefore, the delicate overall balance of the package appears to get distorted in this suggested formula (WTO 2003b). Many other serious concerns were communicated to all participating members by a joint submission mad by 27 countries.

These expected cuts in the new round, in another sense, have their own sensitivity and get reflected in a different manner. For instance, reductions in the final bound rate weighted averages presented in table 2 above keep varying across the test country cases.

Fig. 3: Application of Harbinson's Formula on Developed Country Bound Rates

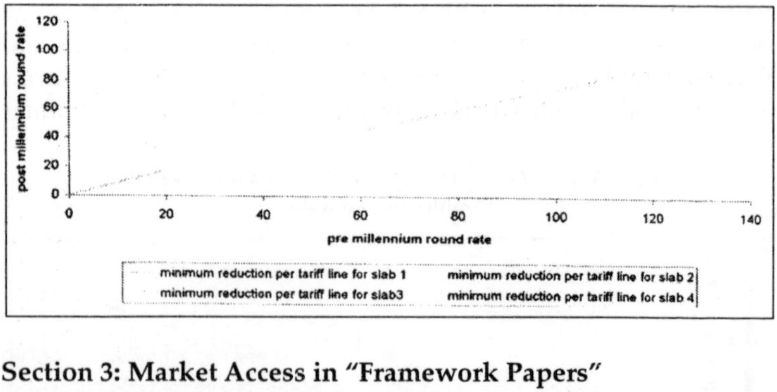

Section 3: Market Access in "Framework Papers"

Having missed the 31 March 2003 deadline for arriving at modalities the Chair of the General Council, Mr. Carlos Perez del Castillo in mid-July proposed a series of initiatives in order to come out with the first draft of a Ministerial text for the Cancun meeting. The EC-US jointly placed a text for members' consideration in order to arrive at a consensus. This joint text is called the "framework paper" and does not specify any numbers. The "joint text" brought a counter response in a series of framework by different coalition groups. The coalition of developing countries, now known as G 20+, in a detailed framework paper succinctly brought out the primary concerns of the developing countries. Among the G-20 countries, India and Pakistan represent South Asia. The G 20 was very clearly arguing for an enhanced market access to the developed country markets for their agricultural produce. This was based on a clear understanding that the tariff profiles are different in different countries. For instance, about 10.1 per cent of the total tariff lines in the US are above 30 per cent. In the case of the EU 27.1 per cent tariff lines and 16.2 per cent tariff lines in Japan have tariffs more than 30 per cent.

EC-US Joint Text

The EC-US framework paper suggested a blended formula approach. The blend was between the elements of linear reduction and Swiss formulae. The framework paper denotes a minimum per centage reduction in "import sensitive tariff lines" subject to a percentage average tariff cut. The coefficient in the Swiss formula is unknown and leads to heavy speculations before any firm commitment. Lastly, certain unknown percentages of tariff lines are to be made duty free. In addition, the members are expected to ensure "effective additional market access through a request-offer process" on certain tariff lines. The joint text not only proposes a blended formula, a combination of tariff cuts and TRQs is also proposed.

The joint text was greeted with dismay as it specifically served the interests of both the members (EC and the US) and was wide off the mark in the context of the Doha Declaration. The skillful use of "import sensitive tariff lines" was against the grain of submissions made by a large number of developing country members, which talked about provision on special products (SPs).

Since, some agricultural tariffs are recorded to be very high; they vary across countries and commodities. As a result, the global average (agricultural) tariff is estimated at 62 per cent with the global median at 40 per cent. It is also estimated that in South Asia, Central America and South America the average tariffs across the commodity groupings are also relatively close to the overall

Box 2
EC-US Joint Framework Text on Agriculture Market Access – 13 August 2003

The Doha declaration calls for "substantial improvements in market access". Negotiations should therefore provide increased access opportunities for all and in particular for the developing countries most in need and take account of the importance of existing and future preferential access for developing countries.

To achieve this, commitments shall be based on the following parameters:

1. The formula applicable for tariff reduction shall be a blended formula under which each element will contribute to substantial improvement in market access. The formula shall be as follows:
   (i) […]% of tariff lines subject to a […]% average tariff cut and a minimum of […]%; for these import sensitive tariff lines market access increase will result from a combination of tariff cuts and TRQs.
   (ii) […]% of tariff lines subject to a Swiss formula coefficient […].
   (iii) […]% of tariff lines shall be duty-free.
2. For the tariff lines that exceed a maximum of […]% Members shall either reduce them to that maximum, or ensure effective additional market access through a request: offer process that could include TRQs.
3. The use of the special agricultural safeguard (SSG) remains under negotiation.
4. A special agricultural safeguard (SSM) shall be established for use by developing countries as regards import-sensitive tariff lines.
5. All developed countries will seek to provide duty-free access for at least […]% of imports from developing countries through a combination of MFN and preferential access.
6. Having regard to their development and food security needs, developing countries shall benefit from special and differential treatment, including lower tariff reductions and longer implementation periods.

regional averages. The European regional coalition (EU 15) along with North America (constituting Canada, Mexico and United States) specifically shows a high dispersion rate across commodity mean (Paul 2001). In this context the use of the phrase "import sensitive" and the unspecified per centage put in the brackets [ ] in the formula becomes very deceptive and therefore the dismay at the blended formula for the agriculture sector.

G-20 Framework Paper

The diverse grouping of countries, called G-20+ tabled the most significant proposal on 19 August 2003 after the EC-US joint text was put on the table preparatory to the Cancun ministerial. This submission came as a counter proposal to the EC-US framework paper for developed countries without any specific numbers. This grouping using the three-pronged EC-US blended framework exclusively for the developed countries, suggested several significant initiatives to enhance market access by the developing country members. For instance it suggested that only linear formula be used for estimating the reduction levels of the developing countries. Some other salient features of the proposal can be gleaned in box 2 below.

For example, given the skewed tariff profile of the developed members the linear cut and tariff escalation was to be addressed in the first band. The term *"import sensitive"* in the first band has been replaced with *"tariff escalation"* as well as an *unspecified factor* to account for processing of primary food products. The tariff rate quota was to be expanded and the in-quota tariffs were to be brought down to zero. In addition it was proposed to discontinue the Special Safeguards (SSGs). It requested the developed countries to provide duty free access to all tropical products and other mentioned in the Preamble of the Agreement on Agriculture (AoA).

Box 3
Agriculture Market Access Framework Proposal by G 20+ – 20 August 2003

The formula applicable for tariff reduction in *developed countries* shall be a blended formula and shall be as follows:

(i) [...]% of tariff lines subject to a [...]% tariff cut. With a view to addressing *tariff escalation, a factor of [...]* will be applied to the tariff rate cut of the processed product, in case its tariff is higher than the tariff of the product in its primary form.

(ii) [...]% of tariff lines subject to a Swiss formula coefficient [...].

(iii) [...]% of tariff lines shall be duty-free.

contd.

Box 3 (contd.)

1. The total average tariff cut of items (i) and (ii) above shall be at least [...] % and, in any event, significantly higher than the tariff cut in i).
2. For the tariff lines that exceed a maximum of [...]% Members shall reduce them to that maximum.
3. Tariff rate quotas shall be expanded by [...]% of domestic consumption and in quota tariff rates shall be reduced to zero. Strict rule for their administration will be agreed to. Larger expansion or creation of TRQs could be the result of a request and offer process.
4. The Special Agricultural Safeguard (SSG) for developed countries shall be discontinued.
5. All developed countries shall provide duty-free access to all tropical products and others mentioned in the Preamble of the Agreement on Agriculture as well as to other agricultural products representing at least [...]% of imports from developing countries.

Special and Differential Treatment

6. Having regard to their rural development and food security needs, developing countries shall benefit from special and differential treatment, including lower tariff reductions and longer implementation periods, as well as from the establishment of Special Products (SP), under conditions to be determined in the negotiations. The formula applicable for tariff reductions shall be as follows:
   (i) all tariff lines subject to a [...]% average tariff cut and a minimum cut of [...]%.
   (ii) There will be no commitments regarding TRQ expansion and reduction of in quota tariff rates for developing countries.
7. Under conditions to be determined in the negotiations, a special safeguard mechanism (SSM) shall be established for use by developing countries, the scope of which would depend on the impact of tariff cuts as per 2.6 above.

Cancun Ministerial Text

As the date for the fifth ministerial came closer efforts by the General Council increased in order to hammer out a ministerial text. Many countries, interestingly in groups, made a number of framework suggestions, albeit, using either the EC-US joint text or the G20+ text. For example, nations from the coalition AU/ACP/LDC(see notes at the end) emphasised measures to tackle 'tariff peaks' and 'tariff escalation' along with ensuring improved market access for agricultural products from the developing countries. AU/ACP/LDC coalition has more than 70 WTO members and observers who are very poor and are reported to be net food importing nations. AU-African Union has a total of 54 member states. ACP-African Caribbean and Pacific group countries consist of about 77 signatories of the Cotonou Agreement with EU. LDC-Lease developed countries, out of a total of 49 LDCs, 30 are members of WTO with Nepal and Combodia as the newly acceded members. This group also requested the developed countries to commit a fixed time schedule for tariff education as well as non-tariff barriers to be addressed in a serious manner. The detailed proposal was submitted in response to the draft text of the Ministerial circulated by the General Council Chair, Carlos Prerez del Castillo. The consolidated written statement by the coalition is significant as many members are looking forward to concluding a type of economic partnership agreement with the EU.

Castillo Draft

A detailed exposition on the agricultural framework for establishing modalities was contained in the Annex A of the revised draft Cancun Ministerial Text. The "Castillo Draft" heavily borrowed from the EC-US joint text and for cosmetic effect incorporated a few points from various other "framework paper texts" circulated by the coalition of members.

The "Castillo Draft" specifically on the market access borrowed everything from EC-US joint text. As an after thought the draft added a best endeavor provision to "effectively address" tariff escalation. Similarly, the G20 provision for duty free access to tropical products was also reproduced. However, the "Castillo Draft" took the initiative of introducing Special and Differential Treatment (S&DT) options under each of the three pillars of AoA. Interestingly, these provisions do correspond with the G20 framework text.

Innovations, though complex, are offered under the market access pillar. The "Castillo Draft" in this respect, provides for two options in an "either/or" format for the developing countries. The first option provides for three band/formula meant for the developing countries as proposed in the Harbinson draft modalities. The second option is a new blend (on the lines of EC-

US Joint Text) of linear reduction and Swiss formulae without a zero duty category choice. However, under both choices and within the linear reduction formula band, the developing countries were given an additional flexibility to denote special products (SP) with a lower reduction commitment.

Box 4
Revision 1 "Castillo Draft" (JOB(03)/150/Rev.1 24.8.03)

Market Access

The Doha Ministerial Declaration calls for "substantial improvements in market access". Negotiations should therefore provide increased access opportunities for all and in particular for the developing countries. To achieve this, commitments shall be based on the following parameters:

1. The formula applicable for tariff reduction by developed countries shall be a blended formula under which each element will contribute to substantial improvement in market access. The formula shall be as follows:
   (i) [...]% of tariff lines shall be subject to a [...]% average tariff cut and a minimum of [...]%; for these import-sensitive tariff lines market access increase will result from a combination of tariff cuts and TRQs.
   (ii) [...]% of tariff lines shall be subject to a Swiss formula coefficient [...].
   (iii) [...]% of tariff lines shall be duty-free.
2. For the tariff lines that exceed a maximum of [...]% developed-country participants shall either reduce them to that maximum, or ensure effective additional market access in these or other areas through a request-offer process that could include TRQs.
3. The issue of tariff escalation will be effectively addressed.
4. The use and duration of the special agricultural safeguard (SSG) remains under negotiation

Special and differential treatment.

5. Having regard to their development, food security and/or livelihood security needs, developing countries shall benefit from special and differential treatment, including lower tariff reductions and longer implementation periods.
6. The formula applicable for tariff reductions by developing countries shall be as follows:

(i) [...]% of tariff lines shall be subject to a [...]% average tariff cut and a minimum of [...]%; for these import-sensitive tariff lines market access increase will result from a combination of tariff cuts and TRQs. Within this category, developing countries shall have additional flexibility under conditions to be determined to designate Special Products (SP) which would only be subject to a linear cut of a minimum of [...}% and no new commitments regarding TRQs.

(ii) [...]% of tariff lines shall be subject to [...]% average tariff cut and a minimum of [...]%.

(iii) [...]% of tariff lines shall be subject to [...]% average tariff cut and a minimum of [...]%.

Or in place of (ii) and (iii) above (iv) [...]% of tariff lines shall be subject to a Swiss formula coefficient of [...].

7. The applicability and/or extent of the provisions of paragraph 2.2 above to developing countries remain under negotiation, taking into account their development needs.
8. A special agricultural safeguard (SSM) shall be established for use by developing countries subject to conditions and for products to be determined.
9. All developed countries will seek to provide duty-free access for at least [...]% of imports from developing countries through a combination of MFN and preferential access total 10 points. Participants undertake to take account of the importance of preferential access for developing countries.

"Derbez Draft" on Agriculture Market Access

The Cancun Conference Chair Mr Luis Ernesto Derbez tabled a draft text on 13 September 2003 attempting to make some so-called "significant modifications" to the "Castillo Draft". The significant modification under the market access pillar is two-fold. Following the strong demand by the AU/ACP/LDCs coalition two parts were added to the market access pillar.

First, members were required to set a "resulting simple average tariff reduction for all agricultural products". Secondly a very limited number of products be designated on the basis of non-trade market access if their tariffs exceeded a certain maximum. The reason and grounds for such provisions apparently suggest that Japan with a very high out-of-quota tariff in Rice would be the major beneficiary. It is important to remind ourselves that the coalition of AU/ACP/LDC was represented by Mauritius, a member country that is also part of the "Friends of Multi-functionality"(MF). The original MF6 members are EU, Japan, Korea, Mauritius, Norway and Switzerland.

Box 5
Revision 2 "Derbez Draft"(JOB(03)150/Rev.2 13.9.03)

Market Access (Significant changes have been emphasised/ highlighted/strike out)

The Doha Ministerial Declaration calls for "substantial improvements in market access". Negotiations should therefore provide increased access opportunities for all and in particular for the developing countries. To achieve this, commitments shall be based on the following parameters:

1. The formula applicable for tariff reduction by developed countries shall be a blended formula under which each element will contribute to substantial improvement in market access *for all products.* The formula shall be as follows:
   (i) [...]% of tariff lines shall be subject to a [...]% average tariff cut and a minimum of [...]%; for these import-sensitive tariff lines market access increase will result from a combination of tariff cuts and TRQs.
   (ii) [...]% of tariff lines shall be subject to a Swiss formula *with a* coefficient [...].
   (iii) [...]% of tariff lines shall be duty-free. *[The resulting simple average tariff reduction for all agricultural products shall be no less than [...]%.]*
2. For the tariff lines that exceed a maximum of [...]% developed-country participants shall either reduce them to that maximum, or ensure effective additional market access in these or other areas through a request-offer process that could include TRQs. *[Within this category, participants shall have additional flexibility under conditions to be determined for a very limited number of [...] products to be designated on the basis of non-trade concerns that would only be subject to the provisions of paragraph 2.1 above].*
3. The issue of tariff escalation will be effectively addressed *by applying a factor of [...] to the tariff reduction of the processed product in case its tariff is higher than the tariff for the product in its primary form.*
4. *I n-quota tariffs shall be reduced by [...]%. Terms and conditions of any TRQ expansion/opening remain under negotiation.*

5. *The use and duration of the special agricultural safeguard (SSG) remains under negotiation.*

Special and differential treatment

6. Having regard to their development, food security and/or livelihood security needs, developing countries shall benefit from special and differential treatment, including lower tariff reductions and longer implementation periods.
7. The formula applicable for tariff reductions by developing countries shall be as follows:
   (i) [...]% of tariff lines shall be subject to a [...]% average tariff cut and a minimum of [...]%; for these tariff lines market access increase will result from a combination of tariff cuts and TRQs. Within this category, developing countries shall have additional flexibility under conditions to be determined to designate Special Products (SP) which would only be subject to a linear cut of a minimum of [...]% and no new commitments regarding TRQs; *however, where tariff bindings are very low (below [...]%) there shall be no requirement to reduce tariffs.*
   (ii) [...]% of tariff lines shall be subject to *a Swiss formula with a coefficient of [...].*
   (iii) [...]% of tariff lines shall be *bound between 0 and 5%, taking into account the importance of tariffs as a source of revenue for developing countries.*

   In implementing tariff reductions under paragraphs 2.7(ii)and 2.7(iii) above, developing countries should benefit from an additional implementation period of [...].
8. The applicability and/or extent of the provisions of paragraph 2.2 above to developing countries remain under negotiation, taking into account their development needs.
9. A special agricultural safeguard (SSM) shall be established for use by developing countries subject to conditions and for products to be determined.
10. All developed countries will seek to provide duty-free access for at least [...]% of imports from developing countries through a combination of MFN and preferential access, *including particularly all tropical and other products referred to in the preamble of the Agreement on Agriculture.*
11. Participants undertake to take account of the importance of preferential access for developing countries. *The further consideration in this regard will be based on paragraph 16 of the revised First Draft of Modalities for the Further Commitments (TN/AG/W/1/Rev.1 refers).*

The failure of member countries to converge on an acceptable ministerial text on agriculture in general and market access in particular after the Derbez Text is not surprising. Both the texts (i.e., "Castillo" and "Derbez") have made the framework very complex with blended formulae and conditionalities in an either/or format. We must recognise the fact that livelihood options indeed, was the issue of greater interest to a majority of member countries.

A complex market access formula, it must be pointed out, diverts the focus away from this primary concern of the developing countries. Therefore, the suggested framework for modalities is neither warranted nor expected for leading to a final decision in a "single undertaking" decision-making framework. The "Derbez Draft" indeed requires simplification and demystifying before the negotiations are started (see notes at the end). We can however, attempt to summarize the core modality of various proposals to market access negotiations discussed above in a tabular format for ease and ready reference (table 3).

Section 4: Simulated Market Access Scenario Based on "Derbez Draft"

As it is know, agriculture is the largest income-generating sector for the developing countries. The coalition of developing countries unequivocally proved that this important sector remained untouched by a number of trade liberalisation initiatives since 1995. The special and differential treatment (S&DT) provisions for developing countries incorporated in the Draft Ministerial text, in fact, was perceived to serve the interests of powerful developed nations. The possible implications of such a complex formula proposed as the market access modality in the agriculture sector can be explained with the help of a few simulations. This is of immense value to negotiators in particular and the populations at large in the country dominantly occupied in farming operations. However, efforts are required to make the methodology of market access calculations more transparent and simple. Although we can enumerate a number of horizontal actions that limit market access to a great extent (Mehta & George 2003).

Methodology

The simulation exercise is based on an analysis of the bound rates of USA selected to represent the case of the developed country.

Table 3
Comparison of Market Access Core Modality for Agriculture Products Proposed in Different Submissions

Proposal	*Core Modality*	*Developed Countries*	*Developing Countries*
Harbinson's Modalities Revised Draft Text	Multi-slab Linear Reduction Formula	$T_1 = T_0 * (1\text{-}A/100)$, Where $A=60$ if $T_o>90$; $A=50$ if $15<T_o\leq 90$; $A=40$ if $T_o\leq 15$	$T_1 = T_0 * (1\text{-}A/100)$, Where, $A=40$ if $T_o>120$; $A=35$ if $60<T_o\leq 120$; $A=30$ if $20<T_o\leq 60$; $A=25$ if $T_o\leq 20$
EC-US-Joint Framework Text	Blend of Linear Reduction, Swiss Formula and Zero Tariffs	$T_1=W_1 * T_0 * (1\text{-}A/100)+ W_2*(B*T_O/B+T_O) + W_3*0$	$T_1=W_1 * T_0 * (1\text{-}A/100)+ W_2*(B*T_O/B+T_O) + W_3*0$
G-21 Framework Text	Blend Formula for developed, and Simple Linear Reduction Formula for developing countries	$T_1=W_1 * T_0 * (1\text{-}A/100)+ W_2*(B*T_O/B+T_O) + W_3*0$	$T_1 = T_0 * (1\text{-}A/100)$,
Castillo Draft Text	Blend Formula for developed and Multi-slab Linear Reduction Formula OR Blend formula for developing countries	$T_1=W_1 * T_0 * (1\text{-}A/100)+ W_2*(B*T_O/B+T_O) + W_3*0$	$T_1 = T_0 * (1\text{-}A/100)$, Where $A=60$ if $T_o>90$; $A=50$ if $15<T_o\leq 90$; $A=40$ if $T_o\leq 15$ **Or** $T_1=W_1 * T_0 * (1\text{-}A/100)+ W_2*(B*T_O/B+T_O) + W_3*0$
Derbez Draft Text	Blend of Linear reduction, Swiss Formula and Zero Tariffs	$T_1=W_1 * T_0 * (1\text{-}A/100)+ W_2*(B*T_O/B+T_O) + W_3*0$	$T_1=W_1 * T_0 * (1\text{-}A/100)+ W_2*(B*T_O/B+T_O) + W_3*0$

Where,

T_1 = proposed bound rate in post-millennium round negotiations
T_0 = base rate of negotiation (i.e., Uruguay Round Final bound rate)
A = a coefficient representing % linear cuts
B = a constant value, commonly known as Swiss Coefficient
W_1, W_2, W_3 = weight of agricultural tariff lines such that $W_1+W_2+W_3=1$.

India has been selected to represent the south Asian country. The base rates (i.e., UR final bound rates) are the same as used for estimating the impact of Harbinson's formula carried out in an earlier section. The contrast in tariff profiles within these two selected countries is unmistakably illustrative of the developed and the developing country approach to the activities typical to the agriculture sector. For instance, the final bound tariffs in the case of India, though high, was reportedly never applied. About 83 per cent of tariff lines were seen to be at least 50 per cent lower than the bound rates (FAO 2003). Similarly, in the case of the USA it has been shown that high tariffs in the agricultural sector caused distortions. It restricted trade in agricultural products, especially those that originated from the developing countries. (Paul 2001b). In addition, it was found that sanitary and phytosanitary (SPS) measures also limit market access. Thus, stringent SPS measures often act like "market access plus" provisions.

The formula proposed in the "Derbez Draft" talks about three slabs of reduction. Although the percentages of tariff lines in each slab are yet to be decided, we conducted our analysis on some assumptions under the alternate scenario. We have taken various combinations for the number of tariff lines on which the first two modes of reduction will be applied. We have ruled out the case of duty free imports from our analysis for simplicity and ease in cognition.

It can be noticed that the first slab is quite similar to Harbinson's three-slab reduction. We have chosen the middle slab of Harbinson's formula with slight modifications. It is important to recall here this middle slab, i.e., *"all agricultural tariffs .... simple average reduction rate shall be [50] per cent ..... per tariff line"*. The 50 per cent cut is applied on all tariff lines that are supposed to fall under the first slab of revised ministerial formula. This is with respect to analyses conducted for the USA.

India being a developing country is obliged to apply provisions of the special and differential treatment. Notably, a separate four-slab tariff reduction formula was proposed in the Harbinson's revised draft modalities. And in this ministerial text also, giving due regard to the developmental and security needs of developing countries, the same formula has been proposed. However, the percentage of tariff lines to be included in at least three slabs would differ. Taking this into consideration, the tariff cutting analysis of

India in the first slab of the revised ministerial text have been carried out by using the second slab of Harbinson's reduction commitments for developing countries. "*For all agricultural tariffs ...... the simple average reduction rate shall be [35] per cent ...... per tariff line*". The modification here pertains to all tariffs to be covered in this slab and have been reduced by 35 per cent. Since the ministerial draft text offers a number of combinations to the developing countries for effecting tariff reductions, we decided to work out certain likely combinations for our simulation exercise.

Combinations

The different combinations of number of tariff lines to be included in first two slabs can be assumed as follows (without taking the third slab of zero duties):

1. Top 10% of high tariffs as per Linear formula and rest 90% of tariffs as per Swiss formula.
2. Top 25% of high tariffs as per Linear formula and rest 75% tariffs as per Swiss formula.
3. Top 50% of high tariffs as per Linear formula and rest 50% tariffs as per Swiss formula.
4. Top 60% of high tariffs as per Linear formula and rest 40% tariffs as per Swiss formula.
5. Top 75% of high tariffs as per Linear formula and rest 25% tariffs as per Swiss formula.
6. Top 10% of high tariffs as per Swiss formula and rest 90% of tariffs as per Linear formula.
7. Top 25% of high tariffs as per Swiss formula and rest 75% tariffs as per Linear formula.
8. Top 50% of high tariffs as per Swiss formula and rest 50% tariffs as per Linear formula.
9. Top 60% of high tariffs as per Swiss formula and rest 40% tariffs as per Linear formula.
10. Top 75% of high tariffs as per Swiss formula and rest 25% tariffs as per Linear formula.

The results of the Swiss formula are calculated by taking different values of the B coefficient. The selected B coefficient values are 15, 20, 25 and 30.

Simulation Results/Observations

It is known that a reduction in tariffs is larger and deeper with the application of the Swiss formula as compared to the linear reduction formula. So if the Swiss formula is applied to a higher tariff, i.e., peak tariffs or import sensitive items, etc., the tariff average gets reduced drastically (WTO 2003c). The expected deeper cut in the case of Swiss formula is a well-recognized empirical fact. This fact is quite evident in our test case of USA. Expectedly, it occurs because there is a high dispersion rate across commodity means in most of the North American countries as also in the EU (Paul 2001c).

The present bound tariff average of USA was found at 9.5 per cent. After applying the Swiss formula for different values of B to the top 10 per cent tariffs and linear reduction to the remaining 90 per cent tariffs, the estimated average was found to range between 2.4 to 3 per cent (table 5). Whether or not the developed countries will accept this option or combination is not worth speculating, as the decline in average is around 70 per cent. Alternatively, when the top 10 per cent of tariffs were reduced by the linear reduction formula for different values of B the average ranged around 5.2 to 5.6 per cent showing (depicted in table 4) the magnitude of decline comes to about 40 per cent from about 70 per cent. Since this is a most likely scenario as sensitive items are the ones with high tariffs, the post-millennium average tariff of the US will be in the range

Table 4
USA: Proposed Bound Averages as per "Derbez Draft" for Agriculture Products: High Tariffs subject to Linear Reduction

	Swiss Formula				
*% of lines used as per Harbinson second slab**	*B=15*	*B=20*	*B=25*	*B=30*	*% of lines used as per Swiss formula*
top10% of lines	5.2	5.4	5.5	5.6	90% of lines
25% of lines	5.1	5.2	5.2	5.2	75% of lines
50% of lines	4.9	4.9	4.9	4.9	50% of lines
60% of lines	4.8	4.8	4.8	4.8	40% of lines
75% of lines	4.8	4.8	4.8	4.8	25% of lines

*Simple average linear reduction of 50% cut per tariff line. (Harbinson's second slab for developed countries)

Note: Total number of lines used for this analysis is 1611.

5.2-5.6 per cent. The choice of tariff lines, if the "import sensitivity" argument of the developed countries is to be upheld, we suspect would be focused on effecting a shallow cut in the tariffs. The developing countries in that case will have to watch out for the actual numbers put on the table during the negotiations.

Table 5
USA Proposed Bound Averages as per "Derbez Draft" for Agriculture Products: High Tariffs subject to Swiss Formula

		Swiss Formula				
	% of lines used as per swiss formula (lines with higher tariff rates)	*B=15*	*B=20*	*B=25*	*B=30*	*% of lines used as per linear formula*
Simple average linear reduction of 50% cut per tariff line. (Harbinson's second slab for developed countries)	Top 10% of lines	2.4	2.7	2.8	3.0	90% of lines
	25% of lines	2.6	2.9	3.1	3.4	75% of lines
	50% of lines	2.8	3.2	3.5	3.7	50% of lines
	60% of lines	2.9	3.3	3.6	3.8	40% of lines
	75% of lines	2.9	3.3	3.6	3.8	25% of lines

Note: Total number of lines used for this analysis is 1611.

An opposite trend was observed in the case of Indian agricultural tariffs. The present bound average of India was estimated at 114.5 per cent. After applying the Swiss formula for different values of B to the top 10% tariffs and linear reduction to the remaining 90 per cent tariffs, the average was estimated to range between 62.1 to 63.2 per cent (table 6). The reduction is around 50 per cent. On the other hand, when the top 10% of tariffs were reduced by the linear reduction formula for different values of B and the rest by the Swiss procedure, the average ranged around 25 to 33 per cent showing a decline of 70 per cent.

The contrasting trends in the decline of averages in the cases of USA and India with the application of the same procedure of tariff reduction can also be explained in terms of degree of skewedness in the tariffs of both countries. In the case of USA the number of lines with high tariffs is very low and a majority of its tariffs, i.e., 1330 out of 1611, lie between the 0 to 10 per cent range. Since most of the Indian tariffs are on the higher side, the reduction of the top 75 per cent of tariffs as per the Swiss formula and the remaining (lower range) tariffs by linear reduction is leading to a drastic 80% decline in the average (see table 6). Remarkably, the decline ranged from 19.8 to 27.9 per cent for different values of B.

Table 6
India's Proposed Bound Averages as per "Derbez Draft" for Agriculture Products: High Tariff subject to Swiss Formula

		Swiss Formula				
	% of top lines used as per Swiss formula	*B=15*	*B=20*	*B=25*	*B=30*	*%of lines used as per linear reduction formula*
Simple average ltnear reduction of 35 % cut per tariff line. (Harbinson's second slab for developing countries)	10% of lines	62.1	62.4	62.8	63.2	90% of lines
	25% of lines	49.6	50.6	51.6	52.5	75% of lines
	50% of lines	32.8	34.8	36.6	38.4	50% of lines
	60% of lines	27.6	29.9	32.1	34.2	40% of lines
	75% of lines	19.8	22.6	25.3	27.9	25% of lines

Note: Total number of lines used for this analysis is 666.

It is noted that a decline in the bound average of Indian agricultural products is around 40 per cent only when the top 75 per cent of tariffs are reduced by the linear reduction formula and the remaining lower range of tariffs by Swiss reduction method (table 7). In this case, averages are lying between 67.4 per cent to 69.2 per cent considering 4 different values of the "B" coefficient. In the same range, when the value of the Swiss formula coefficient was taken as 300 the estimated average is recorded at 76.5 per cent.

A comparison of both the scenarios indicates that the developing countries, no matter which combinations are used, would be required to make larger reductions from their respective average bound rates. The negotiating space appears to have drastically shrunk for the developing countries. For example, the reduction level attained using the Harbinson formula would be reached under the blended formula only if the "B" coefficient is taken to be 300. This implies a 43-per centage point decline in the average bound tariff that was pointed out in Section 2. Fig.1 provides a visual for six other countries.

Table 7
India's Proposed Bound Averages as per "Derbez Draft" for Agriculture Products

	Swiss Formula				
*% of top lines used as per Harbinson second slab**	*B=15*	*B=20*	*B=25*	*B=30*	*% of lines used as per Swiss formula*
10% of lines	25.1	28.2	31.0	33.7	90% of lines
25% of lines	37.6	40.2	42.5	44.6	75% of lines
50% of lines	54.3	55.9	57.3	58.6	50% of lines
60% of lines	59.6	60.8	61.8	62.8	40% of lines
75% of lines	67.4	68.1	68.7	69.2	25% of lines

*Simple average linear reduction of 35% cut per tariff line. (Harbinson's second slab for developing countries) *Note*: Total number of lines used for this analysis is 666.

These tables also provide us with the possible coordinates of the negotiating strategy that would follow if the blended formula as tabled by the "Derbez Draft" is taken up for further discussion. The futility of pursuing this further is empirically demonstrated using the test case of India and the USA. In this context, the pointer from the south Asian country perspective is to carry out this exercise on a wider scale for other countries and to compare it with the obtaining scenario under the G20+ framework.

Agricultural Tariff Peaks and Highs

It is seen in preceding analyses that between Harbinson's revised draft and the "Derbez Draft", a meaningful engagement with the issue of tariff peaks and highs has been consciously obfuscated, in the first instance. The other instance is of unduly emphasizing on the modalities for reduction in final bound tariff averages. As it has demonstrated in Table 2 the tariff averages being a derived element would be dependent on the number of lines. Here, the higher the numbers of lines, the lower the averages. For instance, consider the US tariff peak at 822 per cent. In the event of applying Harbinson's formula, the range of reduction would be 0-452. The 822 per cent peak, however, will be subject to a minimum average reduction and may be estimated at about 328 per cent. In the event of applying "Derbez Draft" and taking the top 10 per cent line to be "import sensitive" for linear reduction the range of tariff cut could result into 0-534 per cent (see table 4 and box 5). The tariff peak of 822 in this case of a minimum average reduction will be reported at 411 per cent. In case the developing countries persuade the US to apply the Swiss formula on the peak, we can notice a sharp reduction to 15-42 per cent depending on the "B" coefficient value. These simulation results have been summarised in the table 8 below.

Table 8
Impact on US Peak Tariffs as per Different Formula

(in per cent)

Present range of US bindings		0-822
Harbinsons multi slab linear reduction formula	Range	0-452
	Average reduction in peak	328
Top 10% of tariffs by linear reduction and rest by Swiss	Range	0-534
	Average reduction in peak	411
Top 10% of tariffs by Swiss with B=15	Peak Tariff	15
Top 10% of tariffs by Swiss with B=45	Peak Tariff	42

Based on the above analysis, the query: what should be the position of India and other developing countries *vis-à-vis* USA and other developed countries in terms of the bargaining terrain on agricultural market access, can be attempted for suitable responses. The bargaining strength of India in particular and of South Asian countries in general lies in steadfastly holding on to the removal of the phrase "import sensitive" from the "Derbez Draft". Secondly, the developed countries must agree to subject their top peak tariff lines to reduction using the Swiss formula. The developed countries, on the other hand, most probably would insist on retaining the "import sensitive" element in the "Derbez Draft" so that these countries could use the linear cut on them. Understandably, the arithmetic of the blend formula favours the developed countries by making the tariff level highly flexible and "sensitive imports" dependent. The interests of the developing (including south Asian) countries, as it is already demonstrated, are severely compromised under such a blended framework

Section 5: Concluding Observations and Policy Recommendations

The post-URAA experience of the developing countries with trade liberalisation and oscillations in the domestic economies notwithstanding, the Doha Development Round negotiations did set an ambitious mandate. The developing countries, undoubtedly, have realized the long-term potential of the trade and reflections of the high-expectations at Doha were found in the mandate.

The Fifth Ministerial (highest decision making body of WTO) during 10-14 September 2003 in Cancun, Mexico did not come out with any decision nor direction. However, the need for a concerted engagement to accommodate the sovereign aspirations of the developing countries was indeed clearly visible at the Cancun meeting. The large number of "framework paper" submissions by different coalitions and the alliances of member countries are pointing towards this aspiration and ambition.

There is no denying the fact that the "Single Undertaking" of the Doha mandate should neither leave anybody unhappy nor be the cause of imbalances in any of the three sectors, namely, agriculture, non-agriculture and services. And, within AoA the pulls and pressures of the three pillars, namely, market access, domestic support and export competition should not be allowed to fluctuate wildly between the developed north and the developing south. The ease with which consumers and producers can be separated in the developed countries is not possible in the developing south where the producer cum consumer category dominates.

The market access of agriculture products, against this backdrop, has gone through a lot of remarkable changes in the past few months. The revised draft modalities of agriculture (WTO 2003d) submitted by the Chairman Harbinson suggested a multi-slab linear reduction formula for tariffs with certain special provisions for developing countries. Simulations conducted on the basis of that formula brought out the fact that the present bound average of India would get reduced from 114.5 per cent to 71.6 per cent. The decline in the average was about 37.5 per cent. The corresponding reduction in average bound rates for Pakistan and Sri Lanka was 35 per cent and 30 per cent correspondingly Bangladesh, being a least developed country, is not required to make any reductions.

A similar exercise conducted for USA showed a decline of 52.3 per cent in the bound average. The weighted average of the proposed bound tariff averages stood at 4.5 per cent while the current bound average of agriculture products in USA is around 9.5 per cent. Since the draft ministerial text (Castillo Draft) was silent on the issue of peak and specific duties on tariffs it was perceived to provide the developed countries a fertile space to aggressively promote their own imbalances within and amongst the three pillars. The position on reduction in peak tariffs and conversion of specific duties into their *ad valorem* equivalents by the developed nations needed to be made clear to meaningfully continue with the engagements.

The WTO Cancun Ministerial Text issued by the Conference Chair, Mr. Derbez leaned heavily on the joint EC-US "framework paper" on agriculture. This bias complicated the negotiation process by mystifying the approach to the agriculture market access pillar. The option for multi-slab linear reduction was removed in this text. Hence, the developing countries are being squeezed to provide better market access to the developed countries' agricultural produce. For example, India will have to reduce her average bound tariff in agriculture anywhere in the range 45-83 per cent depending on the blended combination of the formula (suggested for core modality) and the chosen value of "B" coefficient (for the Swiss element) in the blend formula.

This has severely limited the options for developing countries. In addition, both "Drafts" (Castillo and Derbez) is silent on a number of crucial parameters that go into the formula. The simulated estimates based on this draft suggest varying pictures for developing and developed nations. One of the coordinates emerging from our limited case study shows that in the case of USA the decline in average tariff ranges between 5.1-5.6 per cent depending on the combination. In addition, there will not be a substantial reduction in peak and high tariffs. Based on this study the bargaining strength of India in particular and of south Asian countries in general lies in steadfastly holding on to the removal of the "import sensitive" phrase from the "Derbez Draft". Secondly, the developed countries must agree to subject their top peak tariff (agricultural) lines to reduction using the Swiss formula. For example, the US peak tariff of 822 per cent on application of the Swiss formula will get reduced to about 15, per cent in a case of the "B" co-efficient being 15 and to 42 per cent in case the "B" co-efficient is 45. The lower range of 90 per cent of tariffs should be reduced by a simple linear reduction of 50 per cent per tariff line. There may not be the requirement for the third of the blend formula since the imports of many products are already free of any duty in developed countries.

In the case of developing countries, a multiple scenario is obtained. The proposed average tariff for India declines from 114.5 per cent to a range between 19.8-63.2 per cent depending on the combinations used. Obviously, this is too large a range for any developing country. Notably, the proposed range is dependent on many factors that have not been spelt out, like 'import sensitive items' in the Swiss element of blend formula, the number of lines subject to linear cuts and values for "B" coefficient. Consider for instance, the top 75 per cent of tariff lines that could be subject to a simple linear reduction. The remaining lower range of 25 per cent tariff lines will have to be adjusted using the Swiss formula with 300 as the coefficient to reach the reduction level attained on using Harbinson's formula. Frankly, this asking rate of "B" coefficient is unimaginable and outrageous. The slab, asking for duty free imports, could be deleted from here also since agriculture is the core sector for these countries and it is not feasible, economically as well, for them to allow any agricultural product to be imported freely.

Thus, it is clear that this is not the case cannot acceptable to any developing country. The developed countries on the other hand may insist on retaining the "import sensitive" element in the "Derbez Draft" so that these countries could use the linear cut on them. In which case the peak tariff of 822 in the case of USA may stand reduced at 534 per cent. In the event that they use the first slab of Harbinson's formula, 822 per cent peak tariff may get reduced to 452 per cent.

The analysis of the core modalities formula that is expected to lay the foundation for the post- negotiations commitments bears out that this is the main cause of concern. The caution and restraint shown by the group of developing countries during the series of discussions amply justify that complex formula to address trade distortions are highly impractical and adversely impact the distributional capabilities of the national governments.

The greatest cause of imbalances has been identified in our study to be pivoted on the formula. Expecting the developing countries to peg their commitment levels significantly lower than the currently prevailing unweighted average applied tariff levels because it is much lower than the committed average bound rates is unfair. The averages during the pre-millennium period conceal a great deal of craft and caprice of the developed north. In this limited exercise, we have brought out that the issues of "tariff peak" and "tariff escalations", indeed, are real regressive practices. That they unduly tilt the balance in favour of a few countries in the first instance and therefore the need for a fresh look at the whole issue of special safeguard measures.

It is shown that given the tariff profile, the higher reductions at higher levels of tariffs are deceptive. The preponderance of *non-ad valorem* tariffs in the northern developed country members' schedules is a clever ploy to conceal the ground realities and therefore the intentions. The developing countries are indeed constrained by shallow and almost empty treasury chests to enhance investment in technology and infrastructure in order to garner the benefits of trade in agricultural products. However, with comparable level of applied tariff averages, the developing countries are willing and conscientious players in the agriculture trade arena. In this respect the market access plus scenario in the form of stringent sanitary and phytosanitary (SPS) measures need to be taken on board the discussion table in Geneva.

What should be the position of India and other south Asian countries vis-a-vis the US and other developed countries in terms of the bargaining terrain on agricultural market access during the forthcoming rounds of the WTO General Council?

The much acclaimed value-added agricultural product export models to start with are not feasible in the post-millennium round if the concealed protection currently in vogue in the OECD countries are to continue. The fact that tariff peaks, tariff escalation and specific duties (*non-ad valorem* duties) all find easy and dominant use in agricultural products is not to be taken as residual or insignificant. A pro-active and serious engagement with these issues, at the least, has become imminent at this juncture to redeem the Doha Round to ensure an optimistic outcome to market access in agricultural products. This study indicates that the negotiation must focus on the G20+ framework as this provides for the removal of "import sensitive lines" from the blended formula, for developed countries. The developed countries must be persuaded to commit deeper cuts in their top tariff lines. The market access pillar in the agriculture negotiations plays a crucial role and the bargaining terrain has to impart a sufficient level of confidence and comfort to the developing countries. The G20+ framework apparently leads towards the right coordinates of this bargaining terrain in WTO.

Notes

Fortunately, demystification exercise is not insurmountable as the following helpful leads are available. WTO (2003), "Formula Approaches to Tariff Negotiations", Negotiating Group on Market Access, TN/MA/S/3/Rev.2, 11 April (03-1988) Geneva. Mehta, Rajesh (2003) Industrial Tariffs: Towards WTO Round Negotiations, RIS, New Delhi. UNCTAD (2003), Back to Basics: Market Access Issues in the Doha Agenda, UNCAD/DITC/TAB/Misc.9. Bacchetta, M. and B. Bora (2003). "Industrial Tariff Liberalization and the Doha Development Agenda", WTO Discussion Paper No.1. and Francois, Joseph and Will Martin (2003), "Formula Approaches for Market Access", The World Economy, Vol.26, No.1, January, pp.1-28.

References

FAO (2003), "Agricultural Commodities: Profiles and Relevant WTO Negotiating Issues", Rome. www.fao.org/es/esc/common/ecg/27655_en_profiles.pdf]. Also see FAO (2000), "Country Case Studies: Agriculture, Trade and Food Security: Issues and Options in WTO Negotiations", Rome.www.fao.org/DOCREP/003/X8731e00.htm] and Gulati, Ashok, Rajesh Mehta and Sudha Narayanan (1999), "From Marrakesh to Seattle: Indian Agriculture in a Globalising World", *Economic and Political Weekly*, 9 October, pp. 2931-2942.

Gibson, Paul et al. (2001b), *ibid* and Burfisher, M. et al. (2001) "Options for Agricultural Policy Reforms in the WTO Negotiations", Economic Research Service, USDA, *Agricultural Economic Report # 797*, January: Washington DC.

Gibson, Paul *et.al.* (2001a), "Profiles of Tariffs in Global Agricultural Markets", Market and Trade Economics Division, ERS, USDA, *Agricultural Economic Report # 796*, January; Washington, DC.

Gibson, Paul, *et. al.* (2001c), *ibid.*

Hanumantha Rao, C.H. (2001), 'WTO and Viability of Indian Agriculture', *Economic and Political Weekly*, Vol. 36, No. 36, 8 September, pp. 3453-3457.

Kaplan, Edward S. and Thomas W. Ryley (1994), "Prelude to Trade Wars: American Tariff Policy", 1890-1922, Greenwood Press, Westport, Connecticut & London.

Mehta, Rajesh and J. George (2003), 'Implementation Issues in SPS: A Developing Country Perspective for Development Agenda on the Meandering Pathways from Doha to Cancun', *RIS Discussion Paper # 58*, Research and Information System for the Non-Aligned and Other Developing Countries, September: New Delhi.

WTO (2000), "Committee on Agriculture–Special Session–Market Access–Submissions..." G/AG/NG/W/37, 28 September (00-3944), Geneva, p. 3.

WTO (2003a), "Committee on Agriculture: Special Session Negotiations on Agriculture–Report by the Chairman to TNC", TN/AG/10 (03-3669) 7 July, Geneva. In this respect document number TM/AG/9 dated 8 April 2003 and TN/AG/R/7 dated 24 March 2003 are very informative. However, for details of background discussion that provided valuable inputs to the Chairman see overview in WTO (2002) TNIAG/6, 18 December (02-6943).

WTO (2003b), "The Doha Agenda: Towards Cancun", Trade Negotiations Committee, TN/C/W/13, 6 June (03-2980), Geneva.

WTO (2003c) *ibid*.

WTO (2003d), "Negotiations on agriculture: First draft of modalities for the further commitments", TN/AG/W/1/Rev.1, Geneva, 18 March.

5

Impact of World Trade Organization on Agricultural Trade and Environment

P. Leela

Section 1: Introduction

The Eighth Round of GATT negotiations popularly known as the Uruguay Round and the signing of the Marrakesh Treaty led to the establishment of the World Trade Organisation (WTO) in 1995, with a view to liberalise and expand World trade by bringing down tariff rates and by dismantling the complex system of quantitative restrictions on trade. The Uruguay Round marked a major departure from the earlier GATT rounds of negotiations by bringing under its purview a wide spectrum of areas for the first time like: agriculture, services, textiles, environment, trade related investment measures and intellectual property rights.

Agriculture continues to occupy an important place in the economies of South Asia in terms of its contribution to GDP, foreign trade and in terms of its share in the work force. The Agreement on Agriculture reached in the Uruguay Round of Multilateral Trade Negotiations liberalises agricultural trade and opens up the agricultural sector to international competition.

In recent times, environmental issues are attracting deep concern and increasing attention due to the proliferation of environmental standards and regulations. Trade and environment are interlinked. Trade policies, including agricultural trade liberalisation policies, have an impact on environment and environment policies have an impact on trade. Consequently, towards the end of the Uruguay Round, trade related environmental issues emerged at the centre of attention during the debates on 'green growth', put forward by the environmental groups. Ensuring environmental sustainability has been stated as the Seventh Millennium Development Goal of the UNDP. Against this background, the object of the present paper is to examine the impact of WTO. on agricultural trade and environment, with reference to India, which is an important country in the region of South Asia.

Section 2: Agreement on Agriculture

One of the important Agreements of WTO is the Agreement on Agriculture (AoA). It governs the World trade in agricultural commodities. It aims at liberalising World trade in agricultural commodities. The basic objective is to initiate a process of agricultural trade reforms with a view to establish a 'fair and market-oriented' agricultural trading system. The AoA. increases market-orientation in agricultural trade by providing commitments in the areas of market access, domestic support and export competition. Liberalisation of agricultural trade benefits the agricultural-exporting developing countries of South Asia through the rise in the prices of agricultural commodities consequent to the withdrawal of subsidies to their farm sector by the developed countries. Tariffs on agricultural products are to be reduced over a period of six years by an average of 36 per cent in the case of developed countries and 24 per cent over a period of 10 years in the case of developing countries. Least developed countries are not required to reduce tariffs. The signatories are also to cut domestic and export subsidies in agriculture, patent seeds for commercial uses, compulsorily import a certain percentage of a country's food need (Bhorali 1994). In actual practice, subsidy to agriculture turned out to be a controversial issue.

Trade Problems of Agricultural Commodities

The Agreement on Agriculture of the WTO and the consequent liberalisation of trade in agricultural commodities are expected to increase the agricultural exports of the developing countries in the markets of the developed countries. This, however, did not materialise. In fact, in the post-Uruguay period, exports to Japan and the European Union (EU) from the developing countries of the region declined or remained at the same level (Vyas 2002). This points to the statement of Finger and Schuler that trade liberalisation is not merely an issue of trade barriers alone (Rajan 2002). The major problem faced by the agricultural exporting developing countries is the subsidization of agriculture by the developed countries. Instead of being reduced, this subsidization is being increased by the developed countries under different garbs, apart from various tariff and non-tariff barriers used by them to protect their farm sector.

The opportunities arising from liberalisation of World trade in agricultural commodities can be reaped only when reforms are implemented both in the developing as well as in the developed countries' agricultural sector. All barriers to trade in any form have to be removed. At present while agricultural production is relatively free from controls, marketing of agricultural commodities is still subject to government control.

In the post-WTO scenario, many developing countries experienced:

(a) decline in agricultural trade as a proportion of total trade;

(b) increase in agricultural trade in absolute terms (most of it in the form of agricultural input imports for promoting agricultural production); and

(c) diversification of agricultural exports.

Agricultural Export Performance of India

Agricultural exports of India in terms of value, as shown in table 1, increased from Rs. 21,138 crores in 1995-96 to Rs. 29,312 crores in 2001-2002. During this period, the value of total exports of India increased from Rs. 106,353 crores in 1995-96 to 209.018 crores in 2001-2002. The relative share of agricultural exports in the total exports of India reached a peak level of 20.4 per cent in 1996-97, but declined gradually to 14.02 per cent in 2001-2002.

Thus, during the post–WTO period, agricultural exports of India showed an increase in absolute terms, but experienced a decline as a proportion of the total exports of India. The decline in the relative share of agricultural exports is due to the relatively faster growth of the total exports of India, while the increase in the absolute value of agriculture exports was mainly due to the significant increases recorded by exports of cereals, sugar, oil meals, processed foods, poultry and dairy products.

Table 1
Agricultural Exports of India

(Rs.in Crores)

Year	*Total Exports of India*	*Exports of Agricultural and Allied Products of India*	*Percentage share of Agricultural Exports in Total Exports*
1990-91	32,553	6,317	19.40
1995-96	106,353	21,138	19.87
1996-1997	118,817	24,239	20.40
1997-1998	130,100	25.419	19.54
1998-1999	139,752	26.104	18.68
1999-2000	159,561	25,016	15.67
2000-2001	203,571	28,582	14.04
2001-2002	209,018	29,312	14.02

Source: Government of India (2000-01 and 2002-03), Economic Survey.

The important agricultural commodities exported by India, as shown in table 2, include: coffee, tea, oil cakes, tobacco, cashew kernels, spices, sugar, raw cotton, rice, fish and fish preparations, meat and meat preparations, fruits, vegetables, pulses and miscellaneous processed foods. During the last decade (table 3), there is a decline in the relative share of coffee, tea, oil cakes, tobacco, cashew kernels and raw cotton, while there is an increase in the relative share of spices, sugar, rice, fish and fish preparations, meat and meat preparations, fruits, vegetables, pulses and miscellaneous processed foods in the agricultural exports of India. Thus, during the post WTO period, there is a change in the composition of agricultural exports with India emerging as a net exporter of cereals from being a net importer.

Trade Liberalization and Rice Exports

Rice is the major cereal exported by India. The World rice market has been expanding over the years, particularly from the 1990's. More than 90 per cent of World's rice production of 397 million tonnes in 2001 came from Asia. Rice production and related activities form the lifeline of about 70 per cent of the poor people of Asia.

Table 2
Composition of Agricultural Exports of India

(Rs. Crores)

	1960-61	*1970-71*	*1980-81*	*1990-91*	*1995-96*	*2000-01*	*2001-02*
1. Coffee	7	25	214	252	1503	1185	1095
2. Tea & Mate	124	148	426	1070	1171	1976	1719
3. Oil Cakes	14	55	125	609	2349	2045	2263
4. Tobacco	16	33	141	263	447	871	808
5. Cashew ernels	19	57	140	447	1237	1883	1652
6. Spices	17	39	11	239	794	1619	1497
7. Sugar	30	29	40	38	506	511	1782
8. Raw Cotton	12	14	165	846	204	224	43
9. Rice	-	5	224	462	4568	2943	3174
10. Fish & Fish Preparations	5	31	217	960	3381	6367	5897
11. Meat & Meat preparations	1	3	56	140	627	1470	1193
12. Fruits, Vegetables & Pulses	6	12	80	216	802	1609	1560
13. Misc Processed Foods	1	4	36	213	745	1094	1236
Total value of exports of Agrl & allied prodts	284	487	2057	6317	21138	28582	29312

Source: Government of India (various issues), Economic Survey.

Table 3
Agricultural Exports of India - Relative Share

(Percentage)

	1990-91	*1995-96*	*2000-01*	*2001-02*
1. Coffee	4.0	7.1	4.1	3.7
2. Tea	16.9	5.5	6.9	5.9
3. Oil Cakes	9.6	11.1	7.2	7.7
4. Tobacco	4.1	2.1	3.0	2.8
5. Cashew Kernels	7.1	5.9	6.6	5.6
6. Spices	3.8	3.8	5.7	5.1
7. Sugar	0.6	2.4	1.8	6.1
8. Raw Cotton	13.4	0.97	0.78	0.1
9. Rice	7.3	21.6	10.3	10.8
10. Fish & Fish Preparations	15.2	15.99	22.3	20.1
11. Meat & Meat preparations	2.2	2.97	5.1	4.1
12. Fruits, Vegetables & Pulses	3.4	3.79	5.6	5.3
13. Misc Processed Foods	3.3	3.5	3.8	4.2

Source: Based on Government of India (2002-2003), Economic Survey.

Liberalization of trade in respect of rice, as part of the Agreement on Agriculture of GATT 1994 has multifarious implications. It leads to free trade in rice. Such free trade in rice will have an impact on the pattern of trade flows of the countries concerned and also on the performance of agricultural exports. For example, in the past, both Japan and Korea banned the imports of rice. But under Annexure 5 of the URAA, these countries are committed to provide minimum access quotas.

Apart from WTO Agreement on Agriculture, rice trade flows are determined by a host of other factors like: the supply of rice and the domestic as well as the external policies of all the countries involved in the rice trade. For example, basmati rice is much in demand in West Asia. This demand is met by countries from South Asia including India. On the other hand, most of the demand of South America is for paddy, which is supplied by U.S.A. Indica rice accounts for 75-80 per cent while aromatic varieties like basmati rice account for only 10 per cent of the World rice trade.

Given the competitiveness of different countries, rice trade liberalization will lead to changes in the pattern of trade flows. Rice would flow from poor countries, which have comparative advantage to rich countries where prices of rice are high. This is also predicted by the Arkansas Global Rice Model, which states that in the year 2010, Thailand, Vietnam and India will be the major net exporters of medium and long grain rice followed by U.S., Pakistan and China, while Canada, South Africa, Indonesia and countries of West Asia, East Asia, South America and European Union would continue to be net importers (Gulati and Narayanan 2003).

India has become a net exporter of rice from being a net importer. Rice exports of India accounted for 10.8 per cent of agricultural exports of India in 2001-2002 and for 20.1 per net of total World rice exports in 1999. India has emerged as the second largest exporter of rice and sixth largest exporter of wheat (G.O.I. 2002-2003, p.108). Rice is mainly exported to Saudi Arabia (57.55 per cent), Kuwait (10.66 per cent) and U.K. (10.51 per cent). Together, these three countries accounted for 78.72 per cent of the rice exports of India in 2001-2002.

At the Doha meet, India sought to safeguard the food and livelihood security of its subsistence level farming community by insisting on the reduction in the high tariffs and subsidies prevalent in the developed countries. But the subsidies are being continued in other forms of the Green, Blue and Amber Box provisions.

Section 3: Trade and Environment

The end of Uruguay Round of multilateral trade negotiations saw the emergence of the role of WTO in environment and in trade-related environmental issues. This led to the establishment in 1994 of the Committee on Trade and Environment (CTE.). After the liberalisation of agricultural trade, focus has now shifted to technical regulations such as food safety, health and safety of consumers, health of plants and animals, packaging, eco-labelling, quality standards and environmental norms.

Under WTO, environmental issues are incorporated in a number of Agreements. These include:

- Agreement on Agriculture
- Agreement on Sanitary and Phyto-Sanitary (SPS) measures
- Agreement on Subsidies and Counterveiling Measures
- Agreement on Technical Barriers to Trade (TBT).

In recent times, there has been a global proliferation of environment and health related standards and a rise in environmentally-sensitive goods. It is now widely believed that environmental and health-related standards, rules and regulations in developed countries have the potential to create barriers to trade. They tend to impede the trade of developing countries either implicitly or explicitly (Chaturvedi and Nagpal 2003).

Pesticide maximum residue levels (MRL) permitted in foodstuffs, packaging requirements for fruits and vegetables, emission standards for machines impede the exports of food and agricultural products. Strong consumer movements and stronger concerns for protection of human health, plant health, wildlife and environment exert pressure on exports. There is also the problem of compliance cost in respect of sanitary and phyto-sanitary (SPS) measures. For example, the cost of upgrading the sanitary conditions in the Bangladesh frozen shrimp industry in order to satisfy E.U. and U.S. hygiene requirements is placed at $17.6 million for 1997-98 (Cato 1998). In addition, there is the problem of time element involved in upgrading the facilities. Factories have to be kept closed for long to upgrade the facilities with huge investments.

At present, out of 404 plants in India, only 90 plants are approved on grounds of upgradation for fishery exports to the EU (Cato).

Technical standards necessitate the imports of inputs and technology. They add to the cost of production and price of the final product and thereby reduce the export competitiveness and export performance of the products. Lack of expertise, lack of timely information and the complexity of the system of environmental standards, which may be incompatible with the prevailing systems of production and marketing of the developing countries, may add to the woes of the exporters from the developing countries.

Studies (Rao 2001) indicate that as a result of trade liberalistion the incentive framework for agriculture in India has improved considerably. However, in spite of the favourable macroeconomic environment there has been some slowing down of agricultural growth in the post-economic reforms period. This is due to lack of public investment in agriculture. Therefore, public investment has to be stepped up in agriculture in order to improve productivity. Further, efforts have tobe made to diversify agricultural output in a cost-effective way. Efforts should also be made to tap export potential of agricultural commodities by improving quality, packaging, and eco-labeling and by ensuring the maintenance of the required health and safety standards. The markets of other developing countries also have to be tapped to expand the agricultural exports, taking into account the possible competition from the agricultural surplus developed countries. At the same time, domestic policy reforms and removal of domestic restrictions become important in improving domestic supply conditions for export purposes.

Section 4: Conclusion

The post-WTO scenario has witnessed a shift in focus from food security to food safety and from trade liberalization to environmental concerns. The emphasis is on the fulfillment of technical measures such as regulations relating to food safety, packaging and air-conditioning requirements, quality standards, eco-labelling and emission of machines. Such a shift, even though important and natural from the point of view of health of humans, plants and animals, has been posing problems for the developing countries in reaping the benefits of liberalized world trade. Many of the developing countries are experiencing hardships in expanding their exports to the developed countries as the environmental standards are turning out to be environmental non-tariff barriers to their trade with the developed countries. In addition, there are compliance costs and huge investments, putting pressure on the export competitiveness of the developing countries.

If the agricultural-exporting-developing countries are to reap the benefits of agricultural trade liberalization, in terms of wider markets and higher prices, the subsidization given to their farm sector by the developed countries in various garbs under the Blue Box and Green Box provision has to be removed. Developing countries have to be given government support and technical assistance in helping them cope with the regulatory standards set by the developed country importers for food safety, quality and environmental norms and also to assist them in bringing down the compliance costs. Developing countries, on their part, have to make efforts to produce organic agricultural products, to obtain a greater share of the expanding markets for such products in the World markets.

Public investment in agriculture has to be increased in order to improve efficiency and productivity. Agricultural production has to be diversified in a cost effective manner. Domestic policy performs are needed to remove domestic restrictions so that domestic supply conductions can be improved for enhancing the export performance of the agricultural commodities. Investments are needed to improve the infrastructural facilities. Export markets of developing countries among themselves have to be explored by improving competitive efficiency and exportable surpluses.

References

Bhorali, D. (1994), *GATT Agreement or Dunkel Draft Treaty: Its Impact on Agriculture, Industry, TRIPs and TRIMs and Drug Industry*, Mittal Publications, New Delhi.

Cato, J.C. (1998), *Economic Issues Associated with Seafood Safety and Implementation of Seafood HACCP Programmes*, FAO, Rome.

Chaturvedi, S. and Nagpal, G. (2003), "WTO and Product-Related Environmental Standards: Emerging Issues and Policy Options", *Economic and Political Weekly*, January 4-10, Vol. XXXVIII, No. 1.

Government of India (2002-2003), *Economic Survey.*

Gulati, A. and Narayanan, S. (2003), "Rice Trade Liberalization and Poverty" *Economic and Political Weekly*, January 4-10, Vol. XXXVIII, No. 1.

Hanumantha Rao, C.H. (2001), "WTO and Viability of Indian Agriculture", *Economic and Political Weekly*, September 8-14, Vol. XXXVI, No. 36.

Rajan, R.S. (2002), "Trade Liberalisation and Poverty: Revisiting the Age-old Debate", *Economic and Political Weekly*, December 7-13, Vol. XXXVII, No. 49.

Vyas, V.S. (2002), "Our Agrarian Future: A Medium-Term Perspective on Asian Agriculture" *Economic and Political Weekly*, December 15-20, Vol. XXXVII, No. 50.

PART - III

WTO and Singapore Issues –South Asia

6

Competition Policy in India and South Asia

Smriti Mukherjee

Concerns about competition policy have figured on international agenda since long. Increased market access for foreign firms and restrictive business practices followed by domestic markets could lead to contradictory policy mix. In the 1970s discussions in this regard were initiated under UN auspices towards the concluding stages of Uruguay Round competition policy emerged as a new issue and finally WTO Ministerial Conference at Singapore in 1996 set up a Working Group on the interaction between trade and competition policy.

Competition policy basically means competition law, ie., the laws that are implemented to regulate anti-competitive behaviour in markets. Historically competition laws have dealt with restrictive trade practices of firms in their own countries. By and large countries thought it beyond their capability to try to control anti competitive behaviour in foreign markets. Domestic cartels of exporting firms were in conformity with the principles being followed by countries participating in international trade.

WTO competition policy is relevant in regard to TRIPS, TRIMS and GATS the most important elements of it being non-discrimination, national treatment and market access. It does not ask members to follow a common competition policy and they are tree to adopt any competition law that they wish. Only constraint is that these laws should not come into clash with WTO's declared objectives of market access and national treatment.

This paper argues in two ways: a) Is there any strong economic logic behind lax competition rules following globalization and b) if more competition still seems to be desirable how do the members of a regional economic group (say in South Asia) behave?

Section 1: The Issues in Competition Policy

Government's can be assumed to be maximizing domestic welfare. In a broad sense welfare may be thought of consisting of consumer surplus, public sector profit, corporate profit and profit earned by domestic firms from abroad. Competition policy is looked upon as a tool to maximize this welfare function. The question arises that why different countries should have different competition policies. To that one can say that a government is quite free to attach different weights to different components of the domestic welfare function. In a democracy a government aligned to the left will most likely have a strict competition policy whereas a right wing government will not mind somewhat liberal competition policy. As far as domestic firms are concerned core of the competition policy is to choose the optimum number of firms competing domestically and the tariff rate as well. Given the number of domestic firms if the tariff rate is chosen in such a way that it gives rise to supernormal profits there will surely be incentive for outside firms to enter and profits would be driven down to zero. On the other hand, if number of firms and tariff rate taken together are such that losses are being made there will be exit until non-negative profits become a reality.

Following opening up of the country as number of competing firms go up who are the principal beneficiaries? Obviously the consumers. Increased specialization, large-scale production, intense competition and larger alternatives will surely lead to an augmented utility function. If the pre liberalization utility function consisted of n different commodities the consumers can now have any number of commodities between 11+ 1 and say 2n. Increase in the number of firms might result in differentiated products and so the effect on market price may be less severe. In the case both domestic firms and new entrants are producing homogeneous products aggregate output will increase and market price will definitely come down. This will affect total revenue of both domestic and foreign firms. So market price and profit level of both the firms will depend upon individual output levels chosen by them. If product market equilibrium is to be preserved increase in the supply of output is to be matched by increase in demand and if labour requirement per unit of output remains the same aggregate employment is going to increase in the economy.

It is true that the most important effect of foreign competition will be greater output and lowering of cost. Consumer surplus is definitely going to increase, government revenue will come down owing to lowering of tariffs and if domestic corporate profits show a decline it might be compensated by foreign earnings of domestic firms. Under these assumptions increased competition in the domestic market is conducive to higher welfare. For a developing country inability of the domestic firm to take advantage of foreign markets might lead to dependence on the home market where its share is declining. In this situation it is possible that free entry from abroad will contribute to lessening of domestic welfare and domestic firms might seek protection against national injury. If they try to get the remedy there might be an incentive for the firms to form cartels, which if permitted will definitely have export market implications. Higher prices associated with cartels may augment export revenue provided the commodity involved is either essential or in short supply.

In a domestic market where limited number of firms is competing there will always be an attraction to form cartels. It is one effective way to get out of cutthroat competition for market share. Cartels can very often act against the national interest When new firms seek entry cartels may try to prevent it adopting unfair trade practices. Thus it is possible that domestic cartel will flood the market with previous stocks so that prices come down to abnormally low levels making, it impossible for the foreign firm to compete. This is one instance where one needs an international trade law to ensure free and fair competition. As opposed to this case there may arise situations where the government of the country may have to encourage the coming together of domestic firms by way of mergers and acquisitions. A large number of small firms may be uneconomic in the sense that none of them achieves full capacity utilization as a result of which ruling price remains at a higher level. In order to promote efficiency the government may create conditions facilitating mergers and acquisitions. Regrouping of rums may actually pave the way for them to withstand foreign competition. Shutting out foreign competition is no competition policy. The government must have a strong trade policy to ensure optimum national surplus.

A new dimension to competition policy has been added by the phenomenon of FDI inflow. On the one hand there is the national treatment clause, which requires the host country to offer at least as favourable treatment to foreign investors as that meted out to domestic investors in like circumstances. This clause applies to both pre and post entry situations. Pre entry national treatment enables the foreign firms market access and freedom to move into the factor market. Post entry national treatment takes the form of non- discrimination with domestic enterprises. While developing countries in general welcome FDI inflow they have to be cautious about tile undesirable effects FDI may bring in. The undesirable effects may consist of It restrictive business practices, abuse of dominant position and cross border mergers and acquisitions. When foreign entry is accomplished through cross border M and As, the probability of anti competitive behaviour increases due to two reasons. Firstly because the number of market participants may be reduced and second because there may not be any addition to capacities.

Increase in competition and local capacity building are twin objectives of welcoming FDI. f that is overshadowed by anti-competitive behaviour there is need for regulation by the host county government- International law guarantees a state the absolute right to control the admission and establishment of foreign units into its own territory. Control measures may take the form of exclusion of FDI from certain selected areas, restriction on equity holding, withholding of strategic information etc. Presently no country allows foreign entry as a matter of right, regulatory mechanism is always there. By 2003 some 93 countries have framed competition rules and established separate agencies to implement these laws. But establishing an agency does not contribute to the capacity of poor countries to pursue the anti-competitive behaviour of a large multinational company.

The issue of merger is no doubt an important area of international trade policy. It leads to economies of scale expands market and is supposed to facilitate innovation also. When two firms from two different countries decide to merge they have to think about their own welfare and national welfare as well because otherwise the contending parties might be pulled up by anti-monopoly commissions in their respective countries. Third country where both these parties will contest for market share that country's producer and consumer interest however goes completely unrepresentative. At present however when merger takes place producer interest in both the countries acts as the accessory condition. If increase in producer interest is going to be positive it meets private interest condition and the merger is okayed. At the next stage national interest in both the countries, which consists of producer as well as consumer interest, is taken into consideration. If producer and consumer surplus increase in each country the merger serves national interest and none of the countries where the firms are located is going to suffer a decrease in welfare. There is no scope for anti-trust laws to come into action in either of these countries. In two countries A and B there are two firms each owned by citizens of two different countries. Provided surplus in both the countries increases the merger will be termed welfare augmenting.

Section 2: Competition Policy in SAARC

Among the seven SAARC members' existence of a definite policy to prevent industrial concentration could be found in the ease of India and Sri Lanka only. The consultation of Trade Policy Review brought out by the WTO in 2000 for Bangladesh but there was no mention of any competition policy as such. For Nepal and Pakistan one has to depend on their respective central bank reports but there also there was no mention of any competition policy. Further in the case of Pakistan the following quotation shows that there is no consistent anti-trust policy.

"A side effect for consumers is higher prices and possibly lower quality. For example in Pakistan currently the two brands of tea are being marketed by one single TNC. Before their takeover both these individual brands had their own quality, which was reasonably consistent and distinct. But after the TNC take over, not only has their quality suffered butlhe price has also risen as the TNC enjoys nearly monopolistic control over the local market. Thus the issue of competition and regulation is important and needs to be institutionalized at the international level so that the unbridled economic power of the TNC's can be checked" (Pakistan Development Review, 2001).

For Sri Lanka and India the present status of competition policy is like this:

	Sri Lanka	
Area	*Legislation/Regulation*	*Ministry/Institution*
Competition Policy	1. Fair Trading Commission Act 1987	
	2. Amendment Act, 1990	Fair Trading Commission
	3. Amendment Act 1993	
	India	
Competition Policy	MRTP Act, 1969	MRTP Commission 1970
	Substantial acquisition and Takeover	Securities & Exchange Board, 1997
	Competition Act, 2002	Competition Com.

The two SAARC countries having a well-defined competition policy have one thing in common. "Public Interest' happens to be the most important consideration to initiate action against monopolistic practices. In Sri Lanka however, companies acquiring a market share of more than one third or mergers resulting in a dominant firm status must notify before the Fair Trading Commission. Cartels are not covered by the Fair Trading Commission as a result of which if imports are procured at a higher price and that results in unreasonable domestic prices the commission may recommend tariff adjustments. Trade Policy Review for Sri Lanka published by the WTO in 1995 cites one case of toothpaste imports where import duties were lowered from 35 per cent to 10 per cent in 1995. In India when the MRTP Commission was first set up the emphasis was more on preventing economic concentration as laid down in the Indian constitution? Subsequently however competition policy has become more mature and now it focuses more on any practice that attempts at preventing, distorting or restricting competition in any manner. Market dominance as such is not undesirable until it is accompanied by anti-competitive behaviour.

Why is it that competition policies have suddenly acquired increased importance in recent years? One reason may be greater integration in the world economy in the wake of globalization movement. Mergers and takeovers are taking place in unprecedented scale most of it being in the U.S.A and in automobiles, defence and pharmaceutical industries. Mergers have a tendency of cartelization of markets and introducing increased barriers to entry. Collusion in price fixing is quite common and local subsidiaries of TNCs very often indulge in other forms of anti-competitive behaviour. Another reason why competition policies on the part of developing countries have assumed increased significance is that so far many of them have not felt the necessity of such a policy owing to the powerful presence of a strong public sector. Whatever industrialization under import substitution policy has taken place was to a large extent due to active state support. Public corporations were at the forefront of industrialization in many of these countries and little attention was given to private firm behaviour. Now under the pressure of privatization many of these state owned companies are being privatized and taken over by private sector. Before privatization they were like state monopolies and now it will be easier for them to engage in anti-competitive behaviour. New economic environment marked by privatization requires framing of a suitable competition policy.

Arguments given in support of mergers and acquisitions are familiar: they result in greater economies of scale, lower costs of production and higher R and D expenditure leading to faster technological innovation. Economizing on too much of competition is also another argument given in support of mergers. Now that TNCs are no longer confined in developed market economy countries and developing country, TNCs have become a phenomenon we may note that Japan and South Korea have actively encouraged growth of monopoly corporations by deliberately following lax competition policies at home. The central question is that developing countries have to decide what type of trade related competition policies is conducive to development. And if any international agreement on competition policy is reached the developing countries have to study its impact on development carefully.

It is a well-known fact that European Union is interested in WTO accepting the national treatment clause in competition policy agreement. If it is carried through, competition policy of every country will have to incorporate this provision in an explicit manner. Domestic firms and local subsidiaries of foreign affiliates are to be treated at par; non-discrimination principle will have to be extended between these two groups of competing firms.

Apparently it is just the logical extension of basic GAIT principle, which is applied in the case of trade involving goods. It has been argued in certain quarters that inclusion of this clause will render ineffective tile public interest argument that is most often employed to initiate action against anti-competitive behaviour. Domestic firms will have to suffer due to internationalization of competition policy. It has also been pointed out that many developing countries lack: the initiative to implement their competition laws to safeguard free entry in the presence of MNCs. To this it can be pointed out that developing country exporters also many a time sell their products to oligopolistic firms or cartels who tend to overcharge foreign customers. If reciprocity principle is understood properly there is really no valid ground for denying national treatment to domestic subsidiaries of TNCs.

Section 3: A Competition Policy for SAARC

It is true that while increased market access is being provided by lowering of tariffs throughout the world that opportunity cannot be allowed to be ruined by restrictive policies followed by a few domestic firms. One positive incentive for engaging into this kind of behaviour may be that average cost curves, instead of being U shaped tend to be more like an L. Higher output does not automatically give rise to lower cost instead after a certain stage addition to output does not evoke any response from the side of costs. Output neutral average cost can be offset by technological change but practicing barriers to entry may achieve the desired result more easily. Here the developing countries in general have to be careful and drafting of a competition policy is a must.

Once large scale FDI inflow becomes a reality developing countries will have to devise a comprehensive national policy in this regard- Foreign firms may be more efficient and denying national treatment to them would mean resulting to some thing like the infant industry argument employed in the case of tariffs. So one has to get reconciled to the entry of more efficient competitors. The major post entry problem hosts countries will have to tackle relate to the clout foreign affiliates might enjoy in credit market. They may have access to credit on favourable terms not because they are more efficient but simply due to the fact that their owners are positioned abroad. Banking practices will need to be improved to treat domestically owned sound units at par with foreign ones. The problem appears to be reverse than that discussed in international forums.

Foreign affiliates might soon acquire dominant status in developing country markets and this may serve as all incentive to abuse their market power. This is the real challenge to developing country partners in SAARC. A sound competition policy based to be formulated in order to see that abuse of market power does not pose any threat to efficiently managed domestic firms.

Settlement of disputes between investors and host countries is another key aspect of national competition policy. Host countries can offer a general framework of dispute settlement base don the laws of the land but there is a possibility of divergence between host country law and standard international law. Very often foreign investors might prefer arbitration facilities that ensure quick settlement. Internationalization of dispute settlement may not be a common practice with SAARC members. To ensure FDI inflow an institutional system of internationalized dispute settlement will be necessary. Laws of the land should be amenable to outside settlement of disputes involving foreign investors and host country government whenever there is a need.

While resolution of any investment dispute should primarily be attempted through bilateral and informal amicable means. At present the two international agencies engaged in dispute settlement are (1) International centre for the Settlement of Investment Disputes and (2) the International Chamber of Commerce (ICC) Court of Arbitration. In view of the fact that disputes may multiply in future some institutional changes may be thought of in matters relating to dispute settlement. A three stage dispute settlement machinery comprising of facilities of arbitration at national regional and international level may be useful. Host country being a developing country will prefer national level arbitration. Costs involved will be much less also but major impediment may be reluctance of foreign firms. Here again good offices of UNCTAD may be utilized to prevail upon the developed country entrants to accept this arrangement.

Regional level arbitration facilities are especially relevant for partners of an economic integration. Although formally there may not be any necessity of competition policy coordination among the group members availability of a common forum may prove to be useful. In the SAARC secretariat a cell may be created where any such dispute involving a member and any TNC can be discussed Individual countries can formulate some lowest common denominator type of approach in this regard ie the type of MNC behaviour that will be acceptable to all needs to be defined. In case the MNC is very strong obviously the first choice will be to take the dispute to a global agency where standard procedures will be there for dispute settlement. Successful implementation of competition policy at the regional level will necessitate the creation of a new institutional set up.

Section 4: Conclusion

Globalization and liquidation of government monopolies have meant bold steps towards freer trade. The benefits accruing due to these two policy changes cannot be allowed to be eroded by new barriers to trade and free entry erected by multinationals. Needs of faster development should get the top priority and gains from an international competition policy will have to be studied very carefully. There is one word of caution here. To be too vocal against restrictive trade practices of MNCs or lax competition policies followed by certain countries may not serve the developing country group. There are certain developing countries who are aspiring to be big players in mergers and acquisitions and cross border M&As created by them are a reality. Developing country unity can be preserved by keeping in mind the varied requirements of countries participating in international trade.

References

Bhattacharjea, A. (2000), "Predation, Protection and the Public Interest", *Economic and Political Weekly*, December 2, pp. 4327-4336.

Bhattacharjea, A. (2001), "Trade, Investment and Competition Policy: an Indian Perspective" in Mattoo, A. and R.M. Stern (ed), *India and the WTO*, World Bank and the OUP, pp. 197-234.

Bhattacharjea, A. (2003), India's Competition Policy–An Assessment, *Economic and Political Weekly*, August 23, pp. 3561-3574.

Bhattacharjea, A. (2001), "Competition Policy: India and the WTO", *Economic and Political Weekly*, December 22, pp. 4700-4713.

Bliss, C. (1996), "Trade and Competition Control" in Bhagwati and Hudee (eds.) *Fair Trade and Harmonization*, MIT Press, Cambridge.

Ghous, G., "Pricing in International Markcts: A Challenging Job", *Pakistan Economic and Social Review*, Vol. XXXVI, No. 1, pp. 99-110.

Head, K. and Jolm Rides (1997), "International Mergers and Welfare Under Deccntralized Competition Policy", *Canadian Journal of Economics,* Vol. XXX, No. 4b.

Hockman, B. and Petros C. Mavroidis (2002), "Economic Development, Competition Policy and the WTO", *Policy Research* Working Paper 2917, October, W.B.

Horn, H. and J. Levinsohn (2001), "Merger Policies and Trade Liberalization", *Economic Journal,* 111, April, pp. 244-276.

Levinsohn, J. (1996), "Competition Policy and International Trade" in Bhagwati and Hudce(ed.), *Op.cit.*

Lloyd, P.G. (1998), "Globalization and Competition Policies", *Review of World Economics,* Band 134, pp. 161-185.

Lommerud, K.E. Meland, F. and Sorgard, L. (2003), "Unionized Oligopoly, Trade.

Liberalization and Location Choice", *Economic Journal,* October, Vol. 113, No. 490, pp. 782-800.

Mahmood, M.A. (2001), "Book Review in *Pakistan Development Review,* 40:1, Spring, p. 80.

Pistor, K. and others (2003), "Evolution of Corporate Law and the Transplant Effect.

Lessons from Six Countries", *World Bank Research Observer,* Vol. 18, No. 1, Spring, pp. 89-112.

Richardson, M. (1999), "Trade and Competition Policies: Concordia Discors?" *Oxford Economic Papers,* 51, pp. 649-664.

Reserve Bank of India (2002-2003.), *Annual Review.*

Singh, J. (2000), Monopolistic Trade Practices and Concentration of Economic Power, EPW, December 9, pp. 4337-4444.

South Centre (2000), "Trade Related Agenda, Development and Equity (T.R.A.D.E), Competition Policy-Development and Developing Countries", Working Paper 7, November.

United Nations (2000), *Industrial Development Organization Report.*

UNCTAD 10th Session (2000), *Report of the UNCTAD.*

UNCTAD (1996, 2000 and 2003), *World Investment Report.*

WTO (1995), *Trade Policy Review,* Sri Lanka.

WTO (1998), *Trade Policy Review,* India.

WTO (2000), *Trade Policy Review,* Bangladesh.

7

World Trade Organisation and Core Labour Standards–South Asian Perspective

N. Nirmala

Section 1: Introduction

Core labour standards are international instruments defining a range of human rights at work that provide a guide to a civilized, dignified and sustainable workplace. (ILO 2003) In recent years, a broad international political consensus has emerged concerning the definition and recognition of a set of core labour standards. This has been accompanied by agreement that these standards should not be used for protectionist trade purposes. At the same time, there is evidence of a continuing gap between the recognition and the application of core labour standards. Moreover, the complex and multifaceted nature of the issues surrounding core labour standards has led to Considerable debate in the international community.

Such widely recognized and accepted core labour standards are nothing but the basic conventions of the International Labour Organization which are listed hereunder:

1. *Forced Labour Convention 1930 (Convention 029):* It provides for progressive abolition of forced in all its forms and, pending this abolition, its use only for public purpose and, as an exceptional measure, subject to conditions and guarantees set out in detail in various Articles of the Convention. This Convention was adopted in the background of practices then current in colonial territories.

2. *Freedom of Association and protection of Right to Organise Convention, 1948 (Convention 087):* It provides that the workers and employers, without distinction whatsoever, shall have the right to establish and join organizations of their own choosing without previous authorization. It also provides for guarantees permitting those organizations, and any federations, they may establish, to carry on their activities without interference from public authorities.
3. *Right to Organize and Collective Bargaining Convention, 1949 (Convention 098):* This Convention supplements Convention 87 and is designed to protect workers, against any acts of union discrimination, to safeguard workers and employer's organizations from mutual interference and to promote voluntary negotiation between Management and labour.
4. *Equal Remuneration Convention, 1951 (Convention 100):* It provides that the nations must promote and, in so far as is consistent with the methods in operation for determining wages, ensure the application of this principle of equality, and that this should be done by means of legislation, collective agreement or wage fixing machinery.
5. *Abolition of Forced Labour Convention, 1953 (Convention 105):* This convention supplements Convention 29. It provides for immediate and complete abolition of forced and compulsory labour of political purposes, as a method for mobilizing and using labour for economic development, as a means of labour discipline, as a punishment for having participated in strikes and a means of racial, social national or religious discrimination.
6. *Discrimination (Employment and Occupation) Convention, 1958 (Convention 111):* It refers to grounds of discrimination as diverse as race, sex, political opinion etc. The convention along with recommendation 111 covers discriminatory laws or acts in general, such as "any discrimination, exclusion or preference ... which has the effect of nullifying or impairing equality of treatment" and which can be the result ot not only legislation but also of existing factual positions or practices.
7. *Minimum Age Convention, 1973 (Convention 138):* This Convention provides for the minimum age to be specified by each state when ratifying this convention, and this age may

not be less than 15 years, except countries whose economy and educational facilities are insufficiently development. It also provides that minimum age must not be less than 18 years in dangerous occupations.

Currently, labour standards are not subject to WTO rules and disciplines. For several years the issue of trade and core labour standards has been the subject of intense debate among and within some World Trade Organization member governments. Some WTO member governments in Europe and North America believe that the issue must be taken up by the WTO in some form, if public confidence in the WTO and the global trading system is to be strengthened. Whereas, many officials in developing countries argue that better working conditions and improved labour rights arise through economic growth. They say that if the issue of core labour standards became enforceable under WTO rules, any sanctions imposed against countries with lower labour standards would merely perpetuate poverty and delay improvements in workplace standards.

Section 2: Background

The issue of trade and labour standards has been with the WTO since its birth. At the Ministerial Conference of the General Agreement on Tariffs and Trade held in Marrakesh in April 1994 to sign the treaty that formed the WTO, nearly all ministers expressed a point of view on the issue. (WTO 1999) The Chairman of that conference concluded that there was no consensus among member governments at the time, and thus no basis for agreement on the issue. When the Director- General of the ILO opened the International Labour Conference for a debate on this issue, in June 1994, the developing countries almost *en bloc* made an attempt to put an end to the discussion on the item. The WTO came into being without any consensus on linking trade and labour standards.

In December 1996, the first Ministerial Conference of the newly created World Trade organization was held in Singapore. The Conference attracted considerable attention, particularly the negotiations concerning the controversial issue of the 'social clause' i.e., the linking of labour standards with trade liberalization. The linking of trade and labour standards within WTO was urged most strongly by the United States, France and some other developed countries, and opposed by a substantial number of developing countries and the United Kingdom. Of all the new issues, the developing countries did best in protecting their interests in labour standards. They established in the Declaration (WTO 1996) that the Ministers "renew our commitment to the observance of internationally recognized core labour standards," but included the following points reflecting their interests:

(i) The ILO is the competent body to set and deal with labour standards;

(ii) The use of labour standards for protectionist purposes is rejected;

(iii) The comparative advantage of countries, particularly low-wage developing countries, must in no way be put into question; and

(iv) The WTO and ILO secretariats will continue their existing collaboration.

The inclusion of a reference to labour standards for the first time within an official WTO document indicates the importance that leading trading countries accord to the subject. The US threatened to refuse to sign the Declaration if it did not refer to labour standards. The Dutch and Scandinavian Ministers also supported WTO consideration of labour standards. Developing countries, most notably Malaysia and Egypt, argued strongly against consideration of labour standards by the WTO, reiterating contentions that the trade/labour standards link was a reflection of protectionist tendencies and was aimed at limiting the comparative advantages of developing countries. The Declaration emphasized that the ILO, and not the WTO, is the competent body to set and deal with labour standards, thus rejecting suggestions that the WTO itself might take the lead in setting and enforcing labour standards. The US has been pushing hard for the incorporation of labor standards into the WTO. However, developing countries have successfully thwarted all efforts to create a working party on trade and labor standards. (Khor 1997)

The Second Ministerial Conference of WTO, held at Geneva in May 1998, established a process to prepare for the Third Ministerial Conference and to submit recommendations regarding the WTO's future work program, which would enable Members to take decisions at the Third Ministerial Conference at Seattle. The International Labour Conference adopted a significant *Declaration on Fundamental Rights at Work and its Follow up* on 18th June *1998* declaring that member states of ILO have an obligation to implement certain ILO core conventions which are fundamental workplace rights even if they have not ratified them. These core conventions includes: freedom of association and recognition of the right to collective bargaining; elimination of all forms of forced labour; the effective abolition of child labour and the elimination of discrimination in hiring and employment practices.

In 1999, ILO member governments also agreed to prohibit and eliminate the worst forms of child labour. These practices were defined as all forms of slavery, child prostitution and pornography, the use of children to traffic in drugs and work, which is likely to harm the health, safety or morals of children. ILO member governments said they recognized that child labour is largely a function of poverty and that the long-term solution to the elimination of exploitative and harmful child labour is through sustained economic growth (WTO 2001).

At the 3rd Ministerial Meeting in Seattle in December 1999, the issue of core labour standards was perhaps the most debatable issue on the agenda. At the conference itself, the US, EU and other developed country governments fought to get the issue addressed in a working group and succeeded. Debate in that group was intense and there was strong disagreement among members. Although, officials from both EU members and US said they did not intend to use of trade sanctions in the context of the labour standards issue, developing country governments fiercely opposed both proposals.

Since the Seattle Ministerial Conference, governments from around the world have turned their attention to the ILO as the forum for addressing this question. During the June 2001 meeting of the ILO governing body, the Working Party on the Social Dimension of Globalization reached several agreements on how it might proceed with its work. (i) There was general agreement that trade liberalization and employment and investment, with special emphasis on poverty reduction, should be issues taken up by the Working Party; (ii) There was also general agreement that a permanent forum for exchange of views should be established; (iii) There was further the idea that a global commission of eminent personalities could be formed to examine the social aspects of globalization. (WTO 2001). Despite the negotiating strength of the

US, the developing countries are highly unified against adding labor standards to the agenda and acting with one voice, they have managed to keep the issue out of the WTO in the Doha negotiations.

Section 3: An Overview of Arguments and Concerns

Developing Countries viewpoint

In the case of the controversial core labor standards, many developing countries argue that labour standards are merely another form of protectionism on the part of the developed world. As most of the developing countries' exports are labor-intensive, they believe that restrictions on trade due to labor standards would further restrict their access to the developed world's markets. (Stern and Katherine Terrell 2003).

Developing countries also argue that some forms of child labor are essential to the survival of extremely poor families that rely on the income generated by every family member. These countries fear that permitting the creation of unions will cause multinational companies who are interested in investing in countries with low labor costs and low labor activism to disinvest. (Kimberly Ann. 2003) While most of the 177 ILO member countries enforce these core standards, many of the developing countries are wary of making a legal commitment to upholding labor standards through the WTO. (Grace 2000)

Developed Countries viewpoint

The US, the EU, and Canada contend that the only way to ensure that countries uphold labor standards is with the threat of economic sanctions by the WTO. (Burtless 2001) They also believe that incorporating labor issues into the WTO broadens support for and reduce criticism of the WTO. (Grimaldi 1999).

Trade Union Organizations, NGOs, and Human Rights Organizations point of view

Labour organizations all over the world argue that WTO rules permit the exploitation of labor, the degradation of the environment, and the undermining of national regulations designed to protect the health and safety of citizens. (AFL-CIO 1999) There are many Trade Union Organizations of developing and developed countries, which intend to have linkage between the WTO and Labour Standards. Within the African region, the Congress of South African Trade Unions (COSATU) among others has been strongly advocating this position. Besides Trade Unions, many Non-governmental Organizations, especially those advancing the cause of human and workers' rights, have also been advocating this position. These two sets of organizations have bona fide reasons for wanting to provide a better mechanism for the observance of workers' core labour standards than provided for by the ILO. Workers and rights-based organizations, genuinely believe that placing labour under the WTO purview would further their cause. (Tandon 2002).

These organizations share this view with governments and sections of the private sector that mainly represents the corporate interests of the developed countries, in order to keep away 'cheap imports' from the developing countries, which threaten their industries and jobs. In fact, this argument can be used by any high cost producing country against any other low cost producing country (Tandon 2002).

The rights-based organizations support the unions on this issue. They say that they are not in favour of labour standards being used as a protectionist ruse, nor are they interested in increasing the power and mandate of the WTO. They want the WTO to be human rights sensitive rather than have rights subjected to the trading dictates of the WTO. (Tandon 2002).

Intellectuals' point of view

Globalization Argument: Many are concerned that the present model of trade liberalization is exacerbating developmental inequalities, environmental degradation, workers' exploitation and gender imbalances and demand that it should receive careful consideration based on solid evidence.(Salazar-Xirinachs 1999) Contrary to this argument, another section believes that true improvements in labor conditions will only come about with the assistance of economic growth from globalization. (Burtless 2001).

Development Argument: There is the argument that since poverty, informality and labor market conditions in developing countries are quite different from those of an advanced industrial economy, the strict importation of rules and models of labor-management relations from advanced countries is questionable. (Salazar-Xirinachs-1999)

Efficiency Argument: A majority of countries favor a context of cooperation rather than one of negotiation, not only because of the economic and social damage that limitations to market access could inflict on them, but also because they are convinced that, to an important extent, the source of the problem lies in the lack of capacity to implement core labor rights, linked to limitations in institutional infrastructure and human and financial resources. (Salazar-Xirinachs-1999).

Section 4: Views of International Fora on Implementation of Core Labour

Various reports of International Institutions on implementation of the core labour standards clearly reveal the undermining or denial of the basic rights not only by the developing countries but by the developed countries as well. It is pertinent to note that some countries have not ratified the core labour standards adopted by ILO. The first set of reports of the Follow-up on Declaration of Fundamental Principles and Rights at Work. (ILO 2000) brings out that a number of industrialized countries have not ratified all the core standards (and thus escape ILO supervisory mechanism). New Zealand and the United States have not ratified the Conventions on Freedom of Association (No 87) and effective recognition of the right to Collective Bargaining (No 98); Canada and the United States have not ratified the Convention on All Forms of Forced (No 29) or Compulsory Labour (No 105); Australia, Austria, Canada, Czech Republic, Japan, New Zealand, United Kingdom and the United States have not ratified the Convention on the effective Abolition of Child Labour (No 138); Japan, Luxembourg and the US have not ratified the Conventions (No 100 and 111) on the Elimination of Discrimination in respect of Employment and Occupation. All these industrialized countries have submitted reports to the Follow-up, but by not being members of the Conventions, they escape the scrutiny of the ILO supervisory body on their implementation

The expert-advisers note in their report that with the burgeoning of the informal sector in many countries and new types of labour arrangements in some, questions arise about whether effective protection is in fact being guaranteed by law in relation to the fundamental principles and rights at work. (ILO 2000). A report of Human Rights Watch (HRW 2003) reveals that the link between core labour standards and WTO may lead to trade wars between developing and developed countries in which each accuses the other of violations of labor rights. Addressing the US laws on the rights of workers, the Human Rights Watch report states that millions of workers are expressly barred from the law's protection of the right to organize. Unionization in the US is only 15% of the workforce. The US legal doctrine allowing employers to permanently replace workers who exercise the right to strike effectively nullifies the right. (Human Rights Watch, 2003).

ICFTU in its report has condemned flagrant violations of workers' trade union rights, including violence against trade union activists. The report also highlights "widespread child labour" with approximately 50 million children at work; at least 50% of them are engaged in dangerous professions. (ICFTU 2002) The ICFTU in a way insists on the integration of the roles of the WTO and ILO along with the respective Governments for the protection of core labour standards. It also calls for international pressure for the protection of minimum labour standards. (ICFTU 2002).

General Trade union view point on linkage of CLS to WTO is expressed in the Statement (Trade Union Statement 2000) which states that the unbalanced approach to globalization based on the simple deregulation of markets has led to a questioning of the multilateral trade and investment system. If the system is to have legitimacy then trade and investment rules must be made coherent with wider concerns of public policy such as environmental protection and sustainable development, food and product safety and the observance of fundamental labour rights. Developing countries must be better integrated into the WTO decision-making process and given increased access to industrialized country markets within a framework of adherence to core labour standards.

Another view point of Trade Union is manifested in the Statement (Trade Union Statement 2003) to the effect that priority to protect the fundamental rights of workers against unscrupulous governments or companies which seek to gain an unfair advantage in international trade through the violation of core labour standards. It further proposed a suggestion to establish a formal structure to address trade and core labour standards. Such a body should also address wider trade-related social issues, such as the impact of trade policies on women, and the provision of adjustment assistance for workers displaced by trade. Clearly, such discussions must not result in any arbitrary or unjustified discrimination. In a call given by Australian Council of Trade Unions to Global unions (ACTU 2000 (a) President Sharan Burrow said that cut-throat competition is reducing labour standards around the world. Just as the WTO has rules on trade implementation, it should have rules on labour standards to protect vulnerable workers and share the benefits of prosperity. She also said that women are being drugged to work 70 hours straight in Export Processing Zones set up in developing nations to attract international investment.

In another statement issued by ACTU (ACTU 2000(b) it is said that the cut throat economic competition that is promoted through the World Trade Organisation (WTO), is often depriving workers of even their most basic rights. It is also stated that millions of workers, particularly in developing countries, are being left without any protection against governments and employers who will continue to treat them as disposable resources until the WTO ensures respect for workers' rights in its trade agreements.

The ICFTU's General Secretary, Guy Ryder, said that globalization has the potential to bring prosperity to people across the world, but today's crude, free market globalization is pushing standards down and leading to massive exploitation. (Lobe 2003) An ICFTU report states that in the absence of effective multilateral trade rules to support the standards set by the ILO, the negative downward spiral of lower standards will continue, as governments compete against each other for foreign investment by offering cheaper labor, tax breaks and other concessions. (Lobe 2003). The Regional Conference of ICFTU-APRO\ILO unanimously adopted as one the conclusions that the International Financial Institutions (IFIs) should ensure that trade rules and procedures are in consistence with the ILO Core Labour Standards, and trade unions should ensure those workers' rights are not lost in the pursuit of the expansion of global trade. (ICFTU-APRO\ILO 2003).

Section 5: South Asian Perspective

The trade unions and governments of South Asian countries have been vehemently opposing the linkage of core labour standards to WTO right from the inception of the debate on this issue at the Ministerial Conference of GATT. In an important Asian Meet, renowned economists discussed elaborately on the implications of linkage of CLS to WTO on developing countries came out with some important conclusions, which are as follows:

(i) Linking of labour conditions to trade distorts free trade flows as goods produced by workers not engaged according to internationally recognized labour standards will face restrictions;

(ii) It is likely that the standards eventually set by the developed countries may not be relevant for developing countries;

(iii) Higher labour standards will escalate production costs and renders developing country exports uncompetitive;

(iv) Higher labour costs will jeopardize the flow of foreign investment as relatively inexpensive labour will cease to be an attraction;

(v) The competitiveness of good based on low-tech and labour-intensive production strategies will be eroded;

(vi) There will be a rise in unemployment as exports and investments are hit. (ASIAN MEET 1994).

In a Joint Statement by the SAARC Commerce Ministers on the Third WTO Ministerial Conference it is stated that social clauses like, environment, labour standards, etc. should be placed in the agenda of WTO as they are not trade related and that the use of unilateral trade measures are inconsistent with international law.(SAARC 1999) SAARC countries in another Joint Statement resolutely opposed any linkage of trade with social or other non-trade issues like labour standards. (SAARC 2001).

Reports on Implementation of Core Labour Standards

South Asia has around 10% of unionised workers. General trend of labour market is denial of basic labour rights particularly in informal sector. Further process of informalisation in the industrial sector is increasing day by day. Globalisation of capital has resulted in a steady increase in unemployment & a drastic deterioration in the living & working conditions of labour. It has resulted into privatisation, closures & retrenchments of the company and led to massive job losses. (ICFTU 2000). Sub-contracting of work by companies to small family based, home-based units is also increasing simultaneously with sub-contracting and casualisation of labour. Another impact of the globalisation is de-unionisation in work place. The result is reduction in membership and weakening of the bargaining capacity of the trade unions. This process has intensified exploitation of toiling masses. The rich are becoming richer, and the poor are the poorer. (ICFTU 2000).

In a new report on India, produced to coincide with the 19-21 June WTO trade policy review, the ICFTU has condemned flagrant violations of workers' trade union rights, including violence against trade union activists. The report also highlights "widespread child labour" with approximately 50 million children at work; at least 50% of them are engaged in dangerous professions. (ICFTU 2002). India has ratified neither of the two ILO core conventions covering trade union rights. In addition, 370 million unprotected workers outside the formal economy have virtually no rights at all. The situation is most starkly illustrated in perhaps the most dangerous sectors, those of agriculture, forestry and fishing and plantation work, where out of 191 million workers engaged, about 190 million -99 per cent-are informal. In the 'informal economy' in India, working conditions are poor, exploitation is rife, and violence is common.(ICFTU 20002). Therefore, the central point of trade union demand today is to put an end to the adverse effects of the policies of globalization. The effects such as massive job losses, new job creation in poorly paid informal sectors, restructuring of enterprises to face competition, slowdown in the industrial growth, growth mainly in service sector and growing industrial sickness imposed by the globalsing finance capital.

Certain important suggestions were also made in this context, which are as follows:

> Establishment of basic labour rights in all South Asian Countries in conformity with the 8 ILO core conventions including conventions 102,103,107 and 141; (ii) National need based Minimum wage and the formulation of wage policy in each SAARC country;(iii) Formulation of SAARC Trade Union Alliance; (iv) Inclusion of labour charter, as one of the activities of SAARC area of activities. (gefont 2000).

It has been well established that the central point of trade unions' agenda through out South Asian region has been *protests and struggles* against the globalization policies such as, massive job losses, new job creation in poorly paid informal sectors, restructuring of enterprises to face competition, slowdown in the industrial growth, growth mainly in service sector and growing industrial sickness imposed by the globalising finance.

Section 6: Concluding Remarks

A cursory look of the above observations and views of various international fora reveal that a serious brutalization and denial of basic rights of the workers is going on not only in most of the developing countries but also developed countries. Undermining of core labour standards is taking place in spite of relatively strict labour laws and regulations.

Though most of the International trade unions insisted on the integration of core labour standards with World Trade Organisation rules and regulations and policy review procedure, they were critical of the adverse impact of globalization process on the basic rights of the workers. There is an outright opposition to the linkage of CLS and WTO as far as South Asian countries viewpoint is concerned.

It is historically established fact that formal institutionalization of the basic rights of workers in any country primarily depends on the struggles of the trade unions and the policies of the government. In 1960's and 1970's when welfare state concept was in vogue throughout the world, especially in the developing countries, the working class could achieve and establish certain basic rights, like right to collective bargaining and freedom to form unions or associations, etc. With the advent of globalization era, last two and half decades witnessed a rapid decline in the trade unionism and flagrant violation of basic rights of the workers through out the world and especially in the South Asian region. In view of these historical facts it may be concluded that linkage of Core Labour Standards to WTO is no solution for the overall regulation of basic labour standards throughout the world. It is the balance of power between the capital and labour that ultimately determines the effective working conditions and preservation of fundamental rights of labour.

For the effective protection of core labour standards there is need for strict monitoring mechanism at the international and at the regional levels as well. Secondly, there is need to regulate the globalization and liberalization policies by the respective states in order to protect the basic rights of the workers. Thirdly, the protective labour legislation is to be extended effectively to the unorganized sector. Fourthly, the respective states should ensure job and income security in general. Fifthly, effective measures must be undertaken for strengthening the unionization in both formal and informal sectors.

References

ACTU (2000a), *"Global Unions Push for Workers' Rights at WTO Talks"*, Australian Council of Trade Unions.

ACTU (2000b), *"WTO Ignoring Workers' Rights Inc Face To The Bottom"*, Australian Council of Trade Unions.

AFL–CIO (1999), Executive Council Statement.

Asian Meet (1994), Co- Sponsored by UNLTD, The Malaysian Institute of Diplomacy and Foreign Relations and Malaysian Institute for Economic Research held on 12th September.

Burtless (2001), *'Workers' Rights: Labour Standards and Global Trade'*, Brookings Institute, Fell 2001 Vol. 19 No. 4.

Gefont (2000), Policy Document.

Grace Brewster (2000), *"WTO Trade and Labour Standards"*, Foreign Policy in Fouls, Policy Brief, Vol. 5, and No. 15.

ICFTU (2000), *'Globalising Social Justice: Trade Unionism in the 21st Century"*, International Confederation.

ICFTU (2002a), Condemns Abuses of all Core Labour Standards in India in New Report, online—120/190602/JL, 2nd June.

ICFTU (2002b), Report on *"Abuses of all core labour standards on India"*. Online 120/190060/JL Brussels 19th June.

ICFTU–APRO/ILO (2003), "Regional Conference on WTO and its Economic and Social Impacts in the Region, '8-10 October, Singapore.

ILO (2000), Following Report on Core *Labour Standards* Geneva, 12th March.

ILO (2003), *International Labour Standards: What are they? The form, content and Characteristics*, 11th December.

Khor Martin (1977), "The WTO and the Battle Over Labour Standards", *'Third World Network*, 13th January.

Salazar–Xirinachs M. Jose (1999), "Trade Labour Standards and the WTO", Friedrich *Ebert Stiftung Conference*, Washington DC 15th November.

SAARC (1999), Joint statement by the SAARC Commerce Ministers on *the Third WTO Ministerial Conference* (Seattle) Bandos Island, Maldives: 9th August.

SAARC (2001), Joint Statement by the SAAC Commerce Ministers on *the Forthcoming fourth WTO Ministerial Conference* at Doha, New Delhi, India, 23rd August.

Tandon Yash (2002), "Quest for Labour Standards in WTO", Herald imbabwe, 9th December.

WTO (1996), *Singapore Ministerial Declaration*-para 4 WT/Min(96)/Dec/W, World Trade Organisation.

WTO (1999), *"Trade and Labour Standards, Subject of Intensive Debate"*.

WTO (2001), Doha Ministerial: Briefing Notes on *Trade and Labour Standards*–A difficult issue for many WTO Member Governments.

PART - IV
Health and Intellectual Property Rights

8

TRIPS and Public Health: Opportunities and Challenges for South Asian Countries

Indra Nath Mukherji

Section 1: Background

Given the increasing incidence of HIV / AIDS and other epidemics in the global economy, which is felt more severely in the South, the availability and affordability of life saving drugs has become a critical issue in the context of health security. In view of the lack of clarity and ambiguity of Agreement on Trade-Related Aspects of Intellectual Property Rights (TRIPS) under World Trade Organization (WTO), in relation to public safeguard exceptions and given the possibility of being held hostage to trade sanctions, and considering the limited resources necessary to devote to legal suits and dispute settlement procedures, the Southern countries are in a state of predicament and reluctant to take proactive stance in implementing suitable measures to protect public health. This has raised serious questions about the impact of TRIPS on public health affecting the life and well being of millions of men, women and children living in poverty in the developing world.

At the Fourth Ministerial Conference held in Doha, Qatar (9-14 November, 2001), the WTO took the unprecedented step of adopting a special Declaration on issues related to TRIPS and Public Health (Doha Ministers Declaration 2001). This was the first outcome of an initiative that started in early 2001 when, upon the request of the African Group, the Council for TRIPS agreed to deal specifically with the relationship between TRIPS Agreement and Public Health. The need for providing patent protection to innovation is widely accepted. Nevertheless one of the most contentious issues in the TRIPS Agreement relates to the length of patent protection (which is 20 years from the date of filing) and unfettered rights provided to patent holders without corresponding responsibilities. This quite often induce multinational pharmaceutical companies charging prohibitively high price for their medicines even to consumers of the poorer countries in order to maximize their profits.

The TRIPS Agreement however provides some flexibility by permitting the law of a Member "other use of the subject matter of patents without the authorization of the right holder..."(Article 21) This is permitted when the Member failed to obtain authorization from the right holder on "reasonable commercial terms" or within a "reasonable period of time". This requirement to obtain permission from the right holder by a Member may be waived "in case of national emergency or other circumstances of extreme urgency, the right holder shall, nevertheless, be notified as soon as reasonably practicable (Article 31(b)). Section (f) of the same Article states: "Any such use shall be authorized predominantly for the supply of the domestic market of the Member authorizing such use." Section (h) however ensures that the right holder shall be paid adequate remuneration in the circumstances of each case, taking into account the economic value of the authorization.

In practice however, when Member governments tried to take advantage of some of the flexibility by adopting TRIPS-compatible measures mentioned above, they were hauled up before Dispute Settlement Bodies for infringement of patent right holders in powerful industrial countries, notably the United States. To illustrate, when the South African government introduced a measure to import anti-AIDS drugs at a cheaper price making use of TRIPS- flexible provisions, 39 pharmaceutical companies joined hands together to challenge the South African government to withdraw such measure. Similarly when the Brazilian government started implementing "compulsory licensing "provision to local companies to manufacture low cost generic drugs as patents did not satisfy the "working" requirement, the US government stood firmly behind the country's powerful pharmaceutical MNCs and dragged Brazil to the Dispute Settlement Body of the WTO. These challenges were perceived as manifestations of a conflict between the recognition of IRPs and essential public health objectives.

In both the above-mentioned cases, due to pressures from public interests. NGOs from North to South, the complainants were forced to withdraw the cases. These very NGOs went ahead with their advocacy campaigns and finally backed by a number of other developing countries, managed to get TRIPS and Public Health Declaration adopted at Doha (South Asia Watch 2002). As stated by Carlos M. Correa, the developing countries' move to specifically address public health issues at the Council for TRIPS was grounded on the condition that TRIPS Agreement should not prevent Members from adopting measures necessary to ensure access to medicines and to satisfy other public health needs. Several documents, particularly by WHO and UNCTAD, as well as extensive academic work and NGO statements, had highlighted the flexibility allowed by the TRIPS Agreement, especially in relation to exceptions to patent nights, parallel imports and compulsory licensing. The developing countries sought a declaration, not because of the lack of clarity in the Agreement, but as a result of the obstacles that the authorities in those countries had experienced when trying to make effective use of such flexibility at the national level (Correa M Carlos 2003).

Sectioin 2: Doha Declaration on the TRIPS Agreement and Public Health

As stated earlier, the Fourth Ministerial Conference of the WTO, held in Doha adopted on 4 November 2001 by consensus a Declaration on the TRIPS Agreement and Public Health.

As stated by Aarian Otten, the purpose of the Declaration is to respond to the concerns that have been expressed about the possible implications of the TRIPS Agreement for access to drugs. As stated earlier, even while the TRIPS Agreement enshrines in public international law the right of countries to take various kinds of measures which can qualify or limit intellectual property rights, including for public health purposes, nevertheless some doubts had been expressed as to whether the flexibility in the TRIPS Agreement was sufficient to ensure that it is supportive of public health, especially in promoting affordable access to existing medicines while also promoting research and development into new ones. The doubts related to:

- Different views being expressed about the nature and scope of the flexibility in the TRIPS Agreement for example in regard to compulsory licensing and parallel imports;
- Questions being raised as to whether this flexibility would be interpreted by the WTO and its members in a broad, pro-public health way; and
- Concerns about the extent to which governments would feel free to use to the full this flexibility without the fear of coming under pressure from trading partners or industry.

The special Declaration responds to these concerns in several ways. First, it emphasizes that the TRIPS Agreement does not prevent Members from taking measures to protect public health and reaffirms the right of members to use, to the full, the provisions of the TRIPS Agreement, which provide flexibility for this purpose. The Declaration makes it clear that the TRIPS Agreement should be interpreted and implemented in a manner supportive of WTO Members' right to protect public health and, in particular, to promote access to medicines for all (Article 4). Second, it highlights the importance of the "objectives" and "principles" of the TRIPS Agreement for the interpretation of its provisions. These statements thus provide important guidance to both individual Members, and in the event of disputes, WTO Dispute Settlement Bodies. Third, the Declaration contains a number of important clarifications of some of the flexibilities contained in the TRIPS Agreement, while maintaining Members commitments in the Agreement. It makes it clear the each member is free to determine the grounds upon which compulsory licenses are granted (Article. 5(a). This is a useful corrective to the views often expressed in some quarters implying that some forms of emergency are a precondition for compulsory licensing. The TRIPS Agreement does refer to national emergencies or other circumstances of extreme urgency in connection with compulsory licensing, but this is to only indicate that in these circumstances, the usual condition that first an effort must be made to seek a voluntary licenses does not apply. The Declaration makes it clear that each Member has the right to determine what constitutes a national emergency or other circumstances of extreme urgency and that public health crisis, including those relating to

HIV/AIDS, tuberculosis, malaria and other epidemics, can represent such circumstances (Article 5(c).

In regard to the exhaustion of IPRs (including Members' right to permit parallel imports), the TRIPS Declaration makes it clear that the effect of provisions of exhaustion is to leave each Member free to establish its own regime without challenge–subject to the general TRIPS provision prohibiting discrimination on the basis of nationality of persons (Article 5(d).

In regard to the least developed country (LDC) members of WTO (which includes Bangladesh, Bhutan, Nepal and Maldives in South Asia), the Declaration accords them an extension of their transition period until the beginning of 2016 in regard to the protection and enforcement of patents and rights in undisclosed information with respect to pharmaceutical products. The Declaration instructed the Council for TRIPS to take necessary action to give effect to this pursuant to Article 66.1 of the TRIPS Agreement (Article. 7).

An issue that occurred at the time of drafting the Declaration was that of the ability of countries without or with limited manufacturing capacities to make effective use of compulsory licensing. It is not in dispute that Members can issue compulsory licenses for importation as well as domestic production. However, the concern that has been expressed is about whether sources of supply from generic producers in other countries to meet such demand will be available, particularly in the light of the provision of Article 31(f) to the TRIPS Agreement which states that any compulsory licenses granted to generic producers in those other countries shall be "predominantly for the supply of the domestic market of the Member granting the compulsory license". This concern may become greater as countries with important generic industries, such as India, come under an obligation to provide patent protection for pharmaceutical products as from 2005. In this regard the Declaration, recognizing the anomaly, instructs the Council for TRIPS to find an expeditious solution to it and to report on this before the end of 2002 (Article 6, WTO website).

Section 3: Fellow up of Doha Declaration

The WTO Council responsible for IPR approved a decision in the form of a waiver extending until 2016 the transition period during which LDCs do not have to provide patent protection for pharmaceuticals. The decisions of the Council for TRIPS of 27 June 2002 states: Least developed country members will not be obliged, with respect to pharmaceutical products, to implement or apply sections 5 and 7 of Part II, of the TRIPS Agreement or to enforce rights provided for under these sections until 1 January, 2016 (WTO website).

Following the above decision, the WTO member governments broke their deadlock over intellectual property protection and public health on 30 August 2003. They agreed on legal changes that will make it easier for poorer countries to import cheaper generics made under compulsory licensing if they are unable to manufacture the medicines themselves. The decision settles, the one remaining piece of unfinished business on intellectual property and health that was left over from the WTO Ministerial Conference in Doha in November 2001. Commenting on the decisions, the WTO Director-General Supachai Panitchpakdi stated.

> This is a historic agreement for the WTO. The final piece of jigsaw has fallen into place, allowing poorer countries to make full use of the flexibilities in the WTO's intellectuals property rules in order to deal with the diseases that ravage their people. It proves once and for all that the organization can handle humanitarian as well as trade concerns (WTO website).

The decision takes the form of an interim waiver, which allows countries producing generic copies of patented products under compulsory licenses to export to products to eligible importing countries. The waiver will last until WTO's intellectual property agreement is amended. The eligibility conditions of importing and exporting member countries have been specified to ensure that licensing is undertaken to meet the specific requirements of public health. The eligible importing member in question, other than LDC member, has to notify the Council for TRIPS the names and quantities of products needed for which it has insufficient or no manufacturing capacities and confirms that, where a pharmaceutical product is patented in its territory, it has granted compulsory license. The compulsory license issued by the exporting member under this Decision must ensure that only the required quantities are exported to member(s), which have notified their needs to the Council of TRIPS. Further, the products produced under the license have to be clearly identified as being produced under the system through specific labeling or marking (website WTO int.).

Section 4: Opportunities and Challenges

India

The implications of TRIPS Agreement and Public Health offer different opportunities and challenges for India on the one hand, and other South Asian countries on the other in view of significantly larger and wider pharmaceutical manufacturing base in the former country. The TRIPS agreement requires patent protection to be extended to invention–be they products or processes–in every field of technology. The Indian Patent Act, 1970, however, does not allow product patents for food, medicines, drugs and chemicals. By 1 January 2005 however, the TRIPS Agreement stipulates the transition to product patents for all non-LDCs. This will preclude Indian pharmaceutical industries from making copies of products through what is termed "reverse engineering." Use of patented products could lead to substantial rise in market prices of such products. Manufacturing of new drugs would then entail a scale of expenditure running to hundreds of millions of dollars, which very few enterprises in India could afford to launch. Even if license for manufacturing of such products is obtained from the right holder, licensing fee would have to be paid.

The best option for India under the above circumstances would be to take bold initiative to launch branded generic drugs that are becoming available or likely to become available in the next 4-5 years consequent to "blockbuster" drugs going off- patent. The global generics market is to touch $ 45 billion in 2005 according to Credit Suisse First Boston (CSFB) Ltd., the leading global equity analyst. In its equity research on emerging opportunities for the Indian pharmaceutical companies in the US generics market, CSFB noted that drugs going off-patent were resulting in huge market potential for the generics drugs over 2000-05, while the "immediate opportunity is larger than at any time in the history of pharmaceutical industry"(Sukumar 2001). Mr. Alok Gupta, Director- Head of Rabo India's Life Sciences and Biotechnology Department, points out that by 2005, drugs worth nearly $ 100 billion are expected to go out of patent from 15 out of the leading 35 molecules. In the US alone, the patent on drugs with revenues more than $ 40 billion are expected to expire in the next five years. Indian companies have the potential to corner about 25 per cent of this market, amounting to $3.75 billion, which is nearly the same size of the Indian pharmaceutical industry (Business Line 2003). One positive impact to date, particularly since the implementation of the Indian Patent Act 1970 on the Indian pharmaceutical industry has been to develop cost-effective process technology for bulk drugs and conventional formulations enabling it to confidently tap the newly emerging generics market.

Being a major supplier of generic drugs, India is also well positioned to meet the emergency requirements for patented drugs to its neighboring countries in South Asia as also to other developing countries. It is less clear what its position will be after it moves to product patents by 1 January 2005. Would an emergency situation say in Bangladesh enable India to assign compulsory licensing to a local producer to meet the eligible former country's demand for drugs? Besides would it be commercially feasible for India to meet such demand for a restricted market? With the advent of post-2005 era, as India enters the patent- compliant regime, for the sustainable growth of the pharmaceutical industry India could tie up with MNCs for collaborative research and development. There is a saying: 'if you cannot beat them, join them." Of particular interest would be in the area of clinical research and contract research operations. According to D.S.Brar, erstwhile CEO and MD. Ranbaxy Laboratories, India can emerge a top-level destination for drug discovery and clinical research in less than a decade. For achieving this goal, we have some immediate requirements to meet like adequate infrastructure for carrying on good clinical practices (GCP) trials, proper policies and systems for inspections and auditing of clinical trials, competent ethical committees and safeguards to protect the interests of the subjects who undergo the trials" (Khan Faiz 2003). A large diverse patient population, networks of academic and medical centers/hospitals, well-preserved genetically distinct population groups and a pool of scientists, technicians, and doctors are the distinct advantages India offers.

While a number of opportunities are unfolding for the Indian pharmaceutical industry, a number of challenges are also visible. Apart from the very high cost of developing new-patented drugs, there are problems for even the launching of generics. The multinational pharmaceutical firms are asking the Indian Government to provide for "data exclusivity" for a number of years which would prevent Indian companies from using the test data of patented drugs that have either gone off- patent, or are about to do so in the next few years. This would require the Indian pharmaceutical industries to undertake the same trials on their own which apart from being expensive, would considerably delay the introduction of generics and to that extent reduce market competition and prevent prices from coming down to the benefit of consumers. Besides repeated trials would be unfair on the subjects.

The TRIPS Agreement on protection of undisclosed information contained in Article 39.3 states: Members, when requiring as a condition of approving the marketing of pharmaceutical or agricultural chemical products, which utilize new chemical entities, the submission of undisclosed test or other data, the origination of which involves considerable effort, shall protect such data against unfair commercial use. In addition, members shall protect such data against disclosure, except where necessary to protect the public or unless steps are taken to ensure that the data are protected against unfair commercial use. Even though the above stipulation under TRIPS is quite broadly framed permitting national governments considerable flexibility to interpret "new", "considerable effort", and "unfair commercial use", the Indian Government has yet to formulate an appropriate national legislation to look into this. It has set up a Committee to examine the implications of the concept.

Another challenge facing the Indian pharmaceutical industry as also industries in other developing countries is the attempt being made since mid-nineties, by World Intellectual Property Organization (WIPO) at harmonization of the patent system at a higher level with the backing of the US and other industrial countries. The draft for "Substantial Patent Law Treaty"(SPLT) will now come up for consideration in the Tenth Session of WIPO Standing Committee on the Law of Patent in 2004. Given the plethora of patent applications being received in the US becoming unmanageable, an attempt is being made to subject patentability of inventions to be decided by courts set up in only nine industrial countries. It is anticipated that harmonization of patent law at a higher level is designed to undo the various flexibilities that currently exist under the WTO which has been clearly demonstrated particularly in relation to the Doha Declaration on Drugs and Public Health (Economic Times 2004).

Other South Asian Countries

The LDCs among the South Asian Countries have the advantage of following process patenting until 2016. This is an opportunity for them to develop their pharmaceutical industries by manufacturing generic drugs. To the extent that they do not have the requisite technological capability in this regard, they can seek technical collaboration arrangements with India or even attract Indian joint ventures in partnership with their local firms. In this way India's technological capabilities in drugs and formulations can be passed on to these countries who in turn could become important players in the fast evolving global generics market.

One challenge facing these countries however is an attempt by the US to have bilateral free trade agreements with some of them in which the acceptance of TRIPS-plus patent protection as a prerequisite. The recent attempt of the US to have such an FTA with Sri Lanka is a case in point. In such agreements US is offering its market duty-free fro textiles in return for higher IPR protection. Such bilateral deals will again undo the various flexibilities under the TRIPS Agreement for developing countries. Further, an amendment to the TRIPS Agreement to incorporate the August 2003 deal for improving the access to medicines for poor countries has passed the June 30, 2004 deadline, which is now likely to be extended to March 2005. This clearly reflects the lack of enthusiasm on part of the developed world to concede easily to the most pressing needs of developing countries.

Section 5: Concluding Observations

Ambiguities or lack of adequate safeguards for developing countries for fully taking advantage of the flexibilities implicit in the WTO Agreement on TRIPS prompted many developing countries, non-governmental organizations both in the North and the South to urge WTO to enact enabling waivers/amendments to its provisions on TRIPS so that more transparency is obtained for the developing countries to enact supporting national legislations, without fear of retaliation, protecting health security of their citizens. The Doha Declaration can be considered to be a landmark decision in this regard. This has provided both opportunities as well as challenges for South Asian and other developing countries. However the industrial countries, largely influenced by their powerful pharmaceutical companies, are intending to harmonize patenting norms at a higher level through the WIPO thereby largely undoing the gains the developing countries have made through their concerted efforts to make use of WTO-compatible flexible measures to protect their poor and vulnerable citizens from devastating diseases. When the necessary amendments to the WTO text are brought about and also when the draft SPLT is brought before the forthcoming Tenth Session of WIPO, the South Asian Countries should combine with other like-minded developing countries to speak with one voice to safeguard their hard earned gains.

References

Business Line Bureau (2003), "Good Potential for Export of Generic Drugs", October 15.

Correa M. Carlos (2003), *Implications of the Doha Declaration on the TRIPS Agreement and Public Health, Health Economics and Drugs,* EDM Series No. 12.

"Council Approves LDC Decision with Additional Waiver", Press/301, 28 June, www.wto.org.

Declaration on the Trips Agreement and Public Health, www.wto.org.

"Decision Removes Final Patent Obstacle to Cheap Drug Imports", www.wto.org.

Doha Ministerial Declaration on TRIPS Agreement and Public Health (2001), WT/MIN(01)/DEC/W/2,14 November.

Economic Times (2004), Will Global Patent Courts Work?", 23 March.

Khan Faiz (2003), *Clinical trials can be India's Pride,* www.biospectrumindia.com, November.

Otten Adrian, *WTO Declaration on the TRIPS Agreement and Public Health,* www.wto% 20.

South Asia Watch on Trade, Economics and Development (2002), "On TRIPS and Public Health Declaration", Vol. 1, No. 2, December.

Sukumar C.R. (2001), "Generics Market to Surge to $ 45 by 2005: Outlook Bright for Indian Companies", Business Line, October 20.

For full details of conditions see www.wto.int., "Implementation of Paragraph 6 of the Doha Declaration on the TRIPS Agreement and Public Health".

9

Implications of TRIPS Agreement for Developing and Least Developed Countries

A.R. Bhuyan

Section 1: Introduction and Scope of the Paper

The Uruguay Round Agreement on Trade-Related Aspects of Intellectual Property Rights (TRIPS Agreement) is to date the most comprehensive multilateral agreement on intellectual property. It is also the one, which has aroused more controversy than any other Uruguay Round Agreement. Many developing and least developed countries (LDCs) consider the TRIPS Agreement as a clear case of unambiguous loss for them. Under this Agreement, WTO Member States are obliged to provide in their national laws internationally-agreed norms for protecting patents, copyrights, trademarks, industrial designs, trade secrets, integrated circuits and geographical indications. The accord includes areas–such as pharmaceutical products–not previously protected in many countries.

The provisions of the Agreement that seek to protect these intellectual properties (IPs) are specific, binding, and actionable. Non-compliance with these provisions can be challenged under the WTO's dispute settlement mechanism. In contrast, provisions that have potential to benefit technology consumers (the developing countries), such as technology transfer and technical and financial cooperation, while also binding in theory, are vaguely worded, making them difficult to enforce. There is no penalty for non-compliance of these provisions. The Agreement does, of course, contain exceptions and flexible provisions, which the developing countries need to use, but because these exceptions and flexibilities are amenable to different interpretations, the developing countries can hardly take any advantage of these flexibilities. The Agreement has often been seen to prevent the diffusion of technology and knowledge rather than facilitate their access to developing countries. The consequence is that the perceived benefits of the TRIPS Agreement do not always reach the developing countries.

The Doha Development Round is the first important step towards making the TRIPS Agreement more development-friendly. The Doha Ministerial Conference of November 2001instructed the TRIPS Council to work on specific aspects of the TRIPS Agreement. These are *TRIPS and public health, geographical indications (GIs), Review of the provisions of Article 27..3(b), the Relationship between TRIPS Agreement and the Convention on Biological Diversity, Protection of traditional knowledge and folklore, the general review of the TRIPS Agreement, non-violation complaints,* and *technology transfer.* The issues are now being negotiated in the TRIPS Council. This paper highlights the implications of the TRIPS Agreement for developing countries, in particular the least developed ones (LDCs), keeping in view developments to date in the ongoing Doha Development Round negotiations on the Agreement. Section II presents a brief account of the post-Uruguay Round developments and the lead-up to the Fourth Ministerial Conference at Doha. Section III highlights the progress made in the ongoing negotiations on different issues at the TRIPS Council and their likely outcomes. The implications of the negotiations for the developing/least developed countries and their interests and options in the negotiations are discussed in Section IV. Some concluding observations re made in the Fifth and final Section.

Section 2: Post-Uruguay Round Developments and the Doha Mandate

A lot of the pre- and post-Uruguay Round literature has concentrated on the perceived benefits that would accrue to the world as a whole and to the different groups of countries as a result of the successful conclusion of the Uruguay Round of trade negotiations. Little attention has been given to the speed, the scope, and the difficulties of implementation of the Uruguay Round agreements. However, the first WTO Ministerial Conference, held in Singapore in December 1996, highlighted the serious problems being encountered by developing countries in implementing the agreements. This was particularly so in the case of the TRIPS Agreement, which entails significant changes in the administration of intellectual property rights, judicial procedures and customs administration.

Developing countries had no previous legislation in several of the IPR areas covered by the Agreement. Most of these countries did not provide for specific protection for geographical indications and plant varieties. For some areas covered by the Agreement, e.g., integrated circuits and undisclosed information, there were no international instruments in force before the TRIPS Agreement (Correa, 1998). These countries were to face huge administrative cost in their attempts to fulfill their commitments under the Agreement as the systems to protect IPRs in many of them were rudimentary (UNCTAD, 1996b and 1996c). Developing countries, when they entered into negotiations, also voiced their concerns on the socio-economic implications of a tightened IPR regime, although they finally accepted the Agreement. These concerns still remain and are particularly strong in two areas: the protection of plant varieties and of pharmaceutical products. The TRIPS Agreement opens the door to the patenting of life forms such as microorganisms and modified genetic materials. Many environmentalists are concerned that this will be detrimental to the global environment as the present lack of controls and accountability in biotechnology research and application will likely accelerate biodiversity loss and could threaten natural ecosystems.

For plant varieties, the TRIPS Agreement does permit countries the option to either introduce patents or an alternative "effective" *sui generis* system of intellectual property protection. Many governments, NGOs and farmers' groups in developing countries are concerned that the practice of "biopiracy" (patenting in the North of biological materials and resources originating in the South) will intensify. Moreover, unless appropriate *sui generis* systems (that protect the traditional knowledge and genetic resources of farmers) are established in developing countries, these farmers may be disadvantaged by plant variety protection regulations. Most developing countries are dependent upon their agriculture sector.

While 80-90% of seeds used in these countries are produced by farmers in an "informal seed supply system", the introduction of IPRs on plant varieties may replace better adapted farmers' varieties and reduce the diversity and sustainability of agriculture.

About pharmaceuticals, many studies indicate that the introduction of IPRs will lead to price increases. The problem of the inability of AIDS patients in developing countries to have access to patented drugs due to their high prices has already become a major issue of concern. In a field like pharmaceuticals, with high economies of scale in R&D, patents are very unlikely to stimulate R&D by local or foreign firms in developing countries. R&D costs are not affordable to the former, while the latter tend to concentrate R&D in a few locations in industrialized countries. Production by local firms will be limited to generic drugs. Foreign patent owners will have the choice, in principle, to produce locally or to import the product.

The Road to the Fourth WTO Ministerial Conference at Doha, 2001

The problems encountered by developing country members continued to be discussed since the Singapore Ministerial and discussions intensified after the collapse of the Third Ministerial in Seattle in 1999. The main issues raised in the lead-up to the November 2001 Doha Ministerial were: (1) geographical indications, (2) TRIPS and public health, (3) relationship between the TRIPS Agreement and the UN Convention on Biological Diversity and other issues like the protection of traditional knowledge, and new technological developments, and (4) implementation issues, including current obligations on technology transfer under the TRIPS Agreement and a technical issue known as "non-violation" cases.

The Doha Mandate

After protracted and difficult discussions, Ministers adopted the Ministerial Declaration at Doha in November 2001, which set the agenda for negotiations in the Doha Development Round. The Doha Ministerial mandated the TRIPS Council to work on a set of issues. Contained in three important texts agreed at Doha, viz.,

(i) the Ministerial Declaration,

(ii) the Decision on Implementation Related Issues and Concerns, and

(iii) the Declaration on the TRIPS Agreement and Public Health, the Mandate includes specific aspects of TRIPS and public health, geographical indications, protecting plant and animal inventions, biodiversity, traditional knowledge and folklore, the general review of the TRIPS Agreement, and technology transfer.

The Doha Mandates are reproducéd in the Appendix to this paper.

Section 3: Current State of the Doha Round Negotiations

TRIPS and Public Health

The most important agenda item in the TRIPS Council is 'TRIPS and public health'. The Doha Declaration on TRIPS and Public Health reaffirms the right of developing countries to interpret the TRIPS Agreement through a public health perspective. Specifically, the Declaration states "the TRIPS Agreement does not and should not prevent members from taking measures to protect public health". Paragraph 6 of the Doha Declaration on the TRIPS Agreement and Public Health explicitly recognizes the flexibility within the TRIPS Agreement to grant compulsory licenses and the right of countries to determine the grounds on which these are granted. However, many poor countries and small economies cannot take advantage of that flexibility due to insufficient or no pharmaceutical production capacity to manufacture copies of patented medicines. Their only solution is to import such drugs from other countries that have the necessary infrastructure and know-how. This possibility is compromised by Article 31(f) of the TRIPS Agreement, which requires that production under compulsory licensing must be primarily for the supply of the domestic market of the Member authorizing such use. It was to overcome this limitation that ministers instructed the TRIPS Council to find out and expeditious solution' to this problem by the end of 2002.

The TRIPS Council's post-Doha negotiations on this issue started on 5 March 2002 with proposals from the European Union, the United States, and a large group of developing countries (African Group, Brazil, Cuba, Dominican Republic, Ecuador, Honduras, India, Indonesia, Jamaica, Malaysia, Sri Lanka and Thailand). The Council had two tasks. First, it had to find a solution to the problems in making use of compulsory licensing by countries with little or no pharmaceutical manufacturing capacity. It had to report to the General Council on this by the end of 2002.

Second, the Council had to formally implement a decision of Doha Declaration on the TRIPS Agreement and Public Health extending until 1 January 2016 the transition period during which the least-developed countries will not have to provide patent protection for pharmaceuticals. The TRIPS Council approved this decision on 27 June 2002. It also approved a waiver that would exempt LDCs from having to provide exclusive marketing rights for any new drugs in the period when they do not provide patent protection. Both of these decisions were approved by the General Council in July 2002. This was indeed a significant achievement of the TRIPS Council and a major victory for the LDCs. However, consultations on compulsory licensing and domestic production capacity questions–a principal Doha mandate–failed to produce any result. Despite long and intense negotiations, Members could not reach consensus on the 'expeditious solution' by the 31 December 2002 deadline. The negotiations broke down on the question of disease coverage. Despite three extensions of the deadline, the Council failed to find any solution to the problem.

The draft Decision put forward by TRIPS Council Chair Ambassador Eduardo Pérez Motta (Mexico) on 16 December 2002 was opposed by the United States–arguing that the solution should apply only to HIV/AIDS, malaria, tuberculosis and other infectious diseases of comparable gravity. The 16 December draft text refers to paragraph 1 of the TRIPS and Public Health Declaration, i.e., "public health problems afflicting many developing and least-developed countries, especially those resulting from HIV/AIDS, tuberculosis, malaria and other epidemics." The draft also covers active ingredients used in the manufacture of medicines, as well as diagnostic kits needed for their use, as proposed in particular by the African Group.

The United States, supported by Switzerland, rejected the draft text due to strong pressure from its pharmaceutical industry, which was concerned that the broad scope of the proposed solution–the draft limits neither the disease coverage nor the countries that could benefit–would mean the losses of market share for patented medicines due to generics manufactured in countries such as Brazil and India. On the whole, the Chair's 16 December draft Decision did command universal support with the exception of only one Member (the United States). Outstanding difficulties remained with paragraph 1(a) of the draft Decision as it concerned the so-called "scope of diseases" question. Despite intensive consultations during the last few days of December 2002 and January-February 2003, it had not been possible to find a solution to the problem.

The latest setback came on 18 February 2003, when delegates at the TRIPS Council dismissed the compromise solution proposed by the Chair that would complement the 16 December draft, stating, *inter alia*, that Members regarded the solution as "essentially designed to address national emergencies or other circumstances of extreme urgency." Civil society group Medecins sans Frontieres (MSF) strongly criticized the proposed statement saying that paragraph 6 had never been intended to address only national emergencies and that the 16 December draft did not include any limitations to emergency situations. The adoption of the text, according to them, would put countries without the possibility to produce medicines at a disadvantage over countries that do have the capacity.

The deadlock over paragraph 6 solution was ultimately resolved when an agreement was reached by the General Council (IP/C/W/405) on 30 August 2003 for the implementation of paragraph 6 based on the amendment proposed by the US and four other countries–Brazil, India, Kenya, and South Africa–relaxing the global patent rules to enable poor countries without a pharmaceutical industry to import cheaper generic copies of patented essential medicines. This 'solution' is based on a compromise developed by the Chair of the TRIPS Council and on a 'Statement' by the Chair of the General Council. The deal would be in the form a 'Statement' of the General Council Chair to accompany the 16 December draft. The solution takes the form of an *interim* waiver of the obligations under Article 31(f), which allows countries producing patented products under compulsory license to export the products to eligible importing countries, provided that a compulsory license has also been granted in the importing country and that various other conditions are met. The waiver is set to last until the TRIPS Agreement is amended.

The Decision spells out the conditions under which countries without pharmaceutical manufacturing capacity can import generic versions of drugs still under patent. The Chairperson's Statement allowed the 16 December Decision to be adopted without any changes. The Statement notes Members' commitment to using the system established by the paragraph 6 Decision "in good faith to protect public health" and not as "an instrument to pursue industrial or commercial policy objectives". The Chair's Statement stresses the need for preventing diversion of cheap drugs (including active ingredients) to developed country markets, noting Members' understanding that "in general special packaging and/or special colouring or shaping should not have a significant impact on the price of pharmaceuticals".

Criticisms of the Paragraph 6 solution

The compromise agreement reached on 30 August for the implementation of paragraph 6 has been fiercely criticized by civil society groups as well as academics. They strongly reject the Chair's Statement; denouncing the conditions it imposes as a discouragement for developing countries to use the system. Civil society group Medicines sans Frontiers (MSF) said that the focus of the TRIPS & health discussion seemed to be more on giving comfort to the pharmaceutical industry than on access to medicines. It was also alleged that the conditions established in both the text of the Decision and the Statement for allowing exports of patented medicines were hardly compatible with the idea of an 'expeditious' solution (Correa 2004a).

One may also find fault with the Chair's Statement that the system "should be used in good faith to protect public health and not be an instrument to pursue industrial or commercial policy objectives". This Statement seems to ignore that the only sustainable way of providing a credible alternative to the supply by patent owners is the creation of incentives for other commercial companies to supply the required drugs and, ultimately, the development of a viable domestic industry. It was also said that in order to be effective, a solution to the problem described in paragraph 6 should be economically viable, and not just diplomatically acceptable. The 30 August agreement fails to provide an effective means of increasing competition and lowering drug prices. The Chair's assumption that "special packaging and/or special colouring or shaping should not have a significant impact on the price of pharmaceuticals" cannot go unchallenged. In fact, special packaging/colouring that will be needed to prevent re-export by the country producing medicines under compulsory license cannot but raise drug prices (Correa 2004b).

The dominant view is thus that the compromise agreement does not provide a full-proof solution of the problem and may not promote access to medicines for all, particularly for the poor. Too many conditions will be required to be met in order to qualify for importing drugs under this mechanism. A number of difficult steps will have to be followed before being able to import the drugs, which will be very difficult for the poor countries to fulfill. Also, the adopted solution is so complex and cumbersome for the generic manufacturers that they will hardly be able or willing to comply with its provisions. The adopted 'solution' is thus largely symbolic and in view of the multiple conditions required for its application it is unlikely to lead to any significant increase in the supply of medicines, particularly for the poor.

Geographical Indications

Two issues are debated under the Doha Mandate: (a) creating a multilateral register for wines and spirits; and (b) extending the higher (Article 23) level of protection beyond wines and spirits. Both are as contentious as any other subject on the Doha agenda.

Multilateral System for GIs

Negotiations on a multilateral system of notification and registration of GIs for wines and spirits, required under Article 23.4 of the TRIPS Agreement, are currently underway in the special (negotiating) sessions of the TRIPS Council. They are separate from the question of whether the higher level of protection given to wines and spirits should be extended to other products, although some countries have said that they want the higher level of protection to be extended to other products and the register to cover those other products. The Doha Declaration set the deadline for completing the negotiations by the Fifth Ministerial Conference.

Two sets of proposals have been submitted over the years, representing two main lines of argument. While Members generally agree that the system should not increase the level of protection that currently exists for covered products, they remain divided over whether countries should be obliged to protect the registered terms in the multilateral system or whether it should be left to each country to decide. The US and a few other members seek a non-binding system that does not require Members to protect registered terms. The register would rather function as a database. In contrast, the EU and some other countries stress that all registered terms shall be protected in all WTO Member countries, including non-participating Members.

Progress can now be expected only if the EU waters down its ambition on the register or is prepared to accept a trade-off in other negotiating areas, notably in agriculture. The issue mainly reflects a division between the EU and the US, and developing countries are unlikely to have any influence on the debate (ICTSD, 2003c). However, the last scheduled meeting of the TRIPS Council in November 2003 ended without any narrowing down of the differences of views of these two major opposing groups.

Geographical indications (extension of higher level protection to other products)

The second GI issue in the TRIPS negotiation agenda is the extension of higher levels of protection to other products. At issue is the question of whether the higher level of protection currently given to geographical indications of wines and spirits (Article 23) should be extended to other products. Some countries said that by limiting the higher level of protection to wines and spirits, the TRIPS Agreement discriminated, creating an imbalance between WTO Members.

Members generally fell into two camps, one for and the other against extension. Countries for extension say it would benefit trade and development because geographical indications can be a means for countries–particularly developing countries–to market their products and secure higher prices because of the quality associated with the GIs. They object to other countries "usurping" their terms, and deny that GI extension would necessarily raise costs. Countries against extension argue that the existing level of protection (Article 22) is adequate and that providing enhanced protection would be expensive. They say that geographical indications can be so complex that producing countries to block can use their protection imports, and that the administrative cost of protecting the GIs are too high. They also reject the "usurping" accusation particularly when migrants have taken the methods of making the products and the names with them to their new homes. As a result of the deep division among Members on whether to begin negotiations on GI extensions, the TRIPS Council failed to report to the TNC on 'appropriate action' within the deadline, which was the end of 2002.

The deadlock is unlikely to be broken in the TRIPS Council but would require some bargaining in the agriculture negotiations. Indeed, several countries, including the EU, Switzerland and Bulgaria, have explicitly linked the GI discussions to the agriculture negotiations in both the TRIPS Council and the Committee on Agriculture.

Implementation-related Issues

Non-violation complaints

The first TRIPS item in the Decision on Implementation-related Issues and Concerns deals with the extension of the five-year transition period in Article 64.2 of the TRIPS Agreement, which banned non-violation complaints provided for under subparagraphs 1(b) and 1(c) of Article XXIII of GATT 1994. At issue is whether or not to strike out the Article 64 from the TRIPS Agreement. Post-Doha discussions on the subject in the TRIPS Council made little progress. All WTO Members with the exception of the U.S. agree that the Article should either be dropped, or the current moratorium be extended. The Secretariat had prepared a note summarizing the points raised on this issue so far (IP/C/W/349).

At a consultation in May 2003, the Chair listed four possibilities for a recommendation before the Fifth Ministerial Conference:

1. Outlawing non-violation complaints in TRIPS completely,
2. Scrapping the moratorium and allowing non-violation complaints even if there were no modalities,
3. Working on "modalities" so that non-violation complaints could be made, and
4. Extending the moratorium.

Almost all Members favour (1), because they consider non-violation to be an invalid concept in the TRIPS Agreement. A few – Canada, Australia, Japan, Korea and Chinese Taipei among them – either favour (1) or are reasonably willing to accept it, while the US and Switzerland have blocked consensus on this option. The US said the moratorium should expire immediately. Switzerland could accept an extension of the moratorium but not beyond the next (sixth) Ministerial Conference. No consensus could be reached prior to the Fifth Ministerial Conference. The 13 September 2004 Ministerial draft (not adopted in Cancun) instructed the TRIPS Council to make recommendations to the "first Ministerial Conference to be held after 1 August 2004" (with a dispute settlement moratorium in place until that time). The status of the moratorium is now unclear. This means further work will now be needed in the TRIPS Council on the subject.

Incentives for Technology Transfer to LDCs (Implementation of Article 66.2)

The second TRIPS item in the Doha Decision on Implementation-related Issues and Concerns deals with developed-country obligations under Article 66.2 of the TRIPS Agreement to provide incentives for the transfer of technology to LDCs. Specifically, the mandate requires the developed countries to submit reports to the TRIPS Council (updated annually) on the practical functioning of the incentives provided.

The most significant development in this regard was the adoption of the TRIPS Council decision on 19 February 2003 on transfer of technology to LDCs (IP/C/28 dated 20 February 2003). The decision requires the developed country Members to undertake specific legislative, policy, and regulatory measures for their enterprises and institutions to give effect to Article 66.2 of the TRIPS Agreement. This Article instructs the developed country Members to "provide incentives to enterprises and institutions in their territories for the purpose of promoting and encouraging technology transfer" to LDCs. The 19 February decision of the Council thus fulfills one of the mandates adopted at the Doha Ministerial Conference. The decision is now being implemented, and will be reviewed in regular TRIPS Council meetings. At the same time, the question of technology transfer continues to be raised under various TRIPS headings such as TRIPS and Public Health.

Technical and Financiul Cooperation (Article 67)

Technical and financial cooperation is an important issue for the LDCs. Although the issue is not in the Doha agenda, the TRIPS Council has continued its work in this area on the basis of the procedures agreed in its meeting in February 1996. Article 67 of the TRIPS Agreement requires that developed country Members provide, on request and on mutually agreed terms and conditions, technical and financial assistance in favour of developing and least developed countries. Although the provisions of technical assistance are technically binding, they tend to be difficult to implement because there are few mechanisms to ensure that they are actually implemented. Most technical assistance has failed to address the real needs of developing countries. Part of the reason is that such technical assistance is primarily limited to helping developing countries in complying with WTO provisions rather than helping them build the capacity to trade more, negotiate better or adjust to the demands of increased integration.

Moreover, the provisions of technical assistance are largely open-ended and contingent on future negotiations, with most requiring that technical assistance be provided on "mutually agreed terms" or "if requested". Much of the technical assistance has been intended as a quid pro quo for an expanded negotiation agenda and has been used as a political tool to promote a negotiation mandate (Tandon, 2002). While the terms of the technical assistance provisions are reasonable, they are hard to implement and often require yet more negotiating capacity in developing countries. In order to facilitate implementation of Article 67, the TRIPS Council in its June 2002 meeting agreed that developed country Members would update the information on their technical and financial cooperation activities pursuant to Article 67 of the Agreement in time for the Council's meeting in September (2002). The Council has thus far received updated information on the technical cooperation activities from a number of developed Member countries and intergovernmental organizations, namely the FAO, IMF, OECD, UNCTAD, UPOV, WIPO and WHO, as well as the WTO Secretariat.

Outstanding Implementation Issues

Most prominent of the outstanding implementation issues that appear in the TRIPS Council agenda are: the Review of the Provisions of Article 27.3(b); Relationship between the TRIPS Agreement and the Convention on Biological Diversity; and Protection of Traditional Knowledge and Folklore. The TRIPS Council debated these three items at its meetings in 2002. The essential elements of the debate are whether (i) life forms (i.e., plants, animals, micro-organisms as well as non-biological and micro-biological processes) should at all be patented, and (ii) whether the TRIPS Agreement should be revised to make it compatible with the requirements of the Convention on Biological Diversity (CBD) regarding access to genetic resources and the associated traditional knowledge (TK), as well as the sharing of benefits from their use.

Members' views diverged on both these issues. The developing countries in general answered the first question with a *no* to the patenting of life forms and the second by a *yes* to revising the TRIPS Agreement. Most developed countries did exactly the opposite. The debate has been long and protracted. A group of developing countries in their submission (IP/C/W/356) stressed the need to modify the TRIPS Agreement, arguing that it contained no provisions to prevent biopiracy (illegal access and use) or ensure prior informed consent (PIC) and the fair and equitable sharing of benefits. This group called for a revision of the TRIPS Agreement to require patent applicants to (a) disclose the source of origin of the biological resource and associated traditional knowledge (TK), and (b) provide evidence of prior informed consent (PIC) and benefit sharing.

Most developed countries, including the US and Japan, generally resisted amendments to the TRIPS Agreement, arguing that there was no conflict between it and the Convention on Biological Diversity.. The US, in particular, strongly opposed the inclusion of disclosure requirements in patent applications, maintaining that they would be incompatible with the TRIPS Agreement since they would add another substantive condition on patentability beyond those already provided. The EU, on the other hand, adopted a more flexible approach than many other industrialized countries and signaled its willingness to discuss the inclusion of disclosure requirements in patent applications, but stressed that such requirements should not constitute an additional formal or substantial patentability criterion.

The Africa Group and India in separate submissions (IP/C/W/404 and IP/C/W/403) to the TRIPS Council's 4-5 June 2003 meeting stressed the need for a multilateral solution to these issues. The submission by the Africa group was wider in scope than the India-led proposal. It called for a revision of Article 27.3(b) so as to prohibit patenting of plants, animals and microorganisms. A similar call was made by the LDC group in the Dhaka Declaration of 2 June 2003. On traditional knowledge (TK), the Africa group proposed to classify TK as a category of intellectual property and put forth a draft Decision on TK for adoption by the TRIPS Council.

Developing countries generally supported one or both of the papers. In contrast, the US called for traditional knowledge to be removed from the TRIPS Council's agenda. It stressed that contracts would be more effective than the TRIPS Agreement in ensuring disclosure, PIC, and benefit sharing. The EU welcomed the Africa Group's flexible approach to *sui generis* protection of plant varieties and agreed that small farmers should have the right to re-use seeds, but it rejected the call for a ban on patenting life forms. Switzerland, supported by Japan, Canada and the US, submitted that these issues should be discussed at the WIPO, rather than at the WTO. It proposed an amendment to WIPO's Patent Cooperation Treaty that would enable countries to require patent applicants to declare the source of the genetic resources and TK in patent applications but would not oblige them to establish such legislation (IP/C/W/400)

On the other hand, several developing countries stressed that work on access and benefit sharing regarding genetic resources and TK should be carried out in the WTO rather than left exclusively to WIPO. These issues did not figure in the Fifth Ministerial in Cancun. Members discussed this agenda item in the TRIPS Council's November 2003 meeting, but without any result.

The Review of the TRIPS Agreement (under Article 71.1)

There has been very little discussion and there are no proposals on this item under the Doha agenda.

Other Outstanding Implementation Issues and Concerns

The Compilation of Outstanding Implementation Issues Raised by Members (JOB(01)/152/Rev.1) includes the following issues:

> Tiret 91: The period given for implementation of the provisions of Article 27.3(b) shall be five years from the date the review is completed.
>
> Tiret 93: The transitional period for developing countries provided for in Article 65.2 shall be extended. [Proposal by Least-Developed Countries, 22 October 2001: The General Council agrees that the transition period for LDCs shall be extended so long as they retain the status of an LDC.]

Tiret 94: Articles 7 and 8 of the TRIPS Agreement to be operationalized by providing for transfer of technology on fair and mutually advantageous terms.

None of these issues have so far been explicitly addressed or resolved by the TRIPS Council.

Section 4: Interests and Options for Developing Countries and LDCs

Negotiations on the TRIPS issue have been complex thus far. Opposing views expressed on various issues have not been strictly along developed-developing country lines. The broad group of developing countries, of which LDCs are a large component, should continue to reaffirm their viewpoints in the negotiations and also lend support to the views of other groups or countries if that serves their own interest as well those of the LDCs.

TRIPS and Public Health

The developing country position on the TRIPS and public health issue is clear. The agreement reached on 30 August 2003 to adopt the amended 16 December draft Decision for implementation of paragraph 6 of the Doha Declaration on the TRIPS Agreement and Public Health, no doubt resolved the deadlock in the negotiations over TRIPS Agreement and Public Health but the adopted solution has some inherent weaknesses, which should be removed. In order to obtain a permanent solution to the problems affecting countries with limited or no pharmaceutical manufacturing capacity, the followings suggestions appear appropriate:

(i) The cumbersome provisions of the 16 December Decision and the Chair's Statement that are likely to discourage manufacturers to supply essential drugs should be eased.

(ii) Incentives should be created for the commercial companies to supply essential drugs at lower prices.

(iii) Technology transfer being an integral part of the paragraph 6 solution, emphasis will need to be given on technology transfer so that LDCs can build up domestic production capacity.

Technology Transfer

A major LDC interest in the negotiations is an effective implementation of Article 66.2 of the TRIPS Agreement concerning technology transfer. The LDC group should therefore pursue the matter in the TRIPS Council so that the developed country Members fully adhered to the 19 February decision. They should also press that the mechanism for ensuring the monitoring and implementation of Article 66.2 is established on a permanent, not on an *ad hoc*, basis. The broad group of developing countries should be expected to lend support to the LDC group in this regard.

In this regard, the LDC Consultative Group submitted a proposal in June 2002 to the TRIPS Council about the type of the mechanism that is to be put in place by the Council. The main elements of the LDC group's proposal are that the detailed reports submitted by the developed Member countries should contain information regarding the terms under which the technology is being transferred by the developed country enterprises; that the reports should also contain information on the appropriateness and local adaptability of the technology to the particular circumstances of the LDC to which the technology is being transferred; and that the information should show that the particular incentive regime is not simply within the general overseas development assistance (ODA) that benefits all developing countries but that it is specific to LDCs or, at any rate, the incentive regime is over and above what is provided for developing countries generally.

Technical and Financial Cooperation (Article 67)

Under Article 67 of the TRIPS Agreement, the provisions for technical assistance from the developed to developing and least developed Member countries are technically binding, but the TRIPS Agreement has not established any operational modality to implement the provisions. Therefore, to the extent that the present Round presents an opportunity to the developing/least-developed countries to bring any changes in the TRIPS Agreement, they should make concerted efforts aimed at establishing these modalities and making these provisions obligatory for developed countries.

Extension of the Transition Period (an outstanding implementation issue: tiret 93)

Extension of the transitional period is one of the outstanding implementation issues, which is of great significance to developing countries in general. These countries should therefore insist that the issue is adequately addressed and resolved by the TRIPS

Council. The transition period for developing countries, as provided for in Article 65.2, should be extended further. And in view of the special needs and requirements of the least developed countries, their economic, financial, and administrative constraints, and their need for flexibility to create a viable technological base, the transition period for these countries, as provided for in Article 66.1, should be extended to as long as they retain the LDC status (Dhaka Declaration).

Geographical Indications (GIs)

Developing countries/LDCs should be in favour of protecting their own GIs and adopt appropriate legislation for that purpose. They should expedite the process of registering their GIs as required under Article 23 of the Agreement. The position of these countries regarding the extension of higher-level protection to other products is also clear. As GI protection improves market access, it should be extended to products in which they have commercial interest. Such products for Bangladesh are: Jamdani Saree, Tangail Saree, Dhakai Muslin, Rajshahi Silk Saree, Kataribhog rice, Kalijira rice and Chinigura rice.

Review of the Provisions of Article 27.3(b)

The preferred options for the developing countries and LDCs in the negotiations on the Review of Provisions of Article 27.3(b) could be the following:

(i) Article 27.3(b) should be amended in the light of the provisions of the Convention on Biological Diversity and International Undertaking on Plant Genetic Resources.

(ii) The amendment should clarify and satisfactorily resolve the analytical distinctions between biological and microbiological organisms and processes.

(iii) Plants and animals should remain outside the domain of compulsory patentability. They should, in fact, be totally excluded from patentability. Natural processes that produce living organisms should not be patentable.

(iv) The amendment should ensure the protection of innovations of indigenous and local farming communities, including recognizing traditional knowledge and the rights of farmers to use, exchange, and save seeds, and promote food security.

(v) Article 27.3(b) should be implemented five years after the present review is completed (tiret 91 of outstanding implementation issues).

Non-violation Complaints

Non-violation complaints of the type identified in Article XXIII.1(b) and (c) of GATT 1994 should not be applicable to the TRIPS Agreement.

Other Outstanding Implementation Issues and Concerns

Other outstanding implementation issues as appear in the Compilation of Outstanding Implementation Issues Raised by Members (JOB(01)/152/Rev.1)–tirets 91, 93, 94–should be adequately addressed and resolved by the TRIPS Council.

Section 5: Concluding Observations

The main conclusions of the paper can be discerned in the foregoing sections. In this concluding section some of these are pieced together without making monotonous repetitions. Specifically, some observations about the position of least developed countries (LDCs) in the TRIPS Council negotiations are made in this section. The TRIPS Agreement poses great challenges before the LDCs. They will lose heavily if the outcome of the negotiations does not turn in their favour. On the other hand, these countries may also derive significant benefits from a successful conclusion of the negotiations. This is the reason why more and more LDCs–despite their inherent weaknesses and lack of negotiating skill–are actively participating in the ongoing negotiations in different negotiating groups. Let us look at the challenges first.

First, a major challenge for LDCs is in the area of pátent protection, which provides mechanisms for rent transfer from LDCs to developed countries in some key areas, e.g., agriculture, textiles, agricultural chemicals, and medicines. Despite some provisions for technical assistance and the grace period in the TRIPS Agreement (since extended till 2016), LDCs may lose on account of their inadequate exposure and lack of expertise on international trade involving IPs.

Second, LDCs might be adversely affected in respect of technology transfer, the use of seeds by farmers, and the availability of essential drugs to fight a variety of diseases.

Third, uncontrolled diffusion of IPs may have undesirable effects. Sweeping application of the patent regime even on small or simple processes, products, and technologies, which can be easily copied with indigenous resources, will certainly act a deterrent to technology transfer to LDCs.

Fourth, reverse engineering, as is well known, was employed as an effective tool to develop indigenous technology in many countries, including Japan and the NIEs. Absence of such opportunities will be a hindrance to LDCs' industrial growth.

Fifth, the issue of patenting of plants and animals is of particular importance to these countries. Most LDCs have rich resources of plants and animals. They have to ensure that these resources are not misused or exploited, and that they derive full benefit from the patent or protection system applicable to plants and animals.

Keeping these challenges in mind, the LDCs should pursue the following objectives in their negotiations at the TRIPS Council:

(a) They should press for a more broad-based exclusion from patentability, in particular for essential medicines listed by the World Health Organization. A review of TRIPS Agreement Article 27.1 may be needed for that purpose.

(b) No restrictions should be placed on compulsory licensing and parallel imports.

(c) Plants and animals should remain outside the domain of compulsory patentability.

(d) In developing their *sui generis* systems, LDCs should have the flexibility to be guided by their national objectives, and should not be made to conform to any multilateral standard.

(e) Adequate compensation should be made to source country and the indigenous community, which has nurtured particular plants and animals for a long time if these are put to a new use in the preparation of a patentable product.

(f) Given the inherently weak human and institutional capacities in LDCs, the transition period before full implementation of the TRIPS Agreement for these countries should be extended so long as they retain the status of a least developed country.

Now, let us look at the likely advantages of a successful completion of the negotiations. While LDCs should guard against all possible negative outcomes of TRIPS negotiations, they should not lose sight of the potential benefits. Of course, LDCs have genuine reasons to be apprehensive if the outcome of TRIPS negotiations turns out differently from what the expect. Yet, not everything will be lost.

First, LDCs have now up to 2016 to comply with patents for pharmaceutical products. They can use this grace period to enact necessary legislation in areas of patent protection for pharmaceutical products, in particular to change the compulsory licensing provisions. The transition period till 2016 also provides them the opportunity to keep medicine prices low.

Second, they may also attract investment to the pharmaceutical sector, which will serve the domestic demand for essential medicines as well as cater to markets abroad. In the long run, these countries are likely to gain, as intellectual property protection will provide greater incentive to multinational enterprises to invest and to license patented inventions to entrepreneurs in the respective countries.

Third, the LDCs need foreign investment and the transfer of advanced technology, which are critical for their economic development. With adequate protection of IPRs, the industrialized countries will safely transfer the newest technology to these countries. Without protection, these countries will tend to transfer technologies that are outdated, obsolete, and thus have lost their value.

Fourth, protection of IPR would also provide incentives to promote indigenous technological and innovative activities. Without such protection, technicians, creators and skilled workers will move to countries where their efforts are more fully rewarded (the phenomenon of brain drain).

Last but not the least, sufficient protection of IPR will raise the image of the least-developed countries in the outside world.

References

Correa, Çarlos (1998), "Implementing TRIPS in Developing Countries", *Third World Economics*, No. 189.

Correa, Carlos (2004), "Access to Drugs under TRIPS: A not so Expeditious Solution", in ICTSD. *Bridges*, Year 8, No. 1, January.

Ibid., (2004b).

International Centre for Trade and Sustainable Development, (2003a), *Developments Since the Fourth WTO Ministerial Conference: Intellectual*

Property Rights, Doha Round Briefing Series, Vol. 1, Nos. 1 and 5, February.

Ibid., (2003b), *Bridges,* Year 7 Nos. 2, 4 and 5, March. May and June 2003 issues.

Ibid., (2003c), *Cancun Update,* Doha Round Briefing Series, Vol. 2, No. 5, August.

Oyejide, T. Ademola, (2000), *Interests and Options of Developing and Least-developed Countries in a New Round of Multilateral Trade Negotiations,* G-24 Discussion Paper Series No. 2, UNCTAD, May.

Tandon, Yash. "Evaluation of the WTO and Other Forms of Technical Assistance to Developing Countries in the Context of the Uruguay Round Agreements." *Southern and Eastern African Trade, Information and Negotiations Initiative,* Harare, Zimbabwe.

UNCTAD (1996a), *The TRIPS Agreement and Developing Countries.*

Ibid., (1996b),*The Least Developed Countries Report: An Addendum.*

Ibid., (1996c), *The TRIPS Agreement and Developing Countries.*

Ibid., (1998), *The Least Developed Countries.*

Ibid., (2002), *Trade and Development Report.*

World Bank (2001), *Global Economic Prospects and the Developing Countries.*

World Trade Organization (2001a), *Compilations of Outstanding Implementation Issues Raised by Members (Revision,* JOB(01)/152/Rev.1, 27 October.

Ibid., (2001b), *Doha Ministerial Declaration,* November.

Ibid., (2001c), *Doha Declaration on the TRIPS Agreement and Public Health,* November.

Ibid., (2001d), *Doha Ministerial Decision on Implementation Related Issues and Concerns,* November.

Ibid., (2002), *Annual Report (2002) of the Council for TRIPS,* IP/C/27, 6 December.

Ibid., (2002), *Minutes of Meeting of Trade Negotiating Committee,* 4-6 December.

APPENDIX
The Doha Mandate

(i) Public Health

"We recognize that WTO Members with insufficient or no manufacturing capacities in the pharmaceutical sector could face difficulties in making effective use of compulsory licensing under the TRIPS Agreement. We instruct the Council for TRIPS to find an expeditious solution to this problem and to report to the General Council before the end of 2002." *(Paragraph 6 of the Doha Declaration on the TRIPS Agreement and Public Health).*

(ii) Geographical Indications

"With a view to completing the work started in the Council for Trade-Related Aspects of Intellectual Property Rights on the implementation of Article 23.4, we agree to negotiate the establishment of a multilateral system of notification and registration of geographical indications for wines and spirits by the Fifth Session of the Ministerial Conference. We note that issues related to the extension of the protection of geographical indications provided for in Article 23 to products other than wines and spirits will be addressed in the Council for TRIPS pursuant to paragraph 12 of this Declaration." *(Paragraph 18 of the Doha Ministerial Declaration).*

(iii) Non-violation Complaints

"The TRIPS Council is directed to continue its examination of the scope and modalities for complaints of the types provided for under subparagraphs 1(b) and 1(c) of Article XXIII of GATT 1994 and make recommendations to the Fifth Session of the Ministerial Conference. It is agreed that, in the meantime, members will not initiate such complaints under the TRIPS Agreement." *(Paragraph 11.1 of the Decision on Implementation-related Issues and Concerns).*

(iv) Incentives for Technology Transfer to LDCs (Article 66.2)

"Reaffirming that the provisions of Article 66.2 of the TRIPS Agreement are mandatory, it is agreed that the TRIPS Council shall put in place a mechanism for ensuring the monitoring and full implementation of the obligations in question. To this end, developed-country Members shall submit prior to the end of 2002 detailed reports on the functioning in practice of the incentives provided to their enterprises for the transfer of technology in pursuance of their commitments under Article 66.2. These submissions shall be subject to a review in the TRIPS Council and information shall be updated by Members annually." *(Paragraph 11.2 of the Decision on Implementation-related Issues and Concerns).*

(v) Other Outstanding Implementation Concerns

"We instruct the Council for TRIPS, in pursuing its work programme including under the review of Article 27.3(b), the review of the implementation of the TRIPS Agreement under Article 71.1 and the work foreseen pursuant to paragraph 12 of this declaration, to examine, inter alia, the relationship between the TRIPS Agreement and the Convention on Biological Diversity, the protection of traditional knowledge and folklore, and other relevant new developments raised by members pursuant to Article 71.1. In undertaking this work, the TRIPS Council shall be guided by the objectives and principles set out in Articles 7 and 8 of the TRIPS Agreement and shall take fully into account the development dimension." *(Paragraph 19 of the Doha Ministerial Declaration).*

The mandated deadlines for concluding the negotiations were set as follows:

- 31 December 2002: Members were to conclude negotiations under paragraph 6 of the Doha Declaration on TRIPs and Public Health.
- 31 December 2002: The TRIPS Council was to report to Trade Negotiations Committee for "appropriate action" on intellectual property-related implementation issues.
- Fifth WTO Ministerial Meeting (10-14 September, in Cancun, Mexico): Conclusion of the negotiations on the multilateral system of notification/registration of GIs for wines and spirits; recommendations on non-violation.

10

TRIPS Space for Public Health & Indian Patents (Amendment) Act, 2005

V. Rajyalakshmi

Section 1: Introduction

Right to health is one of the central pillars on which rests the effective enjoyment of human right to life and liberty. Therefore, the newly emerging international and national policies, which are throwing tremendous challenges to the right to health, are viewed as a matter of great concern. This is the reason why not debates are taking place at national and international for a on the implications of global policy of IPR protection on the public health. Introduction of pharmaceutical sector into the international regime of IPR protection is nothing but introduction of formidable challenges to the health care systems around the world.

Access to medicines constitutes an important component of medical care for meeting the health needs. As acknowledged by WHO access to medicines is a human right. WHO estimates that more than one third of the population lacks regular access to the medicines they need. In developing countries 0.3 millions children under five years of age died in 1993 (Asian Workshop Report 2000). 8.6 millions of death could have been prevented if those at risk have had access to essential drugs. (Asian Workshop Report 2000a) Today in 32 countries, more than half population lacks regular access to basic essential drugs.(Asian Workshop Report 2000b) Access to medicines represents a very important measure of the quality of a state's health services and is one of the key indicators of equity and social justice.(Peterson 2000). To raise demands regarding the claims of basic health needs is nothing but to challenge the developmental agenda of the state. (Panda Sowmya 2002).

Section 2: Patents and Medicines under TRIPS

Patent provides a monopolistic right to patent holders, to exclusively reap commercial rewards for their intellectual efforts, an economic incentive is offered to the people for inventing and engaging themselves more in creative efforts. This line of thought is indeed proved right because commercial advantages of patents did provide great economic incentive and did boost the research in drugs. But the counter side of this happening is that the pharmaceutical sector, the source of production of medicines, has come under the greedy avidity of monopoly appetite of drug giants predominantly belonging to developed states which keep the prices of the drugs out of the buying reach of a common man.

TRIPS[1] aims to create a harmonized global system for protection of intellectual property rights, which includes patents. TRIPS seek WTO members to conform within specific period to the minimum standards of patent protection as provided in the agreement. For the purpose of such compliance the WTO members will have to devise new laws or modify the existing ones if necessary. National compliance with TRIPS is ensured through the WTO dispute settlement procedure (which places the burden of proof on the defendant). Countries failing to meet their obligations can be subjected to trade sanctions.

Due to liberalization the drug manufacturers are now free from restrictions on manufacture and export and no doubt, the commercial advantages of the patent system can be utilized by drug industries of the developed as well as the developing states. But in the process, the domestic industries are open to international competition. The drug industries of developing states can be no match to the rich and research incentive drug industries of MNCs or of developed states. Patent regime as it stands today precludes the indigenous production of drugs that can provide drugs at cheaper price. This is the typical understanding of any common man of a developing state about the impact of TRIPS on public health. Therefore, the common man's apprehension is that right to health is no more inalienable as any human right ought to be. Out of this apprehension came the urge to have a continuing discussion on the issue of the impact of TRIPS and public health. Therefore, even before the TRIPS Council began to discuss the issue, various NGOs and civil groups have intensified their attention on this sensitive issue. Apart from this general initiative, there were specific happenings, which provided strong impetus for the global discussions about the link between TRIPS and public health, which ultimately led to the adoption of Doha Declaration. They were, the worsening public health situations across the world as millions of HIV + VE patients in developing states could not access the drugs they needed because of their high cost; the Law Suit brought by Pharmaceutical Industry Associations and 39% of its affiliated pharmaceutical companies against the Government of South Africa[i] for its efforts to procure generic version of AIDS medicines through compulsory licensing; Resol of UN Commission of Human Rights on Access to Medication in the context of endemics such as HIV/AIDS;[2] Resol on Scaling up the Response for HIV/AIDS[3] the Resol 'WHO Medicines Strategy';[4] XI Summit of the Heads of State and the Governments of the Group of Fifteen etc.[5]

Though it is generally felt that TRIPS Agreement is not a completely closed code and that it does contain the space necessary to address public health concerns, the complexities of the issues governed by TRIPS and the possible differences in the interpretation of its provisions are such that it is difficult to decipher the space. Moreover, the efforts of the developing countries to utilize TRIPS space for legitimizing their public health measures have already come under pressure from industrialized and multinational companies. Thus when member countries tried to take advantage of the existing flexibilities of TRIPS, complaints were lodged before dispute settlement body of WTO .The landmark illustration in this regard is the law suit brought by a pharmaceutical associations and 39 of its affiliate pharmaceutical companies against South Africa regarding the compatibility with TRIPS of its legislation "Medicines and Related Substances Control Amendment Act' that allowed import of Anti-Aids drugs at cheaper prices. This case is naked example to show that when it comes to reaping of monopolistic profits, even the measures taken to combat the grave threats to human existence such as AIDS would not be spared to come in the way. Further there are many examples of arm-twisting by the developed states whereby many developing states felt compulsions to forego even the transitional concessions allowed by TRIPS itself. One can cite the revised Bangui Agreement[6], 1999 of OAPI (African Organization of Industrial Property) which has pushed 12 member states that are considered least developed states to comply with TRIPS many years before they are required to do so. The Bangui Agreement 1999 also does not allow compulsory licensing for imports. The resistance as one can see from these examples to the efforts of the developing states to utilize the TRIPS space resulted perhaps in greater resolve to spearhead the process of clarifying deriving and devising the space in TRIPS to address the public health concerns. This resolve abetted by civil group responses resulted in Doha Declaration.

The Doha Declaration is a step forward and toward the directions of deciphering the TRIPS space relevant to public health.

Section 3: Doha Declaration

The Doha Declaration on the TRIPS Agreement and Public Health is adopted on 14th November 2001. During the diplomatic negotiations the developed states did try to narrow down the scope of Doha Declaration.[7] They wanted its ambit to be confined only to the issue of access to medicines. Health as a concept has a larger dimension than mere access to medicines. The Doha meeting ultimately could manage to put together a Declaration on TRIPS and Public Health conceding the principle pursued by the developing states[8] and the civil groups that public health is not just about access to medicines. The unpalatable materialistic efforts to limit the usefulness of Doha flexibilities only to the health crises arising out of select diseases like HIV/AIDS, tuberculosis and malaria etc. also could be successfully stalled so that the Doha Declaration stands to broadly recognize the gravity of the public health problems afflicting many developing and least developed countries, especially those resulting from HIV/AIDS tuberculosis, malaria etc. Therefore, public health problems addressed by Doha Declaration in principle cover all health problems, not just those arising out of AIDS, tuberculosis etc.

Access to medicines does not simply mean the physical availability of medicines. Therefore one of the most effective elements of public health policies is providing adequate access to medicines at affordable prices which can reduce mortality and infection rates.(African Group Statement submitted to TRIPS Council 2001). Access can be limited by factors such as financial hurdles, physical and infrastructure barriers and information gaps among others. (African Group Statement 2001 (a) Some of the most successful public health policies have been possible through provisions of access to generic and patented drugs to those in need. .(African Group Statement 2001 (b) When intellectual property rights are property granted and are exercised, they may meet their objective of contributing to the development of new medicines. (African Group Statement 2001 (c) and therefore IPR system may be supported. However, there should be a common undertaking that confirm the right of governments to ensure access to medication at affordable prices and to make use of the provisions in the Agreement whenever the scope or exercise of such rights result in barriers to access to medicines. (African Group Statement 2001 d) In tune with this expectation the Doha Declaration, 2001 affirmed the right of WTO members to use to the full the provisions in the TRIPS Agreement which provide flexibility for the above said purpose. (pgh 4) Consequent to such affirmation, the Doha Declaration confirmed(pgh 50 that these flexibilities include:

(a) In applying the customary rules of interpretation of public international law, each provision of the TRIPS Agreement shall be read in the light of object and purpose of the Agreement as expressed in particular, in its objectives and principles. (pgh 5 (a))

(b) Each member has the right to grant compulsory licenses and the freedom to determine the grounds upon which such licenses are granted. (pgh 5(b))

(c) Each member has the right to determine what constitutes a national emergency or other circumstances of extreme urgency, it being understood that public heath crisis including those relating to IV/AIDS, tuberculosis, Malaria and other epidemics can represent a national emergency or other circumstances of extreme urgency. (pgh 5(c)).

(d) The effect of the provisions in the TRIPS Agreement that are relevant to the exhaustion of intellectual property rights is to leave each member free to establish its own regime for such exhaustion without challenge, subject to MFN and national treatment provisions. (pgh 5 (d)).

What then are the positive and possible implications that can flow from what has been confirmed by Doha Declaration?

Section 4: Objectives and Principles of TRIPS Agreement

Article 7[9] contains the objectives and Art. 8[10] contains the principles. It is claimed that the biggest gain for the developing countries from Doha Conference lies in the flexibilities provided in the Declaration and in the use of Article 8 of the TRIPS.(Dubey Muchkund 2001).

As per Doha Declaration each provision of the TRIPS will have to be read in the light of object and purpose of the Agreement as expressed in particular in its objectives and principles.

Under Article 7 the protection and enforcement of IPR should contribute to the promotion of technological innovation and to the transfer of and disseminations of technology to the mutual advantage of producers and users of technological knowledge and in manner conducive to social and economic welfare and to balance of rights and obligations. These objectives show that TRIPS does not aim merely to protect the private rights. It also seeks to balance the private rights with public rights that are supposed to benefit the society as a whole. The statement of Article 7 that the enforcement of TRIPS should contribute to the aforementioned objectives and the reiteration in the Doha Declaration that each provision of the TRIPS should be read in the light of its objectives and principles leads us to the conclusion that the TRIPS guaranteed IPRs do not exist in vacuum and that they cannot and should not stand in the way of achievement of these objectives. They rather should complement and when necessary even lose their precedence in the promotion of policies conducive to social and economic welfare, public health policy being one of them. If this does not happen i.e. the patent holders fail to meet the objectives of TRIPS, members can legitimately take appropriate measures to protect public health.

Economic incentive of patent rights encourages creation of new drugs and promotes sustainable and improvised availability of drugs to society and thereby producers and users of drugs enjoy mutual advantage. But, in many situations, the patent holders in order to reap commercial benefits may and in fact do abuse their rights either by keeping drug prices beyond the reasonable margin of profit or do not offer the products in sufficient amount to meet public demand. As one could see Article 8 recognized the possibility of misuse of IPR and did provide space to members for taking appropriate measures. Article 8 which contains principles recognizes that the members may in formulating or amending their national laws and regulations, adopt (1) measures necessary to protect public health and nutrition, and to promote the public interest in sectors of vital importance to their socio-economic and technological development, provided that such measures are consistent with the provisions of the Agreement. (2) appropriate measures, provided that they are consistent with the provisions of the Agreement may be needed to prevent the abuse of intellectual property rights by right holders or the resort of practices which unreasonably restrain trade or adversely effect the international transfer of technology.

The Doha Declaration reiterates that TRIPS should be read in the light of its principles amounts to reiteration of the right of the members to take appropriate measures in case of abuse of IPRs as allowed under Article 8. So far as this space is concerned, Doha Declaration made a step forward than being a mere reiteration of Article 8. It is a forward step for the following reasons.

1. Article 8 speaks of abuse of IPR not with special reference to drugs obviously for the fact that it is a general principle. Doha Declaration provided specific dimensions to this principle by recording its recognition of the effect of IPRs on prices of medicines. (pgh 3).
2. From Article 8 it is not clear whether members are entitled to take appropriate measures individually or collectively. Also, Article 8 used permissive language by lightly pointing out that appropriate measures may be needed for preventing abuse of IPRs. On the other hand, the language of Doha Declaration suggests that it is the right of the members. Very specifically, it speaks of WTO members' right to protect public health and in particular to promote access to medicines and emphasizes that the members should not be prevented from taking measures to protect public health (pgh 3). The tenor of this language and the proceedings of Ministerial discussions that preceded the Doha Declaration suggest the individual power of member states to take appropriate measures when necessary.
3. Art 8 provided for leeway for adoption of appropriate measures in case of abuse of IPR. But this is subjected to the

rider that such measures must be consistent with provisions of TRIPS. This restriction is viewed as quite paradoxical and the needy members developed pessimistic attitude about the utility of the so-called space for appropriate measures granted under Article 8. It is generally understood that TRIPS provisions enjoy primacy over appropriate measures. But the vigour and tenor of the language of Doha Declaration suggests a reversal of this understanding. It categorically says TRIPS Agreement 'does not and 'should not' prevent members from taking measures to protect public health. (pgh 3). The affirmation that the Agreement can and should be interpreted and implemented in a manner supportive of WTO member's right to protect public health and in particular to promote access to medicines also suggests shift in primacy from conformity of TRIPS Agreement to member's right to protect public health and in particular to promote access to medicines to all.

Compulsory Licensing

Compulsory licensing helps the governments to balance the public interests with the claims of patent holder. The developing countries have insisted that compulsory licensing is an important instrument to protect public health.[11] Compulsory license provides the ability to override a patent by authorizing a compulsory license for production of drug. A compulsory license is an authorization, which is granted by the government without the permission of the patent holder. Governments are permitted to grant compulsory license provided that is justified by the general public interest.

Patent owners are expected to provide to the their patented medicine. Where this is not done, for e.g. when patent holders fail to provide enough medicines in the domestic market and refuses to voluntary license the production of their patent, public health could be at stake. Therefore, governments may deem it necessary to grant compulsory license to allow interested third parties to produce the medicines in order to ensure that it will be more readily available or more affordable to the general public.(African Group Statement 2001 e)

TRIPS[12] and Paris Convention, 1967 (5 A(g)) allow compulsory licenses. The right of the members to use compulsory licensing system is reaffirmed in Doha Declaration also. (pgh 5 (b)) Neither

TRIPS nor Doha Declaration lists out any specific grounds on which compulsory license may be issued. Such freedom to be drawn out in individual national legislations. However TRIPS (Art. 31(b)) ordains that compulsory licenses can be granted only after the proposed user has made efforts to obtain license from patent holder on commercial terms. Failed in such efforts, compulsory license can be issued but the patent holder has to be compensated. (Art. 31(b)) This position has not changed in Doha Declaration.[xiii] The above-stipulated conditions can be waived in case of national emergency or other circumstances of extreme urgency or in the case of public non-commercial use. (pgh 1 of Aug. 30th Decision 2003). In this regard the Doha declaration clarified that each member has the right to determine what constitutes a national emergency or other circumstance of extreme urgency. (pgh 5(b)) it being understood that public health crises including those relating to HIV/AIDS, tuberculosis, malaria and other epidemics can represent a national emergency or other circumstances of extreme emergency.

To have the best advantage of compulsory licensing, a state needs to have a reasonably sophisticated pharmaceutical industry in order to produce the medicines concerned and must be able to achieve economies of scale to bring the price down to affordable levels many developing countries fail on both counts. Doha Declaration recognized that WTO members with insufficient or no manufacturing capacities[14] in the pharmaceutical sector could face difficulties in making effective use of compulsory license. (pgh 6) so, Doha Declaration instructed TRIPS Council to find expeditious solution to this problem and report before the end of 2002. (pgh 6).

Section 6: Parallel Imports

The concept of parallel imports applies in a situation where the patent holder sells the same product in different countries with different prices. In such a case if the buyer from the country where patent holder sells the product at a cheaper price exports the product to another country at a price higher than what he has secured for but at a price cheaper than what the patent holder offered his product in that country. As a result of this, the profit of the patent holder is effectively reduced. Parallel imports thus would be an effective policy instrument that can check the higher prices of the product.

TRIPS provides exclusive rights (Art. 28) to the patent holder to prevent third parties from making, using, offering for sale or importing the patented product to member countries where a patent holder has obtained patents for the same. But the issue here is once the patented product has already been placed in the market for sale whether the patent holder is further unable to use his exclusive rights to sell or dispose the same-patented product. If he is unable, it means that he is not in a position to prevent any act of import by third party buyers. If his exclusive right is exhausted with the first sale or disposal of patented drug it apparently allows the developing and least developing counties to import this drug from other counties. Therefore, the issue of parallel imports revolves around the interpretation of the doctrine of exhaustion of IPRs and the question whether domestic or international principles of exhaustion are to be followed. (Deviah) This issue was discussed at Doha and the Declaration clarified. (pgh 5(d)) that the effect o the provisions in the TRIPS Agreement of that are relevant to the exhaustion of intellectual property rights is to leave each member free to establish its own regime for such exhaustion without challenge but subject to MFN and national treatment provisions of Articles 3 & 4. So now countries can take advantage of this independence and can legitimize parallel imports.

Section 7: Doha

Paragraph 6 of Doha Declaration mandated the WTO TRIPS Council to find expeditious solution to the problem of compulsory license. Following up the Doha mandate WTO Council responsible for IPR approved a decision in the form of a waiver extending until 2016 the transition period during which LDCs do not have to provide patent protection for pharmaceuticals. The TRIPS Agreement requires (Art. 31) that compulsory licensing must be predominantly for the supply of the domestic market. This has an indirect impact upon those countries which do not have adequate capacity to manufacture drugs and therefore would want to import generics from third country parties which obtained compulsory license.(Jain 2003) But they would find it difficult to find countries that can supply with drugs made under compulsory license because of the condition of 'predominant supply to domestic market'(Jain 2003a). Members were deadlocked over this problem of compulsory license. As a result no decision could be arrived at by the original deadline of 31st December 2002. Ultimately agreement was reached by 30th August 2003. By virtue of 30th August 2003 decision, doubts regarding utilization of compulsory license system for exporting drugs to needy states have been cleared. According to this decision, interim waiver from relevant obligations of TRIPS has been provided (pgh.2) whereby countries are allowed to produce generic copies of patented drugs under compulsory license to export the same to the eligible importing members.(pgh.1) By virtue of this agreement any country can export pharmaceutical products (includes active ingredients and diagnostic kits) manufactured under compulsory licenses but the same must be done in accordance with the terms set out (pgh.2)in the decision. The terms include (a) specification by importing member of names and quantities of the products needed (b) confirmation by the eligible member that the eligible member excepting LDC has established that it has insufficient or no manufacturing capacity in pharmaceutical sector (c) production and export by exporting member should be only in the amounts needed by the importing state (d) distinct packaging for identifying the exports as under compulsory license system etc.

Doha Limitations[+]

Doha Declaration has made a positive contribution in highlighting the issue of public health so far as the access to medicines is concerned. This could happen solely due to the cohesive stand taken by the developing states. Especially, the cohesion yielded as significant result of strengthening the SDT (special but differential treatment) in all the documents adopted in the Doha meet. (Dubey Muchkunda) This appreciation cannot however camouflage the gap between theoretical assertions and practical directions of implementation. Few misgivings about the same have been noted below.

1. Though there is diplomatic victory for the Third World in managing broader title to the Declaration, namely, TRIPS & Public Health' instead of TRIPS and Access to Medicines, the content of the Declaration is largely aimed at providing better Access to Medicines. The larger aspects of public health are not really addressed except by way of rhetoric statement. Doha Declaration did not define pubic health: This lack of any attempt to define pubic health leaves large filed of legal battles

between pharma companies and the individual states that can threat the expeditious use of Doha Declaration. The possibility of narrow interpretation of the term pubic health could render many public health initiatives futile.

2. Though Doha Declaration makes broad references to public health, specific mention of problems like AIDS, Tuberculosis and Malaria etc gives scope for pharma industry to interpret narrowly and try to omit importance to other diseases even though they represents serious public health concerns.
3. Also, the reference to health crisis might undermine the importance of preventive approach, which is very vital for avoidance of public health crisis.
4. The member countries are theoretically empowered to decide as to what constitutes a national emergency or other circumstance of extreme urgency. However, the possibility of narrow interpretation of what constitutes an emergency by the WTO panel still remains.
5. The original intention behind the August 30th 2003 decision was to find expeditious solution to the problem of the countries, which cannot avail the advantage of compulsory license system due to lack of or insufficient capacity for local manufacture. The decision, no doubt, has given green signal for the import of generic medicines but this facility is subject to such conditions compliance with which may render the facility a non-viable economic proposition. For e.g. The necessity of specifying and supplying only the amount of demand and the additional costs to be incurred for distinctive packaging (pgh. 2(b)(ii)) might discourage the compulsory license holder to export of drugs.
6. The August 30th decision leaves unclear whether or not economic efficiency is a ground for determining the lack of manufacturing capacity in the importing country. The lack of clarity on this issue has been defended as a matter of creative ambiguity but we have to note that US is already telling Philippines and other countries that they will oppose economic efficiency as a ground for allowing a country to import generics. (Oxfam Report Sept. 2003).
7. The new deal introduces an element of uncertainty by stating that the system should not be an instrument to pursue

industrial or commercial policy objectives, creating ambiguity over the role that will be played by the businesses that manufacture and sell generics. (Oxfam Report Sept. 2003a).

8. Despite the positive features of the Doha Declaration, one has to remember that it is a Declaration that contains a set of principle. Therefore, it is felt that technically it has only moral force whereas amendment to TRIPS Agreement would have been legally binding.(Dubey Muchkund 2001b).

The overall situation of TRIPS++ is that positive directions laid down by Doha and Doha+ can be waylaid by new legal economic and political obstacles. Enough opportunities are there for big powers to pressure and stop developing countries from using flexibilities, especially the chance for using compulsory licensing system. Developing Countries will have to be vigilant and try hard for bringing amendment to TRIPS, which has long lasting effect than the temporary waiver. They should be vigilant enough to draft an amendment that simplifies and clarifies the procedure and removes unnecessary obstacles to the country's sacred right to protect public health.

Section 8: Caution to Developing Countries

Developing countries in order to protect their public health should also be quick and efficient in using the available flexibilities in TRIPS++. Their legislative and economic policies must be such as to derive maximum benefit from the flexibilities. This is very vital keeping in view that rich countries are regrouping under WIPO to have in place a uniform patent law that can defy sovereignty of nations. Global patenting system apparently to do away with the backlog of patent applications can do away with national phase and jurisdiction. Rich countries are also pushing for *'sui generis'* protection of data basis, which can claim 15-25 year period of protection. Them the patentability, bolar exception, data exclusivity, when determined under SPLT (Substantive Patent Law Treaty) will take away power of national governments to use IPR as a tool fro development. Unfortunately ignorance,[xv] sluggishness, political hindrances, economic and technological backwardness, lack of political trusts, external political pressures[xvi] etc. are jeopardizing the prospects of developing states from efficient use of available opportunities. Regarding the technical assistance, which the countries can have from WIPO, there are misgivings about the genuineness of its advice. For eg. Victor Van Spengler a Legal Advisor to MSF in Cambodia alleges that the draft legislation of patent protection supplied by WIPO to Cambodia did not contain all the flexibilities available under TRIPS. (Oxfam Report 2002).

Therefore, the developing countries should realize that they might lose the advantage of Doha gain unless they make positive efforts to retain it.

Brief mention of the conclusion and recommendations made in the Regional Consultation held at Colombo in 2003 on WTO Agreement and Access to Medicines may be made here to point out the mindset of the Asian region to make the maximum use of Doha Declaration. The workshop held jointly by Health Action International-Asia Pacific, Sri Lanka Ministry of Health and Regional WHO (South East Asia) Office made the following recommendations.

Each country in the region should give the highest priority to formulating appropriate policies, policy measures and laws or legal provisions regarding patents and access to medicines. In so doing, each country should maximize the use of the rights that the country has to protect and promote the health of its citizens and to provide affordable medicines for all. In particular, policy makers in each country should take the following steps (i) limit the scope of approval of patent applications to patents that are genuinely novel or involve an inventive step, and to reject applications that are not novel or do not satisfy the criteria of an invention, or that involve minor developments (such as slightly different dosage or formulation); (ii) examine existing legislation and determine whether there are inadequacies and weaknesses, and if so, to amend these laws and introduce provisions that maximize the rights of the country to be able to adopt policy measures and options such as compulsory licence, parallel imports and government use; (iii) examine the national situation regarding patents and prices of medicine in relation to the diseases in the country, and devise measures such as government use, compulsory licensing and parallel imports in order to effect importation or medicines; (iv) examine and resolve the practical and administrative measures required, such as establishing institutions or competent authorities or an interagency committee, appropriate appeal procedure and appropriate systems and rates of compensation for the patent holder; (v) establish institutional arrangements for coordination of polices and measures between different government departments involved in the issue (i.e. Ministry of Health, Ministry of Industry and Trade, the Patent Office, Attorney General's Office of the Ministry of Law) and (vi) governments should also establish consultative mechanisms with NGOs, social movements and private sector local generic drug producers or potential producers so that a coordinated national response can be effectively made.

Section 9: India's Response to TRIPS–Special Reference to Patent (Amendment) Act, 2005

Public Health Policy of India

India has recently amended its patent legislation to suit the TRIPS regime. Before analyzing the merits on legislation, a brief projection of India's Health Policy and its pharmaceutical competence is worthy of reference.[17]

National Health Planning in India began much before its independence when the National Planning Committee (NPC) of Indian National Congress was set up in 1938. (Benerji 1985) This Committee set up a sub-committee on National Health, which made a penetrating assessment of the then existing health situation and health services in the country and recommended measures for their improvement. (Panda Sommya 2002a). The Report sought the integration of curative and preventive function in a state agency and it stressed that the maintenance of the health of the people was responsibility of the state. In 1943, Health Survey and Development Committee, famously called Bhore Committee, conceptualized a comprehensive health care service satisfying the criteria viz. provision of adequate integrated preventive, curative and promotive health care services, be as close as possible to the beneficiary, the service availability to all irrespective of their ability to pay, looking after specifically the vulnerable and weaker sections of the people etc. (Bhore Committee Report 1948) It suggested for creation of an integrated preventive and curative services and importantly stressed on preventive and social medicine for churning out the so called social physicians. (Bhore Committee Report 1948) During the first two five year plan periods government remained only rhetoric. Gradually over the sixties, the vision of Bhore got progressively diluted. (Panda Sowmya 2002 b) In the Third Five-year Plan priority was given only for family planning.

The private sector grew at a fast pace. It also received government subsidies and state support. Terms and conditions for drug production, which had all along been dictated by foreign firms were made further convenient for the private sector and MNCs. (Sen 1994). By the end of 60's drug prices in India were one of the highest in the world. In 70's there was change in rhetoric largely due to influential statements of global bodies like World Bank, WHO, UNICEF etc. By the mid seventies, it was apparent that hi-tech medical care could not be made accessible to all. Rural Health Scheme was launched in 1977 following Reports of Kartar Singh Committee and Shrivatsav Committee. In 1978 Ama-Ata Declaration was adopted at WHO/UNICEF Conference, which declared the goal of 'Health for All' by 2000 AD to be achieved by primary health care. But in no time, the concept of, 'selective primary health care' caught up limited to technological interventions to areas that ensure quick monitory returns by emphasizing the cost effectiveness principle. The technological approach, which glossed over the socio-political coordinates of health problems, could hardly produce the desired results. The Sixth Five Year Plan signified the coming of age of the private sector to which medical care was opened up.

The National Drug Policy, 1986 has set the clock back from what 1978 policy has done. There is diminution in the range of pubic health services. Now, in the health services, along with rampart privatization, globalization etc. Thus managed health care[18] promises to be the feature of the future. Thus there is an unfortunate trend in India that views health as private matter and health care as a private good.

The government first revised the Patent Act, 1971 and then constituted Health Committee in 1974 to undertake a through analysis of Indian Drug Industry. (GOI Report 1975) Hailhi Committee Report Committee decried the role played by the MNCs in the industry for their reluctance to produce bulk drugs in the country, their reluctance to produce essential drugs. By a unanimous resolution, Hailhi Committee recommended immediate dilution of foreign equity in drug firms to 40% and progressively to 26%. It recommended nationalization of all foreign drug companies and further recommended a leading role for the public sector and a sectoral reservation in the industry to encourage the growth of the indigenous sector. But subsequently, the National

Drug Policy of 1986 reversed all the progressive aspects of 1978 policy reducing in one sweep the span of price control from 347 balk drugs to 166 drugs, decreasing the number of controlled categories to two and increasing the mark of profit up in these to 75 per cent 100 per cent. (Sen Gupta 1976) The Drug Price Control Order in pursuance of National Drug Policy of 1978 bore the imprints of Hathi Committee however partial they were. It contributed to a remarkable growth of Indian drug sector leading to phenomenal rise in capacity in producing essential drugs and a drop in drug prices so much so UNIDO in 1980 identified India as one of the countries with the capacity to produce all essential drugs indigenously. But the implementation of Drug Price Control of order of 1987 based on 1986 policy led to an immediate hike in drug prices. With the government's first attempt at liberalization in 1985, India for the first time began to be integrated into the world economy and had to abide by the rules of global trading which required amending patent legislation.

The coordinated approach adopted by Indian Government in utilizing Indian Patent Act, 1970, Drug Price Control Order[19] and Foreign Exchange Regulation Act[20] provided good boost to Indian Drug industry. India exports more than its imports and supplies 500 bulk drugs, out of which are made domestically 70 per cent of total production is now being carried by local companies. There are 4,000 units in the organized sector and around 13000 units in the small sector. On average, drugs in India are between 1000 and 4000 per cent cheaper than the same product in U.S. pharmacies.[21]

The Indian Patent Act, 1970 by recognizing only the process patents and not product patents effectively served to legalize copying of drugs that are patentable enthused the indigenous production of pharma industry. The Act fostered the protection of public interest by restricting the scope of patentability and the rights of patent holder. It was one of the most balanced statutes in the world. But by virtue of Indian becoming party to TRIPS, amendments to Patent Act are obligated. The process of complying with the provisions of the TRIPS Agreement started with the enactment of the Patents (Amendment) Act, 1999 to provide for a Mail Box for National Patent Offices to start entertaining product patent applications for pharmaceutical and agro chemicals. Thus 1999 Act of our Country also provides for grant of EMR to the patent applications in both sectors on satisfaction of stipulated conditions. The Government further introduced in Parliament in Dec.1999, the Patent (Second Amendment) Bill to comply with other provisions of TRIPS. A joint Parliamentary Committee was established. Meanwhile Doha Declaration was adopted providing for significant, flexibilities and also clarified the doubts about the flexibilities in interpreting TRIPS. Later Patents Amendment Act, 2002 (25th June 2002 enforced on 20th May 2003) read with the Patents Amendment Rules (enforced on 20th May 2003) was passed. Later the Patents Amendment Ordinance 2004 was promulgated followed by the passing of Patents (Amendment) Act 2005 and Patent Amendment Rules 2005.

Indian Patent (Amendment) Act 2005

Having become a member of WTO, it has become inevitable for India to concede to the pressures of WTO and bring about the changes is its patent law so that the same is in tune with its international obligations. The question here is whether India has availed or not the existing flexibilities in TRIPS which have been bargained at Doha and Doha + to protect the public health.

The two most important flexibilities, which are useful for the protection of public health, are compulsory licensing and parallel importing. Compulsory licensing is an important tool to promote competition and increases the affordability of drugs, which is allowed by TRIPS and further reiterated by the Doha Declaration. The new Act 2005 has provided for grant of compulsory licensing (S.84). India by its amendment has specified grounds on which compulsory licensing may be granted. These grounds though are broad and are generally capable of meeting the public health needs nevertheless have reduced the general scope of discretion left by TRIPS[22] and Doha to individual countries. The three major grounds are:

(a) Not meeting the reasonable requirements of the public with respect to patented invention.

(b) Unaffordable pricing of drug.

(c) Non working of patent.

What are the criteria for determining the reasonably requirements of the public have been further specified (S.84 (7)). Patent Act, 2005 has introduced a time limit of 6 months within which the patent holder should consider the applicant for license for manufacture of patented invention. Earlier according to the 2004 Ordinance, the license seeker will have to wait for a "reasonable period" to elapse before he applies for compulsory licensing. The specified time limit helps in making quick decisions for allowing compulsory licensing to local manufacturers.

The Patents Act 2005 (92 A) allows the grant of compulsory license for exporting the patented pharmaceutical products in certain exceptional circumstances. Export is allowed to any country, which has, insufficient or no manufacturing capacity in the pharmaceutical sector provided the compulsory licensing has been granted in such country. Actually Patent Amendment Ordinance 2004 established a system (S.92A(1)) whereby the Indian pharmaceutical manufacturer with compulsory licensing could not export the drug to other countries as a matter of right 2004 Ordinance (29A(1)) required the Indian authorities to examine whether the importing country has complied with the TRIPS obligations or not. So it was widely opposed and argued that it should not be for the exporting country to judge the compliance of the importing states with TRIPS obligations. But now after the passing of Patent Act 2005, compulsory licenses are available both for the manufacture and export of patented pharmaceutical products to any country having insufficient or no manufacturing capacity in the pharmaceutical sector for the concerned product to meet public health problems provided that compulsory licenses have been granted by the importing country or such country has by notification or otherwise allowed importation of the patented pharmaceutical product from India. This compulsory licensing mechanism provided by the patent legislation no doubt reduces the scope of a patentee to misuse the patent power in a monopolistic fashion. However, the Indian legislation leaves in place a procedurally a very laborious and inefficient compulsory licensing scheme. Also any one can oppose the grant of compulsory licensing. This might cause unnecessary delays.

So far as parallel imports are concerned following the Second Amendments in 2002 to the Patents Act (1970), parallel imports of patented products were allowed, subject to the condition that the foreign exporter was authorized by the patentee to sell and distribute. Under the New Amendment Act (2005), the foreign exporter need only be "duly authorized under the law". This change is tantamount to allowing sale of generic products without the consent of the patent holder. Another point of encouragement for generic drug producers is that under the Amended Act 2005 which allowed Bolar provision, the generics can gain entry immediately and just at the time of expiration of patent term. Such an entry of generics hopefully allows affordable access to medicines.

Art 8 containing the principles of TRIPS left the liberty to member states to promote the public interest in sectors of vital importance to their socio-economic and technological development provided such measures are consistent with the provisions of the Agreement. India also repeated the provisions in the general principles applicable to the working of the patent. Apart from keeping 'public interest' in the ambit of general principles, India should have utilized the broad concept of 'public interest' as a ground for issue of compulsory license. This could have taken care of those situations, which are not specified as grounds for issuing compulsory license but nevertheless involve public health concerns.

Non-working of the patent is recognized by India as a ground for revocation. The criticism is that it is not clear whether not manufacturing of the patented products locally amounts to non-working of the patent according to Indian Law. Many countries have specified non-local manufacture as a ground of revocation. But perhaps this criticism is misplaced. This local manufacturing requirement is impliedly taken care of by providing that if specification of patent is not sufficient to enable a person in India possessing in, and average knowledge of, the art to which the invention relates average skill to work the invention or if the specification does not specify the best method of working, patent may be revoked.

*Regarding the practice of ever greening of patents i.e. fresh grant of patents to new indications (uses) of currently patented products, the 2004 Ordinance has allowed such practice. It thus widened the scope of patentability, which is a great advantage to companies, which bring about small change to medicine and seek new patent. In response to this concerns the Patents (Amendment) Act 2005 has reformulated. It adopted a stricter standard according to which "a mere discovery of a new form of a known substance which does not result in the enhancements of the known efficiency of that substance (emphasis added) or the mere discovery of any new property or new use for a known substance or of the mere use of a known process, machine or apparatus is also excluded from patentablity unless such known processes result in a new reactant (S.3(d)). This is a welcome step because people will not be burdened with ever–green patented drugs. Also of relief is the fact that the 2005 Act excludes any process for the medicinal, surgical, curative, prophylactic, diagnostic, therapeutic or other treatment of human beings or any process for the similar treatment of animals excluding plants to render them tree of disease-from the realm of patentability (S.3 (d)).

The 2002 Act also provided that inventions, the primary or intended use or commercial exploitation of which would be contrary to "public order" or "morality" or which cause serious prejudice to human, animal or plant life or health or to environment are not patentable (S. 3b). India has incorporated the qualifier of " serious prejudice to human, animal or plant use or health and has not adopted the standard of "necessity" to protect "order public" or "morality" as is done in the case of Art 27.3 of TRIPS (Mahima Puri, Anjali Varma 2005).

So far as biotechnology is concerned, everybody is aware that there is a great race towards biotech applications. Biotechnology promises many benefits to human health. Eg. Gene therapy. It also carries as many complications. The commercial gains involved in the biotech applications have led to the mad rush towards the patenting of the bio inventions. In this mad rush the boundary between mere discovery and innovation has become a blur. Advanced countries liberally grant patents to biotech products and processes. They grant patents even to naturally occurring genetic material and life forms. But the Indian legislation allows patenting only for microorganisms (53 (F)) and not to gene sequence which is patentable in many advanced countries. However, the benefit to the public in making 'gene sequence' non-patentable is however nullified by the Draft Guidelines issued for patent examiners (Draft Manual of Patent Practice and Procedure, 2005). These Guidelines hold the key to how the Act is actually implemented. While the law embodies in the Patents Act provides the framework, the actual implementation is often determined by how it is interpreted through guidelines provided to patent examiners. (Sen Gupta 2005) The major problem with the Draft Manual is that substantial portions of it are based on documents and understanding of patents law that are quite different from the Amended Indian Patent Law, especially with reference to biotechnology. Gene patenting is a practice, which the Patent Act and India seeks, to prevent. But unfortunately, the Draft Guidelines are so drafted that it is implied that a new gene sequence is patentable.

Regarding protection to our indigenous technology, it is taken care to a certain extent i.e., if the invention was anticipated having regard to indigenous knowledge available in India, patent granted to such invention might be revoked. This right should have been supplemented by other procedural safeguards. Eg, throwing onus of proof on the patent claimant to prove that his invention is not based on indigenous knowledge, at least when there is prima-facie evidence that such knowledge is available in India. Also instead of mere revocation, heavy penalties also should have been imposed when patentee is proved guilty. On the whole it can be said that India has not fully utilized the scope available under TRIPS.

The Act has expanded the grounds to invoke pre grant opposition to patents. On the whole it can be said that the Indian Patent (Amendment) Act 2005 has made itself broadly in tune with the TRIPS Agreement. Yet, through the Act the government has attempted to preserve a larger public domain or patent free zone around the existing state of art than what was provided for under the Ordinance (Mahima Puri, Anjali, Varma, 2005a).

Presently, the government to look into issues related to establish Mashekar Committee;

1. Whether India would still be deemed to comply with TRIPS if it limited the grant of patents for pharmaceutical substances to new chemical entities or to new medical entities involving one or more inventive steps and
2. Whether it would be TRIPS compatible to exclude micro-organism form patentability.

Implementation of the Act with a consciousness about the need take care of public health concerns will be a great service to the general public. Though the powerful drug companies of India who desire strong patent protection are considering the new Act as a disincentive we should understand that India as a leader of South Asia has to conduct itself with a broader perspective and promote those practices that ultimately meet the public health concern of South Asia.

The 30th August, 2003 Decision is seen as promising a great boost to the Indian pharma industrial base thriving on manufacture of generic drugs.[23] Rather than worrying about existing price controls, the Indian pharma industry is now trying to earn profits in the international market by falling in line with international practices (Devraj 2002) and thereby our drug industry is becoming a strong avenue for development of Indian economy. However, the other side of the story is that too many people are spending far too more then what they can afford on health care. Medicines are getting out of the reach of the poor. Therefore, India should consciously try to balance its two vital interests of safeguarding its economic potential of its pharma industry while at the same time securing of affordable access to medicines to its entire people.

India has the good track record of being a most vociferous representative of the interests of the developing states. However, India should remember that as the upcoming leader of most of the international affairs and in whose representative leadership many third world states repose their trust, it has the solemn responsibility to look beyond the short-term diplomatic gains. In the larger interests of the human society it is necessary for India seriously try to route the international thought to ponder over the most basic questions such as whether the discussions on TRIPS and Public Health should merely be a one-off event and should it not be a part of a process which would ensure that the TRIPS agreement does not is anyway undermine the legitimate right of WTO members to formulate their own sound public health policies to suit their needs and implement them by adopting measures as are appropriate to protect public health? Can the drug that makes it possible to exercise a fundamental right to health be bound by rules, which thwart its access for 20 years? Should not essential drugs be global public goods? Can global goods be patentable so that a few have a monopoly over them to the disadvantage of millions? (Jain 2003c) How can research and development of new drugs be organized so as to ensure that they are immediately accessible to all who need them? How can the pharma industry be reoriented towards goals compatible with improving health and the quality of life rather than barrier less economic expansions and profit? (Jain 2003d) While pondering over all these questions relating to the issue of access to medicines, no country should ever lose sight of the fact that public health is not just about mere access to medicines. It is centrally about the most basic right to live with dignity.

Notes

1. The original name Trade Related Intellectual Property Rights Agreement has now become misnomer because even though it was originally that the agreement would cover only trade effects of IPRs, gradually the negotiations came to include even substantial matters related to IPR, for eg, the standards of protection.
2. The Law Suit is a landmark ease instituted by Pharma Industry Association regarding South Africa's Medicines and related substances Act. This Suit illustrates the tension between the interests of drug industry and general public. In this case, the patents, for medicines for HIV/AIDS were held by MNCs who were exclusively marketing the drug at exorbitant prices. CIPLA of India offered to supply drug at a price, which was 3.5% of the price imposed by MNCs. Though this case is withdrawn due to public pressure the case assumed international significance because of the fundamental issue of the implications of patents to pubic health concerns.
3. This Resol 2001/33 adopted in 2001 was approved by overwhelming majority of the members of the Commission.
4. This resolution recognized the access to medicines as an essential human right.
5. The South World Assembly in this Resolution (WHA 54.10) adopted on 21st May 2001 has recalled efforts to make drugs available at lower prices for those in need and urged member states in order to increase access to medicine to cooperate constructively in strengthening pharmaceutical policies and practices including those applicable to generic drugs and intellectual property regimes, in order to further promote innovations and the development of domestic industries consistent with national laws.
6. The World Health Assembly in the resolution (WHA 54.11) notes that "the impact of international agreement on access to or to local manufacturing of essential drugs and on the development of new drugs to be further evaluated". Further the resolution urges members to cooperate with respect to resol 2001/33 of UNCHR and "in order to increase access to medicines and in accordance with the health needs of the people, especially those who can least afford the costs and recognizing the efforts of the members to expand the access to drugs and promote domestic industry, cooperate constructively in strengthening pharmaceutical policies and practices including those applicable to generic drugs and intellectual property regimes, in order to further promote innovations and the development of domestic industries consistent with international law.

7. Held in Jakarta (30-31 May 2001) the Heads of States and Governments stated that the implementation of the TRIPS should in no way prevent developing states from taking measures such as compulsory licensing and parallel imports to ensure access to ......saving drugs at affordable price to overcome hazards to public health and nutrition accused by HIV/AIDS and other diseases.
8. Stuart Harbinson issued First Draft Declaration on Oct 21, 2001 entitled 'Elements for Draft Declaration on Intellectual Property and (Access to Medicines) (Public Health). The square brackets indicate the disagreement between WTO members even about the title of the Declaration.
9. See proposals of developing states submitted on October 4th 2001 by 54 countries which was circulated and non paper at the TRIPS Council Special Discussions on September 19th 2001.
10. Article 7 of TRIPS; The protection and enforcement of intellectual property rights should contribute to the promotion of technological innovation and to the transfer and dissemination of technology, to the mutual advantage of producers and users of technological knowledge and in manner conducive to social and economic welfare, and to a balance of rights and obligations.
11. Article 8 of TRIPS;
    (a) Members may, in formulating or amending their national laws and regulations, adopt measures necessary to protect public health and nutrition, and to promote the pubic interest in sectors of vital importance to their socio-economic and technological development, provided that such measures are consistent with the previsions of this Agreement.
    (b) Appropriate measures, provided that they are consistent with the provions of this Agreement, may be needed to prevent the abuse of intellectual property rights by right holders or the resort to practices, which unreasonably restrain trade or adversely affect the international transfer of technology.
12. See the proposal of Developing Countries submitted on Oct. 4th 2001 by 54 countries at TRIPS Council Discussion on September 19th 2001.
13. See Article 31 of TRIPS read with Article 7, 8 & 40:

    Under Article 31, Where the law of a Member allows for other use of the subject matter of a patent without the authorization of the right holder, including use by the government or third parties authorized by the government, the following provisions shall be respected:

    (a) Authorization of such use shall be considered on its individual merits;

(b) Such use may only be permitted if, prior to such use, the proposed user has made efforts to obtain authorization from the right holder on reasonable commercial terms and conditions and that such efforts have not been successful within a reasonable period of time. This requirement may be waived by a Member in the case of national emergency or other circumstances of extreme urgency or in case of public non-commercial use. In situations of national emergency or other circumstances of extreme urgency, the right holder shall, nevertheless, be notified as soon as reasonably practicable. In the case of public non-commercial use, where the government or contractor, without making a patent search, knows or has demonstrable grounds to know that a valid patent is or will be used by or for the government, the right holder shall be informed promptly;

(c) The scope and duration of such use shall be limited to the purpose for which it was authorized, and in the case of semiconductor technology shall only be for public non-commercial use or to remedy a practice determined after judicial or administrative process to be anti-competitive.

(d) Such use shall be non-exclusive.

(e) Such use shall be non-assignable, except with that part of the enterprise or goodwill which enjoys such use;

(f) Any such use shall be authorized predominantly for the supply of the domestic market of the Member authorizing such use;

(g) Authorization for such use shall be liable, subject to adequate protection of the legitimate interests of the circumstances, which led to be terminated if and when the circumstances, which led to it, cease to exist and are unlikely to recur. The competent authority shall have the authority for review, upon motivated request, the continued existence of these circumstance;

(h) The right holder shall be paid adequate remuneration in the circumstances of each case, taking into account the economic value of the authorization;

(i) The legal validity of any decision relating to the authorization of such use shall be subject to judicial review or other independent review by a distinct higher authority in that Member;

(j) Any decision relating to the remuneration provided in respect of such use shall be subject to judicial review or other independent review by a distinct higher authority in that member;

(k) Members are not obliged to apply the conditions set forth in sub-paragraphs (b) and (f) above where such use is permitted to remedy a practice determined after judicial or administrative process to be anti-competitive. The need to correct anti-competitive practices may be taken into account in determining the amount of remuneration in such cases. Competent authorities shall have the authority to refuse termination of authorization if and when the conditions which led to such authorization are likely to recur;

(l) Where such use is authorized to permit the exploitation of a patent ("the second patent"), which cannot be exploited without infringing another patent ("the first patent'). The following additional conditions shall apply:

(i) the invention claimed in the second patent shall involve an important technical advance of considerable economic significance in relation to the invention claimed in the first patent.

(ii) the owner of the first patent shall be entitled to a cross-license on reasonable terms to use the invention claimed in the second patent; and the use authorized in respect of first patent shall be non-assignable except with the assignment of second patent.

14. See Pgh. 2 & 3 of the Decision of the General Council of 30th Aug, 2003 on implementation of paragraph 6 of the Doha Declaration on the TRIPS Agreement and Public Health.

15. A 1992 UNIIDO Study indicated that as many as 60 states do not have the capacity for either active ingredients or populations).

16. For example, Cambodia not being aware that it does not have to grant patents till 2016, hastened up its national laws few grant of patents.

17. For example by virtue of Bangui Agreement 1999, 12 member stated which are LPCs could not avail the benefits like compulsory licensé and transition period granted to them until 2016.

18. The Author's projection of evolution of India's Health Policy is largely drawn from Soumya Panda, Evolution of India's Health Policy 1947-2001; An Appraisal, Indian Academy of Social Science, 2001.

19. Managed Health Care can be defined as health care services under the administrative control of large private organization with capital financing which means that an employer- private or public agency prepays the managed health care organizations (MNCs) a negotiated sum of money per covered person per unit of time, typically a month.

20. Price Controls acted as disincentive to invest in the Indian market.

21. FERA severely limited the investment of companies whose investment foreign equity exceeded 40%.

22. For eg. in Boston Rantidin costs 42 cents for 150 mg. The same product in India costs 1.79 cents. See, David Scondras, 'A visit to India, Drug prices, research and Global Access, Articles and views, People's Health Movement, Jan, 1999.
23. In fact, the developed states, particularly USA wanted to delimit the scope of discretion for issuing compulsory license only to two situations of national emergency and an adjudicate violation of competition laws. However, the final text of TRIPS does not contain any specific grounds.
24. Today over 70 per cent of pharmaceuticals consumed in pharmaceuticals consumed in the country are locally produced. India has some 250 large pharmaceutical firms and 16,000 small producers.

References

Abrol Dinesh, Researcher working on the issue of S &T Institute of Science, Technology and Development Studies, New Delhi in his *Spread the World Communiqué.*

African Group Statement on TRIPS (2001), Public Health submitted by to TRIPS Council on 18th June.

Banerji D. (1985), "Health and Family Planning Services in India; An Epidemiological, Socio-Cultural and Political Analysis and a perspective", *Lok Prakash,* New Delhi.

Dubey Muchkund (2001), "Implications of Doha for India-II", *The Hindu,* 25th December, p. 12.

Deviah H. Vishwas, "TRIPS and Public Health, Infochang India News & Features Intellectual Property Rights", *TRIPS and Public Health.*

Devraj Ranjit (2002), Health India; Drug Companies Profit but Medicines out of the reach of the Poor, *People's Health Movement,* Issue, 16th December.

George Peterson (2000), WHO Representative to Indonesia at ASEAN Workshop on the *TRIPS Agreement and its Impact on Pharmaceuticals* held at Jakarta 2-4 May.

Jain Ranjit (2003), "Drug Patents, Knowledge, Economy and Pubic Health", *Health Care Management,* 1-15 October.

Mahima Puri and Anjali Varma (2005), "Patents Legislation and International Obligations: India, working paper No. 158 submitted to *Indian Council for Research On International Economic Relations,* March.

Panda Soumya (2002), "Evolution of India's Health Policy 1974-2000–An Appraisal", *Indian Academy of Social Science,* p. 46.

Sen Gupta (1994), "A World Development Report, 1993, Implications for Infrastructure Development in healthcare and the pharmaceutical industry", *Social Scientist*, 22 Sept.-Dec.

Sen Gupta A. (1996), "Economic Reforms, Heath and Pharmaceuticals; conferring legitimacy to the Market", *Economic and Political Weekly*, Nov. 30.

Sen Gupta (2005), *Peoples Democracy*, Vol. XXIX, No. 38 Sept. 1.

11

Cancun 2003–IPR and Issues of Health in Relation to India

M. Chandrasekhar & C. Praseeda

Section 1: Introduction

The standard of health of a nation is the primary indicator of the quality of life enjoyed by the people therein. Health care as a common service to be provided by a central agency to its citizen may also be described as the basic human right of every citizen. This year's budget allots health first place in the category of the "Panch Priorities" enumerated by the Finance Minister (Sankar, Kathuria 2004) The primacy of place occupied by the health sector in the agenda of a nation is reiterated by the myriad trials undertaken by various nations across the past half century, especially by the developing nations to combat the challenges of burgeoning population, achieving food security, providing adequate employment opportunity and above all ensuring necessary provisions of health of its people. The twin objective of achieving economic development and enhancing health and nutrition are the basic foundations of the sustainable development program being pursued by the government of India. Health as an item on agenda in the overall development is to be discussed in relation to other variables like per capita income, socio cultural background, rural urban location, status and literacy of women and overall consumption habits of the population. This underlying relationship is the basis for the development of a policy which aims to improve the per capita income of the population which would automatically trigger improvement in education standards leading to increased employability, and thus finally resulting in enhanced calorie intake. However some research conclusions have challenged this theory. Research studies conducted in Kerala, and Tamilnadu indicate surprising outcomes. These states, which record a fairly high per capita income and low per capita food intake, display low malnutrition levels. Where as states like Rajasthan and Utter Pradesh with low per capita, income and high calorie intake, ironically have high incidence of Malnutrition (Radhakrishna 2002). Thus health as an area of investigation requires deeper in sights into all the related dimensions. The Asia Development Outlook 2000 as described aspects of human deprivation like illiteracy malnutrition, poor health etc., as "Social Challenges" proving serious impediments in the path of attaining sustainable development of a nation. The present study makes an effort to draw attention to issues of health in India and tries to highlight the effort need to enhance the health sector in the light of Cancun 2003. The issues raised in the study to this effect are:

1. Sustainable development–The task of the Indian State.
2. Emerging Trends in disease and health care
3. Health–The Indian Experiment
4. Quo Vadis Cancun–Implications of Para 6.
5. Designing a Road Map for Cancun Dilemma

Section 2: Sustainable Development

Implementing sustainable development is a complex task which needs active and Spontaneous participation of both government and non-government agencies. Despite the various measures adopted to obtain balanced growth and development, a lopsided development effect is observed all over the world due to certain inherent evolution based disparities caused by resource availability, positive political and environmental conditions etc., In countries like India these disparities are observed more in relation to rural and urban areas. The Indian Policy makers though, initially considered health as State responsibility, are presently engaged in providing positive and active role to the private sector.

The early 90's ushered in the policy of liberalization and economic reform, which enhanced the scope of private participation in many areas including health. This development is in tandem with the global trend of marketisation of health care (for profit), and is also a reaction to wide spread multinational competition. The negative aspects of this competition especially in the area of medical cloning by generic industry has been the focus of heated debate in various national and international forums. This issue has also dominated the recent sessions of Cancun without culminating in any amicable solution. The larger implication of Article 28 of TRIPS might jeopardize the access of health facilities to large sections of people living below poverty line especially in South Asia as seen in figure 1.

People living on less than $1 per day
(percentage of total population)

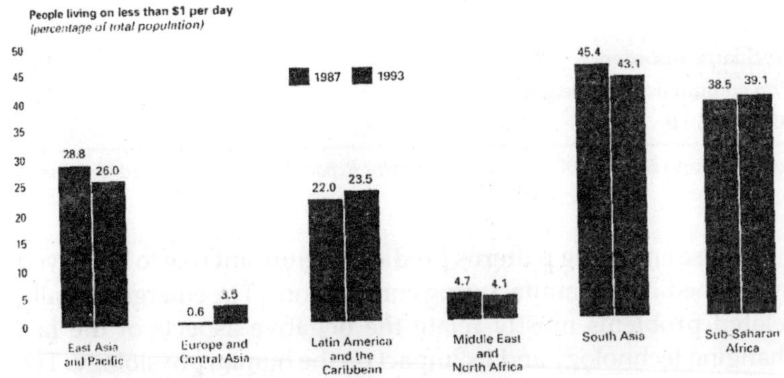

Source: World Bank (1995) *World Development Indicators.*

One of the most noticeable and surprising fact in the figure provided is in relation to the percentage recorded by sub Saharan African countries, indicating that these countries stand second in the list of people living on less than 1$ per day. Though it is to be simultaneously accepted that the combined population of South Asian and other countries is much higher than sub Saharan countries, yet it must also be realized that the former countries are much more developed in terms of their infrastructure when compared to the later. These inferences require deeper study into the reasons behind the facts as there will be and undeniable impact of the Cancun discussions on these countries more than the others.

Section 3: Emerging Trends in Disease and Health Care

The World Bank 2000 report presents a mixed picture of the emerging trends in types of disease. In concurrence with the other environmental challenges the traditional epidemiological diseases that had scourged most of the developing nations are slowly being replaced by non-communicable disease like cancer, injuries neuro-psychiatric conditions. While the former were the result of lack of sanitation and clean drinking water, the later are the results of urbanization, stress due to high levels of competition, irregular sleeping habits (call centers) and changing diet modes (fast foods).

Table 1
Disability Adjusted life years (DALY)
(Loss of active years due to disability)

Injuries	16%
Psychiatric disorders	10%
Non communicable diseases	10%
HIV AIDS TB	7%

Source: World Bank (2000), *World Development Report*, New York: Oxford University Press.

These emerging patterns predict a significant role to be played by the medicine-manufacturing corporations. The emerging health related problems mostly relate the negative aspects of the fast changing technology and its impact on the human physiology. The changing trends of life styles of the generation are also one of the major reasons. In this scenario the implications of the WTO deliberations in relation to product patents and related issues represents a potential threat to the development of pharmaceutical industry of the developing and under developed nations which are presently being swayed by the changing trends.

Section 4: Health- The Indian Experiment

India, which had occupied 115 ranks on the human development index, has since slipped to 124 in 2002 and 127 in 2003, due to inclusion of countries like Botswana, which is a major cause for concern. This fact calls for a stringent review of the health planning under taken by the nation for the past five decades. A review of the patterns of investment on health, family welfare and water supply in relation to the total plan outlay shows that that the investment on health has never gone beyond 1.9 per cent of the total plan outlay up to 8th five year plan.

Table 2
Pattern of Investment on Health, Family Welfare and Water Supply Etc. (Plan Outlays) in Different Plan Periods in Public Sector-Center, States and UT's (Rs. Crores)

Sl. No.	*Period*	*Total Ptan Investment Outlay (all Head of Dept.)*	*Health*	*Family wel-fare*	*Sub-Total*	*Water Supply Sani-tation*
1	2	3	4	5	6	7
1.	First Plan(Actuals) 1951-1956	1960	65.2	0.1	65.3	11.0
		(100)	(3-3)	(-)	(3.3)	(0.6)
2.	Second Plan (Actuals) 1956-1961	4672	140.8	5.0	145.8	74.0
		(100)	(3)	(0.1)	(3.1)	(1.6)
3.	Third Plan (Actuals) 1961-1966	8576.5	225.9	24.9	250.8	105.7
		(100)	(2.6)	(0.3)	(2.9)	(1.2)
4.	Annual Plan (Actuals) 1966-1969	6625.4	140.2	70.4	210.6	102.7
		(100)	(2.1)	(1.1)	(2.2)	(1.6)
5.	Fourth Plan (Actuals) 1969-1974	15778.8	335.5	278	613.5	458.9
		(100)	(2.1)	(1.8)	(3.9)	(2.9)
6.	Fifth Plan(Actuals) 1974-1979	39426.2	760.8	491.8	1252.6	1091.6
		(100)	(1.9)	(1.2)	(3.2)	(2.8)
7.	Sixth Plan (Out lav)	97500	1821.0	1010.0	2831.0	3922.0
		(100)	(1.9)	(1.0)	(2.9)	(4.0)
8.	Total Sixth Plan 1980-1985	109291.7	2025.2	1387	3412.2	3996.9
		(100)	(1.8)	(1.3)	(3.1)	(3.6)
9.	Seventh Plan(Out lav) 1985-1990	180000	3392.9	3256.3	6649.2	6522.5
		(100)	(1.9)	(1.8)	(3.7)	(3.6)
10.	Total Seventh Plan 1985-1990	218729.6	3688.6	3120.8	6809.4	7093.1
		(100)	(1.7)	(1.4)	(3.1)	(3.2)
11.	Eight Plant 1992-1997	434100	7582.2	6500.0	14082.2	16711.0
		(100)	(1.7)	(1.5)	(3.2)	(3.8)
12.	1994-1995 (out lay)	112197.1	1819.1	1430.0	3249.1	588.3
		(100)	(1.6)	(1.3)	(2.9)	(3.2)

Source: Planning Commission, Internet.
Note: Figures in brackets Indicate percentage.

An in-depth observation of the above statistics doesn't show any marked improvement in the outlay for health and related services since the 1st Plan Period. Though successive governments have spared no efforts in launching different schemes and projects in their agenda of obtaining higher levels of health, these efforts do not seem to have resulted in positive returns except may be the electoral returns. It may be noticed that the percentage of outlay for health has never exceeded 1.9 per cent up to 8th five year plan Another conclusion that may be drawn is in terms of implementation blockades due to lack of efficient infrastructure support more so in the rural areas. To strengthen the health sector in India the government not only needs to develop infrastructure but also requires more and more private participation in the areas of rural health, which may be affected in the wake of Cancun resolution and the government policy has to be designed to this effect. The life expectancies at birth in India also do not show very high improvement when compared with to other countries of the world in the similar percentage groups.

Table 3
Comparative Table of Life Expectancies and Health Expenditure in selected South Asian Countries.

Countries	*Under five MR/1000 Live births 1999– 2001*		*IMR/1000 Live births 1999 – 2001*		*MMR 10000 Live births 1995*	**Public % of GDP*	*Private % of GDP*	*Total per-capita expen-diture*
Bangladesh	144	77	96	51	600	1.4	2.4	14
Bhuttan	166	95	75	74	500	-	-	-
Pakistan	128	109	96	84	200	0.9	3.2	18
Sri Lanka	23	19	19	17	60	1.8	1.8	31
India	123	93	80	67	400	5.1	1.7	315
Maldives	115	77	80	58	390	-	-	-
Nepal	145	91	100	66	880	0.9	-	-

Source: UNDP (2003), *Human Development Report*, New York: Oxford University Press

* Expenditure on health, World Bank (2004), *World Development Report*, New York: Oxford University Press.

Note: MR – Mortality Rate.
IMR – Infant Mortality Rate
MMR – Maternal Mortality Rate

A study of the mortality rates in relation to health expenditure provides some specific conclusions. A close observation of mortality rates shows Sri Lanka in a better position than India or other South Asians countries. But a simultaneous study of the related Public and Private Expenditure on health in respective countries shows higher expenditure by India. This may be analysed in terms of difference in population between the two countries and other socio-cultural aspects. In India the statistics show higher expenditure by the public sector in the area of health. Here it may also be realized that the government expenditure on medical education training and research in 1996 – 97 which was around 2,95,700 (inclusive of Aurvedic and Homeopathy) his at present been increased to 6,66,03,300 in 2002. This shows marked improvement in the government allocation in research and development but in view of the present Cancun deliberation this may not suffice.

Table 4
Life Expectancy at Birth by Sex in India, 1991-96

Sl. No.	*India/State/Union Territory*	*Life Expectancy at birth (1991-1996)*	
		Males	*Females*
	India	60.6	61.7
	States		
1.	Andhra Pradesh	61.4	64.5
2.	Arunachal Pradesh	NA	NA
3.	Assam	58.7	58.5
4.	Bihar	60.8	60.1
5.	Goa	NA	NA
6.	Gujarat	60.9	62.7
7.	Haryana	65.2	64.2
8.	Htmachal Pradesh	NA	NA
9.	Jammu &.Kashmir	NA	NA
10.	Karnataka	64.2	65.3
11.	Kerala	68.6	75
12.	Madhya Pradesh	59.2	58
13.	Maharastra	64	65.9
14.	Manipur	NA	NA
15.	Meghalaya	NA	NA
16.	Mizoram	NA	NA
17.	Nagaland	NA	NA
18.	Orissa	60.1	58.4
19.	Punjab	66.6	66.5
20.	Rajastan	60.5	61.3
21.	Sikkim	NA	NA
22.	Tamil Nadu	62.3	63.1
23.	Tripura	NA	NA
24.	Uttar Pradesh	57.1	52.8
25.	West Bengal	61.9	61.9

Source: Registrar General, India, SRS Estimates.
Note: Statistics related to union territories not available (NA)

State wise analysis of life expectancy rates in India also does not show any significant improvement. Highest life expectancy is noticed in the state of Kerala. This may be due to higher levels of education and awareness. It may also be mentioned that there exists very high presence of generic industry providing cheaper medicines to compliment the high levels of health awareness in an average Keralite. This scenario is bound to be effected by the present pattern of Cancun discussions.

Table 5
Estimated Infant Mortality Rates-1993,1994 And 1995
(State-Wise And Rural/Urban Wise, Per 1000 live births)

State	*Infant Mortality Rate (per 1000 livebirths)*							
	1993			*1994*			*1995*	
	Rural	*Urban*	*Com-bined*	*Rural*	*Urban*	*Com-bined*	*Rural*	*Urban*
1	2	3	4	5	6	7	8	9
Andhra Pradesh	70	46	64	68	48	63	73	43
Assam	84	60	81	75	67	77	78	59
Bihar	73	41	67	68	78	66	74	57
Gujarat	65	42	70	70	51	64	68	47
Haryana	70	53	58	70	57	67	69	66
Himachal Pradesh	65	36	66	70	57	67	64	39
Karnataka	79	42	63	73	45	65	69	43
Kerala	15	8	13	16	14	16	17	1
Madhya Pradesh	113	67	106	105	57	98	104	61
Maharashtra	67	32	50	67	36	54	66	34
Orissa	115	69	110	108	65	103	107	65
Punjab	60	39	55	59	35	53	58	39
Rajasthan	88	54	82	87	61	84	89	62
Tamil Nadu	66	38	56	64	48	59	61	43
Uttar Pradesh	98	67	94	91	71	88	89	67
West Bengal	64	33	58	64	48	61	62	45
All India	82	45	74	79	51	73	80	49

Source: Registrar General, India, *Sample Registration System.*
Note: #Excludes Jammu & Kashmir.

A comparative study of the infant mortality rate has not shown any notable variations during the periods of 1993, 1994 and 1995. These statistics point out to the acute dearth in the area of health services. Though the health sector in India provides equal scope for combined participation of government, private (for profit) and non-government agencies, a marked disenchantment is noticed with regard to government health services (Mathiyazhagan 2003) Research has shown that due to poor maintenance of public health services people are going for Private Services. Here it may noticed that their for cheaper alternative medicines, is being catered to by the indigenous generic pharma manufacturing units producing native alternative for cheaper price. It is this segment of consumers, which may be expected to suffer in case of realization of the Cancun Declarations, as it will lead to closure of hundreds of such concerns establishing monopoly of the pharmaceutical giants. Absence of generic industry will automatically raise prices of drugs in some countries, which will have to invest on Research & Development and required technology to develop the drugs. Whereas countries which do not have manufacturing capability and have to depend on a friendly neighboring country are placed in a more difficult predicament (Srinivas 2003).

Sectoin 5: Quo Vadis Cancun

Implications of Para 6 of the Doha Declaration on Health Sector

The last quarter of the 20th century has witnessed the corporatisation of the health sector in India. Globalization has paved way for domination of multinational companies on the world market. These multinational giants are resorting to direct and indirect methods of influencing the national policy (Baru 2003) The sops provided to the pharma industry under Budget 2003 serve as ample examples of their mechanisms. The general investment of the government in the health sector, which was 1.3% in 1990 has fallen down to 0.9% in 1999, adding to the already existing inadequacy of the public health services especially in rural areas. In contrast the tax exemptions provided to the private hospitals and pharma industry are manifold, like:

1. Reduction of customs duty on life saving equipment.
2. Scrapping of customs duty on samples required for clinical testing.
3. Abolition of duty on equipment used for R & D.

The finance minister has referred to these measures as imperative to face the new IPR regime (Sankar Kathuria 2003). But are these measures meant for protection of health sector or for protection of multinational profit bottom lines, is the question being raised in different quarters.

Article 28 of the TRIPS confers exclusive right on the patent holder to produce the goods or permit others the sale or import the patented process or product (Srinivas 2003). Though the provision of compulsory licensing is provided under TRIPS, by the way of which the exclusive rights of the patent holder may be moderated, yet TRIPS does not specify conditions for granting them. In case of a country which does not have the know how to develop the drugs even with the help of compulsory licensing it will be allowed to import only in cases of national emergency. The implications of these provisions of article 28 require nations like India, to develop indigenous capacity of alternative production arrangements.

Section 6: Alternative Arrangements-The Road Map

In this context 2005 may be considered as a watershed year in the history of pharmaceutical industry. The answers to the many questions raised on the ways and means to combat the challenges requires a multidimensional approach. An attempt has been made presently to chalk out some steps, which may be adopted to provide a holistic answer to the present situation.

Suggestions for Improvement

1. International level negotiations to protect the rights of developing countries against differential treatment, which was realized in Doha and resented in Cancun (Bhatta Charya 2003). Newer coalitions need to be established, as the needs of developed and developing nations are not symmetrical. Technological collaboration may be established for knowledge sharing in pharmaceutical industries (Chanakya 2003).
2. Intensive development of internal research and development in pharmaceutical areas by introducing government funded research institution on the lines of IITs needs to be developed.
3. Policy support in terms of relaxations to argument private efforts in Research & Development needs to be enhanced.
4. Bio-diversity legislation to protect traditional knowledge should be strengthened (Mathur 2003). There is a need to define the subtle difference between discovery and innovation to protect traditional knowledge (Lakshmikumaran 2004).
5. Design Policy and take necessary steps to involve non-government organsiations as strategic partners in the area of

health via financial support and provision of adequate infrastructure facility.

6. Implementation of the proposed National Health Insurance Policy to develop individual capacity to enjoy health benefits.
7. Strengthing the grass root level health functionaries and involvement of local bodies and Panchayat Raj institution in administering health facilities (Sekhar 2003).
8. Sensitizing the general public on health related issues to improve the general Health standards of the nation.

These suggestions need a multidimensional implementation, which automatically requires synchronized effort between the government, local bodies, non-government Organsiations and the private sector. These efforts again should be coordinated with the concerted international movement for the advantage at both levels–national international.

References

Arnold, F., Praveen N., Umesh K. (2002), "Indicators of Nutrition for Women and Children", *Economic and Political Weekly*, Feb. 14.

Baru, V.R. (2003), "Privatisation of Health Services, A South Asian Perspective" *Economic and Political Weekly,* October, 18-27.

Bhattacharja, B. (2003), "The Cancun Ministerial: Beginning of the End or End of the Beginning" *Focus WTO,* Sept–October.

Chanakyya (2003), "Economic Development Post Cancun" *The Financial Express,* Sept. 29 pg. 6.

Lakshmikumaran, V. (2004), "Patents in Biotechnology" *Yojana,* March.

Mathiyazhagan, M. (2003)" People Choice of Health Care: Providing Policy Options for Rural Karnataka", *Journal of Health Management,* Sage Publications: New Delhi.

Mathur, A. (2003), "Who Owns Traditional Knowledge", *Economic and Political Weekly* October, 10.

Radhakrishna, R. (2002), "Food and Nutrition Security" *India Development Report,* Oxford University Press.

Sekhar, T.V., Tendulkar (2003), "Sensitising Grass Root Leadership on Health Issues", *Economic and Political Weekly,* November 21.

Shankar, D., Vinishi Kathuria, (2003), "Health Sector in 2003–2004 Budget" *Economic and Political Weekly,* April 12.

Srinivas, K.R. (2003), "Interpreting Prag: Patents and Access to Drugs" *Economic and Political Weekly,* Sept. 20.

Rajan. S.I., K.S. James (2004), "Second National Family Health Survey Emerging Issues", *Economic and Political Weekly*, February 14.

World Bank, (1999/2000), *World Development Report*, New York: Oxford University Press.

Asian Development Bank (2000), *Asian Development Outlook*, New York: Oxford University Press.

World Bank (2004), *World Development Report*, New York: Oxford University Press.

12

Indian Pharmaceutical Industry A Post 2005 Scenario

R. Anita Rao & R. Rajiv Thakur

The Indian Pharmaceutical Industry is a successful, high technology based industry that has witnessed consistent growth over past several years and holds a great potential for future too. At the time of independence, the total market for the pharmaceutical industry was Rs.10 crores and the industry was primarily dominated by the MNCs. As one of the earlier initiatives, the Hindustan Antibiotics Limited (HAL) was set up in collaboration with WHO and UNICEF and Indian Drugs and Pharmaceuticals Limited (IDPL) got established with the help from Soviet Union with the objective of manufacturing penicillin. With the entry of these public sector units in production of the essential drugs, a new thrust and strength was built up in the private sector of the Indian pharmaceutical industry.

The government during 1970 took initiative to build up a coordinated approach involving Indian Patent Act (IPA) 1970, Drug Price Control (DPC) orders and Foreign Exchange and Regulation Act (FERA) which provided good boost to the industry's growth. Consequently, a drastic reduction in the market share of MNCs was witnessed from 80 per cent in 1970 to 48 per cent in 1982. On the other hand, an increasing trend in the share of the domestic private sector share could be noticed, its share increasing from 10 per cent to 50 per cent in 1970 and 66 per cent in 1991 (Palanichamy 2004).

1970

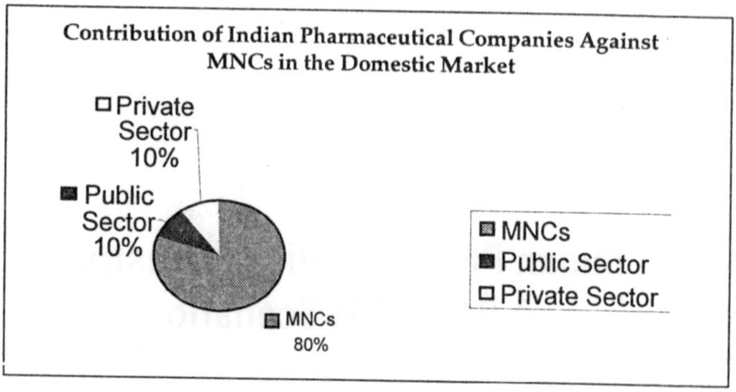

2002

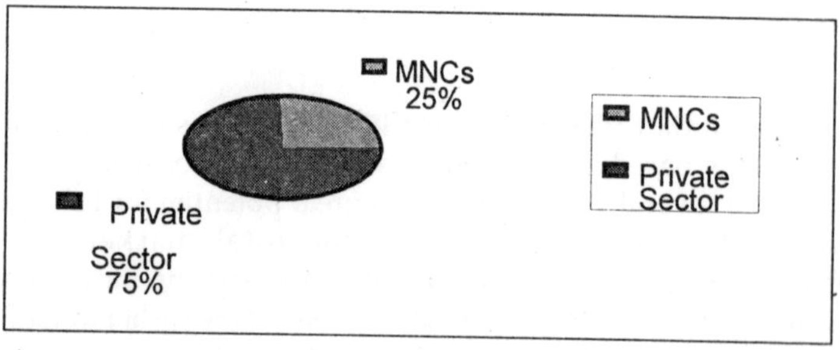

Under the new Industrial licensing policy the quantitative restrictions were lifted, and the pharmaceutical industry is free to export. As a matter of fact, today, pharmaceutical industry exports comes only next to software industry exports from India. A major proportion of revenue generation of the top pharmaceutical companies is from exports and a steady increase in this is expected, particularly after 2005.

The WTO Agreement and the inclusion of Intellectual property rights (IPRs) brought about significant changes in the pharmaceutical industry. The Paris Convention of 1983 left the countries concerned to decide the terms of patent, the duration of patent etc., This gave a wider scope of choice to the countries either to go for process or product patent. The 1970-1990 phase is considered to be significantly important for pharma industries as the Indian Patent Act 1970 gave protection only for process manufacturing.

Few significant points could be highlighted as:

- Product patents to be allowed in all fields of technology without exception.
- Uniform duration of 20 years for patents in pharmaceuticals, food products and agro chemical.
- Compulsory licensing to be given by the government on merits of each case. Compulsory licensing to be granted without the authorization of the patent holder besides those that have already been set forth.
- No discrimination between exported and domestic product.
- For process patent the burden of proof will rest with the party that infringes.

India a signatory to WTO has amended in the year 2002 laws and provided for product patents in pharmaceutical sector. Mention must be made here that this transition is to be completed by 2005. The exclusive marketing rights (EMR) and the mailbox provision have been provided to suit the transitional requirements. The moot point now is how these changes would affect Indian Pharmaceutical industries and what is the preparedness of the pharmaceutical companies to meet the upcoming challenges.

There are two divergent views expressed on the effects of the new regime. The first emphasizes that it would lead to monopoly status and adversely affect the growth rate and that the twenty-year period of patent protection would restrict the technology development in the country. The domestic not so big industries would vanish due to increased competition from the giant MNCs. Once the product regime comes, the cost of the drugs will make the drugs inaccessible for common man. The other side of the arguments is that it gives a greater edge to Indian pharma companies to improve quality and intensive research and development.

The key provisions of the TRIPS Agreement when read in the light of objectives and principles set forth in Article 7 and 8, clearly establish that the protection and enforcement under IPRs do not exist in vacuum. They are supposed to benefit society as a whole and not mere protection of private rights.

Article 6 of the TRIPS agreement is extremely relevant for members, especially developing countries, and particularly the least developed and smaller economies among them. Article 6 provides that Members are free to incorporate the principle of international exhaustion of rights in national legislation. Consequently, any member can determine the extent to which the principle of exhaustion of rights is applied in its own jurisdiction, without breaching any obligation under the TRIPS Agreement.

Article 7 is particularly relevant to ensure that the provisions of TRIPS do not conflict with health policies, the promotion of technological invention and transfer and dissemination of technology. Also the mutual advantage of producers and users of technological knowledge social and economic welfare and balance of rights and obligations are maintained (Arun Goyal).

Article 8 of the TRIPS affirms that the members may adopt measures to protect public health, where the owners of the patented pharmaceutical products may be abusing their exclusive rights by selling or offering for sale drugs at prices beyond reasonable margins of profit, thereby preventing adequate access to medication by the general public. Another situation would be when the owners of patented pharmaceutical product do not offer their product in sufficient amounts to meet the demands of the market. The TRIPS agreement provides the safeguards like parallel imports, compulsory licensing.

Most relevant provisions of the TRIPS agreement with respect to compulsory licenses are article 31, 7, 8 & 40 and an integrated approach to the provisions allow scope for the members to ensure that the regulatory policies can be exercised by governments to promote public health policies.

Article 31 of TRIPS agreement defines the grounds upon which to issue compulsory licenses, however, it has kept open the procedural requirements to be followed by members. Members are free to determine the grounds upon which the compulsory licenses can be granted.

The post patent regime of 2005 is a matter of great curiosity and concerns for many as how the Indian pharma Industry can face this new shift of process to product patenting, taking advantage of the safeguards (parallel imports, compulsory licensing) as mentioned in the Indian patent act of 1970 and as amended in 2002.

Key strengths

The low cost of manufacturing coupled with large pool of English speaking scientists are major sources of strength of Indian pharma industries. The bulk drug production and expertise in process capabilities to produce drugs that are still patented are the positive aspects. The patented drugs are being produced within a short period of time, for example in case of Ranitidine and Ciprofloxacin, there were about 3250 producers in India in 1996 while the patent Regime was still on. The most successful strategy would be to produce or develop indigenous version and make a close substitute to the original one. The other example could be Viagra (Sidenafil citrate) introduced by Pfizer. It took 13 years and huge amounts of investment to prefect this product. In India there are 6 branches available and surprisingly out of 30 raw materials used 26 are available in India (Lalitha 2002).

Certain drawbacks

Relatively low level of research and development and lack of funding from sources other than the parent firm is a set back in Indian scenario. The process patent, which made drugs affordable with low cost, however, had an indirect impact on the research and development areas. The Research, Development and Trials take enormous time, while the process of reverse engineering made the product available with less cost in faster manner. The quality of drugs is a major issue in the global markets. For example, in case of Ciprofloxacin, an antibiotic where more than 70 firms were engaged in its production, two were able to export to USA, since only they could meet the necessary regulatory standards in US.

The Preparedness of the Indian Companies

The development in the last years do reflect positively the preparedness of the Indian companies like Ranbaxy, Cipla, Wockhardt and Dr. Reddy who have already taken initiatives in NDDS (New Drug Delivery Systems).* American home product, Pharmacia and Upjohn, Bristol Mayor Squibb and Glaxo-Wellcome are some of the global companies who have selected India as their out sourcing base. Ranbaxy, Lupin labs and Nicholas Peramel are the first few Indian companies to obtained these contracts. MNCs have started looking at India for research and development collaboration with Pfizer already taking lead in setting up a few member teams to assess the possible collaboration and development in India. Besides, these above collaborations the in-built mechanism in TRIPS agreement under para 6 provision of the Doha declaration regarding the compulsory license is an added advantage and an opportunity to Indian Pharmaceutical industry. The most recent development of CIPLA receiving orders under the above provisions from Malaysia for exports for four specified Anti retroviral (HIV/AIDS) formulation is a convincing beginning in this regard. This deal under compulsory licensing empowers Cipla to sell these medicines under fixed ceiling prices to Govt. of Malaysia, for exclusive supply to government hospitals for two years. Compensation to patent holder as per the deal will be paid within two months from the date of import.

Outsourcing

The outsourcing of clinical trail segment in order to cut short the cost price is an opportunity for Indian pharma Industries. The cost of conducting the trails is comparatively low in India. It is mentioned, that in India the contract research organizations takes about $ 3000, whereas it costs about $ 5000 per patient in USA. The global market is growing at 6 per cent - 7 per cent per year and is expected at around $ 480 billion by 2005 and is further projected at $ 680 billion by 2010. In generics for the next ten years, about $ 80 billion worth of drugs are patented and this too opens a greater opportunity for producing off patented drugs.

Boost for Generics

WHO and UNICEF recognize that the generic pharmaceutical industry has a vital role to play in producing safe and effective medicines at low cost to improve health and life saving drugs. For essential drugs a basic generic legislation, ensuring fast track registration is very essential. Major Indian companies are looking for enormous production facilities in US as this country accounts for nearly 50 per cent of the world market. The US generic market is very large and already Dr. Reddy, Ranbaxy and Cipla have received the US–FDA for generic marketing. Brazil is aggressively promoting generic drugs to increase the availability of drugs to suit the requirement of 17 crore population. However, only 50 per cent of total population has access to pharmaceutical and only can afford to buy prescribed drugs. Indian companies including Ranbaxy, Cadila Pharmaceuticals, Aurobindo Pharmaceuticals and Lupin are interested in Brazil, as it is a gateway to other Latin

American countries. The success of an Indian company bagging the first ever order in the world under the compulsory licensing is a confirmation to the optimism shown by Indian pharma Industry.

To conclude, the options available for Indian pharma industry are:

- To compete with the MNCs by producing their own inventions.
- To produce under license.
- To make drugs that are free from patents.

The success of implementing these options would depend on:

- The strategic approach to global markets of the companies.
- Strong R & D and enhancing of the skills in product development.
- Competitive pricing.
- Diversification of research options in Bio-pharmaceuticals and intensive research in biotechnology.
- Good infrastructure facilities in pharma and chemical engineering areas.
- High competitive work force to meet the demands of the global market.

The strength of Indian Industry should be utilized by adopting various strategies, The new initiatives in R & D, outsourcing clinical trials, acquiring the compulsory licenses and collaborating with MNCs in both manufacturing and marketing would be a step forward to meet the post 2005 scenario.

Note

* Means is a process of modifying the delivery of the drug once it is consumed. It addresses the sustained release of the drug in the body for the effective defusion of drug.

References

Arun Goyal Noor Mohd, "WTO in the New Millennium", *Academy of Business Studies*, p. 565.

Lalitha, N. (2002), "Indian Pharmaceutical Industry in WTO Regime A Swot Analysis", *Economic and Political Weekly* Aug. 24, p. 3547.

Palanichamy, P. Lt CDR G. Shanmugasundaram (2004), *Business and Economic Facts for your March*, p. 20.

Selected Readings

Cullet Phillippe (2001), Patent Bill TRIPS and Right to Health Economic and Political Weekly, October 27 Vol. XXXVI, No. 43.

Ganguli Prabhuddha (2001), Intellectual Property Rights, Unleasing the knowledge Economy. Tata Mccrew Hill Publishing Company Limited, New Delhi.

Keyla B.K. (1994), Patent Protection and the Pharmaceutical Industry in K.R.G. Nair and Ashok Kumar (eds) Intellectual Property Rights Allied Publication, New Delhi.

Watal Jayshree (1996), Introducing Product Patents in Indian Pharmaceutical Sector, Implications for Price and Welfare, World Competition, Law and Economics Review, December.

PART - V
China's Entry into WTO and Other Trade Issues

13

China's Accession into WTO: Opportunities and Challenges for South Asia

T. Nirmala Devi

Section 1: Introduction

The developing world in particular need to play a key role in the WTO negotiations, as multilateral trade liberalization is an indispensable part of development, in view of its provision for export opportunities and domestic reforms. Currently, trade agenda is linked to poverty reduction and economic development in the event of removal of distortions to agricultural trade and of import restrictions on industrial goods, which would benefit the farmers and petty traders. There is a growing concern among the developing countries about the expected benefits, stemming from the completion of the Doha Development Round, not withstanding the little perception on its fulfillment (Michael Finger J. 2002). The developing countries, particularly the low income countries of South Asia were not benefited much from the growth of the World economy, owing mostly to their import substitution development strategies in the past decades and to the formulation of 'new clauses' that are totally outside the ambit of trading system in the current decade. Hence, they are left with the hope of strengthening their current trade through access to new markets. China's accession into the WTO has brought a slight change in the perception of these countries. So far, India as the largest developing country enjoyed some advantage in the negotiations of WTO. From now onwards, it would jointly share the responsibility of championing the cause of the developing world with China, besides a few other countries. However, some analysts expressed the risk of isolation to be faced by India, in the event of the presence of a strong economic performer and major trade competitor, China in the WTO. Against this background, the paper takes the comparison of the impact of WTO on China and South Asian countries in general, with a special focus on India while addressing the development issues under the WTO content. The accession of China into WTO provides opportunities as well as poses challenges to the South Asian countries and in this backdrop, the objective of the paper is essentially about exploring them in a broader perspective. The paper is arranged into five sections. Besides the introduction in section 1, section 2 deals with the performance of growth, trade, FDI along with the policy framework. This section examines how foreign trade plays a significant role in driving growth in China, which in turn drives trade; and the passive role of trade in the overall growth of South Asia. Section 3 focuses on the opportunities for significant expansion of bilateral trade and investment flows between China and India. The challenges of competition from China to the South Asian countries in the international markets as well as the current initiatives for cooperative agreements between China and India are discussed in section 4, while the section 5 provides the concluding note.

Section 2: Growth Performance

China has made its mark in the economic restructuring through successful reform process during the past two and a half decades. This tremendous economic performance also owes to the influence of its strategic presence on the global stage, besides other factors. The country's growth performance can be viewed in the light of the effects of its economic reforms in 1978. The role of the State is vital in the economic transformation of the country. The economy started performing well from the 1980s, in spite of the political turmoil in the late 1980s and early 1990s, which caused an economic slow down (Asian Development Bank 2002). The SAARC countries on the other hand, initiated the package of economic reforms in the early 1990s, despite the presence in a piece meal way from the mid-1980s. The implementation of economic reforms has not brought out the expected improvement in these countries in general however, India achieved a significant progress in its growth rate i.e., a robust 7.7 per cent growth averaged during 1994–96 and again in the recent period, while registering a fluctuation in the growth in between. The country was able to grow at an average rate of 5.5 per cent during 1997-2000 and 5.0 per cent during 2000-2002, in spite of the industrial recession and domestic problems (RIS 2004). In the Asian region, China remained as one of best performing economies in the 1990s, notwithstanding the global economic slow down. The SAARC countries experienced only a modest growth in the pace of economic activity in this decade however, India recorded an impressive economic performance. There is a wide variation in the growth performance of China on the one hand and the SAARC countries altogether on the other. The economic activity of China is far above that of the SAARC countries in general as per table 1, witnessing a significant growth of GDP in total and per capita terms during the period 1965-1999, compared to the South Asian countries. The decadal growth rates of GDP for the periods 1980-90 and 1990-2000 also showed that South Asia's growth in general and India's growth in particular was in no way comparable with China's robust growth rate during the above two periods.

Table 1
GDP Growth Rate (in per cent)

Country	*1980 90*	*1990-2000*	*1965-99*	
			Total	*Per capita*
China	9.5	10.3	8.1	6.4
South Asia				
Bangladesh	4.3	4.8	3.8	1.3
India	5.8	6.0	4.6	2.4
Nepal	4.6	4.8	3.7	1.2
Pakistan	6.3	3.7	5.6	2.7
Sri Lanka	4.0	5.3	4.6	3.0

Source: World Bank (2001), *World Development Indicators*, Washington, DC.

The structural transformation of China has been characterized by a gradual shifting from industry to the service sector from the year 1980 to 1990 and from agriculture to industry from the year 1990 to 2001 with more or less stagnation in the agriculture in the first decade and in the services in the second, as shown in table 2. The share of agriculture value added which was slightly above one-fourth of GDP in the years 1980 and 1990 had declined to a

Table 2
Structure of Output (as a per cent of GDP)

Country	Agriculture value added			Industry value added			Services value added		
	1980	1990	2001	1980	1990	2001	1980	1990	2001
China	26	27	15	52	42	52	23	31	33
South Asia:									
Bangladesh	54	38	23	13	15	25	33	46	52
India	37	31	24	26	29	27	37	40	48
Nepal	57	60	38	13	14	23	30	26	39
Pakistan	31	26	25	25	25	23	44	49	51
Sri Lanka	28	26	19	30	26	26	42	48	55

Source: World Bank (various years), *World Development Report*, New York: Oxford University Press.

less than one-sixth in 2001. On the other hand, the share of industry value added fell from above a half in 1980 to a well above two-fifths in 1990 and regained the earlier share of 1980 in 2001. The service sector, which accounted for less than one-fourth share in 1980 increased to less than one-third in 1990 and registered a marginal improvement to reach to exactly one-third share in 2001. Considering the structural variation in their status among the countries and the services has emerged as a key sector of growth. It is evident from the table that the loss in the share of agriculture value added in India, Pakistan and Sri Lanka in the two decades indicated the gain of service sector, leaving the industry sector remain more or less unchanged. However, Bangladesh and Nepal recorded a sizeable growth in the share of industry value added at the cost of agriculture sector. If the importance of these sectors is judged in terms of employment generation, China's lower share of agriculture in GDP has been able to create jobs to a significant size of population, owing to its high farm productivity, in contrast to South Asian countries in general and India in particular. Likewise, China's relatively lower share of services successfully provides higher employment than India or any other South Asian country, which have sizeable share of services in GDP. Despite substantial share of industry in GDP in China, the employment creation in this sector is above one-fifth of population. There are limited chances of absorbing people in industry due to the adoption of modern production technologies. The diversification of industrial structure is also critical in the structural transformation and the move towards more value added and more advanced industries is revealed by the composition of manufacturing. The share of manufacturing of China changed markedly from 1990 to 2000 i.e., an expansioin in the category of machines and transport equipment and a contraction in other manufactures whereas the decline in the share of textiles and clothing in India followed by the share of food and beverages has been shown as an addition in the category of chemicals (World Bank 2003).

(i) Trade Dependency

Trade liberalization and greater integration with the global market are determined by the proportion of trade to GDP. China has become a very important player in foreign trade and its trade share in GDP has been increasing significantly, i.e., from a less than one-fourth in 1985 to above two-fifths from 1994 onwards. Another important characteristic of China's trade is that the share of exports in GDP exceeded that of imports, unlike most of the developing countries. The share of exports registered a significant increase from 1990 to 2000, compared to the considerable growth of imports during the above period as shown in table 3. Taking a note of the size of economy, the share of exports in China was relatively lower than some of the SAARC countries, for instance, Sri Lanka. The sharc of the total trade has been substantial in Sri Lanka i.e., above three-fourths in the 1980s and four-fifths in the 1990s, except for the marginal fluctuations from 1982 to 1992. The share of exports in this country was also remarkable, witnessing an increase from a less than one-third in the former period to a nearly two-fifths in the second decade, however, it was outnumbered by the share of imports and causing a trade imbalance, unlike China. In India, the share of trade in GDP is not significant, in view of the less importance to external trade in the past decades. However, there was an impressive increase, viz., doubling of its share from 1985 to 2000. The country registered the lowest share of exports and imports in the SAARC region from 1980 to 2000. In the remaining countries of the region, viz., Bangladesh, Nepal and Pakistan the exports recorded a lower share relative to their imports. The current account balance as a percentage of its GDP also revealed a thorough performance of China on the external sector from 1990 to 2000, notwithstanding the modest fall in the surplus in some of the years.

In contrast, a current account imbalance was experienced by the SAARC countries, however, it was at the minimum in India (IMF 2002).

Table 3
Share of Trade in GDP (in per cent)

Country	*Exports*				*Imports*			
	1985	*1990*	*1995*	*2000*	*1985*	*1990*	*1995*	*2000*
China	9.4	15.0	21.0	25.9	13.6	12.2	19.3	23.2
South Asia:								
Bangladesh	8.5	7.1	11.7	15.9	19.1	13.6	20.0	21.3
India	6.1	7.1	10.4	13.2	9.0	9.1	13.2	16.2
Nepal	12.5	12.0	24.4	24.3	21.9	23.7	38.5	33.4
Pakistan	11.8	17.3	17.2	17.1	23.8	25.8	23.9	20.3
Sri Lanka	26.1	28.5	35.4	39.1	38.4	36.9	45.9	49.6

Source: IMF(various years) *International Financial Statistical Year Book*, Washington, DC.

The growth of trade, as visualized by the average annual growth rate of the volume of both exports and imports of China registered a decline from 1980-1990 to 1990-1998, particularly in imports in the latter period, whereas the value of exports had increased relative to imports during the above periods. In contrast, the volume of exports and imports in India improved from the negative rates from the first to the second period, especially in imports. The growth rates of the value of imports of India increased significantly to above one-tenth in the latter period, as against the moderate increase in exports. The progress in the growth rates of exports, as seen from table 4 was quite visible in China from 1990 to 2000, witnessing nearly one and a half times hike. India also experienced a significant growth during this period, in contrast to Bangladesh, Pakistan and Sri Lanka. The decline in exports was substantial in Nepal from 1990 to 1995.

The growth rate of manufactured exports in China registered a sizeable increase of 16 percentage points from 1990 to 2000, experiencing a shift from the share of food, fuels and raw materials to manufactured items in this decade. India too witnessed a rise of eight percentage points in the share of manufactured exports in the above period as a consequence of a drop in the share of food and agriculture and raw material categories. In the share of manufactured exports in the total exports of the SAARC region,

Bangladesh registered a higher per cent, owing to the tremendous growth in the exports of readymade garments followed by Pakistan Among the manufactured exports, the share of high technology exports constituted 19 per cent in China in the above year while there was no contribution from SAARC countries in this category with the exception of India and Sri Lanka with the modest shares of 4 and 3 percents respectively (World Bank 2003). Following the change in the outlook, the share of service exports has been increasing from 1990 to 2000 in China as well as in South Asia. The share of transport in commercial service exports has gone down significantly in China in this period in favour of travel and others category, which included IT services. While in India, the substantial growth in the others category in the second decade was at the cost of transport and travel categories.

Table 4
Performance of Exports

Country	*Growth rate of exports (per year)*			*Share of manufacturing in exports (%)*	
	1990	*1995*	*2000*	*1990*	*2000*
China	19.2	24.9	27.9	72	88
South Asia:					
Bangladesh	28.2	20.2	17.3	77	91
India	9.0	20.3	19.6	71	79
Nepal	35.2	-9.7	—	83	77
Pakistan	12.2	16.1	8.8	79	85
Sri Lanka	23.1	18.6	19.8	54	75

Source: Asian Development Bank (various years), *Asian Development Outlook*, New York: Oxford University Press.

The concentration of exports towards industrial countries is a common characteristic of the developing countries, as seen from the share of Chinese exports to the US, which had increased more than three times from 1985 to 2000 and less than a double in the case of EU during the same period. Japan, as the export destination has lost its priority in China during this one and a half decades. This is also true in the case of SAARC countries in which the EU has emerged as a major market during this period and the share increased roughly three times in Bangladesh, nearly double in Nepal and approximately one and a half times in India, Pakistan and Sri Lanka each. As a single export destination, the US also registered a significant absorption of the share of exports from the SAARC countries during this period (Asian Development Bank). The above analysis of trade orientation clearly indicates that the effective policy framework of the country plays a crucial role in enhancing the share of exports/imports. If the country is in a better performing position, for instance, China, the overall growth has driven the opportunities for external trade, particularly the exports which, in turn, create a favourable environment for inducing further growth. In the low-income countries of South Asia, where growth rate is not optimal, barring India, the domestic environment is not conducive for further encouragement of exports. Though the share of exports is high in smaller countries due to their narrow domestic markets and higher outward orientation, they are overshadowed by the higher share of imports and causing imbalance in trade and current account, as in the case of Sri Lanka.

India's external sector performance to some extent is constrained by the lack of emphasis on trade in the past. In this context, the significant GDP growth in recent years is unable to achieve substantial export performance in the short run particularly, in the absence of special measures. In the event of slow down of the world economy, the liberalization of trade regimes to the major extent and the other positive steps to boost exports are required to attain a significant level of exports, commensurate to the size of the economy. The Chinese government, in order to minimize the adverse impact of the slow down of the global economy, adopted several measures in 2001 to encourage exports such as speeding up the export-tax refunds and customs procedures and granting permission to private companies to enlarge its external trade etc.(Asian Development Bank).

(ii) Role of FDI

The efforts made by the capital-scarce developing countries to raise domestic savings and attract FDI for capital formations are often not met with success, and thus facing the macro economic instability. Before examining the bearing of FDI inflows on the economies, the level of domestic savings are also to be considered in this background. The domestic savings roughly constituted two fifths of GDP during the 1990s and the share of resource balance in GDP was consistently positive, witnessing a surplus of 3 per cent in 1990 and 2 per cent from 1995 onwards. (Asian Development

Bank). In contrast, the resource balance in GDP terms had been negative in the SAARC countries in both the decades, as a result of the lower proportion of savings to investment. However, the resource imbalance was in control in India in the 1980s and 1990s and in Pakistan in the latter decade. The significant size of this imbalance in Nepal in the latter decade and Sri Lanka in the former (World Bank) was pointing out to the dire need of raising the level of domestic savings.

In view of the multiple benefits such as market-access and organizational skills and more importantly the technology transfer, higher emphasis has been placed on the FDI inflows especially from the second half of the 1990s. To lure the foreign capital, certain conditions viz., transparency, liberal regimes, repatriation facilities, tax concessions and other incentives, besides sound macro economic fundamentals are required. The country's decision about the magnitude, pattern and conditions of private foreign investment also matters. India still suffers from several constraints in terms of policy and regulatory framework coupled with weakness in accelerating the reform process, which acted as bottlenecks in attaining the FDI inflows. In other words, India remains as a marginal player in FDI as it has been bypassed in favour of more attractive destinations like China and South-east Asia (Niti Sury 2004). China's share in FDI inflows increased tremendously in the developing world in the later half of the 1990s. Being a small destination of FDI, the South Asia registered a less than 5 per cent of the inflows of the developing Asia. From the table 5, it is seen that a growth of $5 billion was recorded in the stock from 1995 to 2000. Out of the limited share of FDI stock in the SAARC region, India recorded a modest increase of over $150 million in the second half of the 1990s, notwithstanding a drop of $ 1 billion from 1997 to 1998. Sri Lanka, which also registered a decline in the above year, showed a modest increase while Pakistan registered a gradual decline from 1996 onwards in its FDI stock. The share of FDI inward stocks of China as a proportion of GDP was also not comparable with South Asian countries, owing to its well above one-fourth share in 1998, despite having lower share to Sri Lanka in the year 1990. Though the figures of FDI inflows between India and China are not comparable for technical reasons, India's inflows of about $ 3.4 billion in 2001 are too small and represent a mere 1.7 per cent of total inflows of the developing world, in contrast to China's $46.8 billion of inflows, representing nearly 23 per cent of total developing country's' inflows (RIS). The share of FDI inflows as a per cent of gross fixed capital formation was also significant in China, in relation to the SAARC countries in general and India in particular.

Table 5
Foreign Direct Investment

Country	*Inflows (US $ million)*			*Inward stocks (as % of GDP)*		
	1990	*1995*	*2000*	*1990*	*1995*	*1998*
China	3,487	35,849	40,800	7.0	19.6	27.6
South Asia:						
Bangladesh	3	2	170	0.5	0.5	1.5
India	162	2,144	2,300	0.5	1.7	3.4
Nepal	6	8	13	0.3	0.9	2.1
Pakistan	244	719	308	4.8	9.1	14.4
Sri Lanka	43	65	217	8.5	10.0	13.2

Source: UNCTAD (various years), *World Investment Report*, Geneva.

India needs more open and liberal policies for investment besides strengthening the institutions aimed at enhancing foreign investment. As per the evidence, the growth of India so far achieved is not driven by any foreign investment, because the key drivers of productivity change and economic growth viz., infrastructure and exports, face serious investment constraints. On the contrary, FDI has been playing a critical role in China's overall growth rate and the influence of FDI over several key sectors is significant. China in recent years is viewed as more business-oriented nation in which the decision- making is faster and it has more FDI–friendly policies. The official attitude towards FDI in this country is more liberal from the highest level of government to the lowest level of government bureaucracy due to the multi-faceted benefits arising from FDI. In tune with China, India should simplify and modernize certain laws, rules and regulations, elimination of controls and other policy reforms in order to achieve increasing flows of FDI into the country, as its present domestic policies and regulations are not providing the right environment for private investment–both domestic and foreign.

China is growing in importance and is now in the top 15 international trading entities. But it is difficult to generalize about the country, in view of having the characteristics of a developing country and at the same time possessing significant technological and intellectual property capability (Graeme Thomson 2003). The role of private sector in the economic transformation is quite significant in the country, particularly in enhancing employment in a number of ways. The entry of China in WTO is inevitable, taking a note of the economic gains associated with the accession, besides the diplomatic gains. Hence, its gradual transformation into a market economy through reform process is imperative, otherwise the value for Chinese market for WTO members will be marginalized (Graeme Thomson). The adverse implications will be more, if it stays outside the WTO, particularly for its textiles and clothing sector (Ian Dickson 2003).

Section 3: Bilateral Trade

The expanding economic relations between China and South Asia on one hand and between China and India on the other reveal the growing engagement in the form of the comprehensive steps of economic cooperation taken in the recent period. The economic indicators reveal that there is a wide scope for significant expansion of trade and investment flows between China and India. The opportunities provided by the economic expansion of China in Asia and in the World, as well as the mutual trade engagements are dealt with in this section. China's share in the total imports of the SAARC countries is seen in table 6. There was an increase in Bangladesh's imports from China in the 1990s, particularly from the year 1994 and reached the peak in the subsequent year, notwithstanding the fluctuations thereafter. India also recorded a rise in its imports from China from 2000 onwards. The share of China in Nepal's imports which ranged from 5 to 10 per cent in the 1980s, increased to 15 per cent in 2000, while the share was consistent at 4 per cent in Pakistan and varied between 3 and 4 per cent in Sri Lanka. Except in India and Pakistan, the share of China in the total exports of SAARC countries was not considerable, as shown in table 7. Its share in Bangladesh's exports declined from 2.4 per cent in 1981 to a minimal share of 0.1 per cent in 2001, while India was able to raise the share of exports to China from 0.1 per cent in 1990 to 3.5 per cent in 2001. Pakistan, Sri Lanka and Nepal, which had earlier exported a sizeable share to China, witnessed a significant decline in 2001, barring the former country, which retained 2 to 3 per cent share from 1997 onwards.

Table 6
Share of China in the total Imports of SAARC Countries
(in per cent)

Country	*1981*	*1985*	*1990*	*1995*	*1996*	*1997*	*1998*	*1999*	*2000*	*2001*
Bangladesh	4.28	3.28	3.29	9.25	9.24	9.06	7.42	6.39	7.41	8.51
India	0.54	0.64	0.13	2.35	1.95	2.72	2.68	2.68	3.25	4.05
Nepal	5.20	6.47	10.18	7.83	4.15	3.23	4.67	15.14	15.12	12.26
Pakistan	3.20	2.45	4.58	4.41	4.74	5.05	4.53	4.38	4.97	4.75
Sri Lanka	2.06	3.86	4.29	3.38	2.94	2.90	4.52	2.69	3.43	3.68

Source: UN ESCAP (various years), *Statistical Year Book of Asia and the Pacific*, Bangkok.

Table 7
Share of China in the total Exports of SAARC Countries
(in per cent)

Country	*1981*	*1985*	*1990*	*1995*	*1996*	*1997*	*1998*	*1999*	*2000*	*2001*
Bangladesh	2.39	1.26	1.50	0.58	0.58	1.60	0.78	0.18	0.18	0.10
India	0.73	0.25	0.10	0.93	1.68	1.94	2.36	1.95	2.78	3.46
Nepal	4.11	1.48	2.30	—	—	—	—	0.41	0.94	0.70
Pakistan	9.44	2.10	1.20	1.49	1.28	1.70	1.80	2.12	2.64	3.14
Sri Lanka	4.43	1.34	0.16	0.08	0.29	0.17	0.19	0.07	0.09	0.10

Source: As in table 1.

Table 8 provides the share of the SAARC region in China's imports at section level. China's imports from SAARC countries were considerable in section 2, i.e., crude materials, ranging from 2 to 3 per cent. The other sections did not register any significant growth except in food and beverages–ranging from 3 to 7 per cent–followed by animal and vegetable oils, fats–ranging from 1 to 3 per cent–and basic manufactures–ranging from 1.5 to 1.9 per cent. On the other side, China's exports to SAARC countries witnessed a sizeable acceleration (table 9). The share of Chinese exports in section 9, i.e., goods not classified by kind was significant and ranged between 29 and 48 per cent from the year 1992 to 2000, and reached the peak in 1994 and 1995, however, declined to 30 per cent in 2000. Growth was also registered in chemicals (sec. 5), followed by crude materials (sec. 2), mineral, fuels etc (sec.3) and basic manufactures (sec. 6), particularly in the second half of the 1990s, in contrast to the growth in machines and transport equipment (sec. 7) in the first half of the decade.

Table 8
Share of the SAARC Region in China's Total Imports by Section of SITC. Rev. 2
(in per cent)

Section Description	*1990*	*1991*	*1992*	*1993*	*1994*	*1995*	*1996*	*1997*	*1998*	*1999*	*2000*
All commodity	0.40	0.35	0.35	0.51	0.44	0.51	0.79	0.95	0.95	0.75	0.84
0. Food & live ani.	0.29	0.37	0.60	1.39	1.07	0.71	3.37	5.38	6.92	2.59	3.03
1. Beverages&tobacco	0.08	0.93	0.65	0.77	0.75	—	0.31	0.02	0.02	0.05	0.03
2. Crude mat.. ex. fuel	3.19	2.84	2.76	2.72	2.17	2.08	2.92	3.30	3.34	2.82	2.72
3. Mineral, fuel etc.	1.53	0.84	0.20	0.78	1.01	0.36	0.28	0.45	0.13	0.66	0.14
4. Animal, veg. oil, fat	0.01	0.02	0.09	0.02	0.10	1.11	1.36	1.05	2.27	2.25	3.16
5. Chemicals	0.31	0.24	0.13	0.20	0.17	0.35	0.27	0.28	0.25	0.44	0.88
6. Basic anufactures	0.11	0.13	0.33	0.94	0.83	0.98	1.54	1.77	1.88	1.74	1.86
7. Machines, trnport eq.	0.08	0.05	0.07	0.01	0.01	0.03	0.02	0.02	0.02	0.04	0.60
8. Misc.manfd goods	0.03	0.02	0.04	0.08	0.07	0.09	0.10	0.22	0.24	0.24	0.28
9. Goodsnot lassified	—	—	0.11	0.44	0.64	0.13	0.09	0.14	0.10	0.01	0.00

Source: UN ESCAP (various years), *Foreign Trade Statistics of Asia and the Pacific*, Bangkok.

Table 9
Share of the SAARC Region in China's Total Exports by Section of SITC. Rev.2 (in per cent)

Section Description	*1990*	*1991*	*1992*	*1993*	*1994*	*1995*	*1996*	*1997*	*1998*	*1999*	*2000*
All commodity	1.23	1.22	1.26	1.51	1.43	1.67	1.45	1.43	1.39	1.49	1.51
0. Food & live ani	2.28	1.15	0.68	0.64	1.90	0.57	0.57	0.74	0.57	1.62	1.09
1. Beverages & toba	2.50	1.66	1.50	1.10	0.85	0.08	0.01	0.10	0.45	0.07	0.15
2. Crude mate.ex. fuel	1.49	1.39	2.34	2.35	2.73	3.02	3.03	2.50	3.77	4.89	5.53
3. Mineral, fuel etc.	0.45	0.32	0.52	0.53	1.50	2.18	2.04	2.70	2.90	2.41	3.63
4. Animal, veg. oil, fat	0.17	0.05	0.58	0.30	0.15	0.72	0.08	0.24	0.33	2.05	0.79
5. Chemicals	3.18	3.37	3.14	4.18	4.94	5.44	5.16	5.08	5.46	5.87	5.50
6. Basic manufactures	1.07	1.48	1.25	1.51	1.77	2.03	2.21	2.41	2.45	2.67	2.66
7. Mach., tranp eqp.	2.14	2.23	3.03	3.70	1.71	2.09	1.71	1.41	1.11	1.15	1.09
8. Misc. manfd goods	0.20	0.24	0.10	0.20	0.19	0.18	0.18	0.19	0.29	0.27	0.29
9. Goods not classifd.	0.00	0.00	28.75	37.16	47.30	48.32	40.61	33.55	32.90	28.59	29.57

Source: As in Table 3.

Tables 10 and 11 present the list of the top five commodities and their respective shares in India's trade with China from 1990-91 to 2002-03.Electronic goods; organic chemicals; coal; coke and briquettes; medicinal and pharm products and raw silk have been the regular items of imports from China, besides silver, non-electrical machinery and inorganic chemicals during this period. The share of electronic goods in the total imports from China registered a significant growth from the year 1995-96 to the year 2002-03, particularly in the latter, while the organic chemicals shared above 15 per cent of the total in the first three years under consideration and witnessed a modest decline in the later years. India imported a sizeable share of coal, coke and briquettes during the above periods. The consistent items grew at 5.5 percentage points from 1995-96 to 1996-97 and again from 2001-02 to 2002-03.

The role of the world trading system is critical in the developmental process of South Asian countries, since the Uruguay Round. China's accession into the WTO is an important event for these countries in the context of their future trade potentialities. These countries are of the view that the membership of China in the WTO has some favourable as well as adverse implications on their domestic economies. On the positive side, the accession of China to the WTO norms and procedures etc., will bring its trade policy under surveillance and hence state subsidies will be regulated and consequently it will become difficult for the Chinese exporters to dump their products in the world market. Moreover, the Chinese market may become more open and accessible for the South Asian countries (RIS 2001-02). Its entry would bring some positive outcomes for the South Asian countries because these countries, in line with the other members of the Third world are permitted to control imports, if there is a market disruption caused by Chinese exports of textile products in the event of the completion of quotas on textiles ending December 2004, following the continuation of special safeguard mechanism until the end of 2008 (Jeffery L. Gertler 2003). This type of positive outcomes may arise from China's accession to the WTO. In India's global engagement, the political and economic relationship with China plays an important role. The expanding and deepening economic partnership with China in the recent period indicates a paradigm shift in the country's policy. The dramatic expansion of bilateral trade in recent years–starting from a few hundred million dollars

Table-10
Top Five Products in India's Imports from China

1990-91	*1995-96*	*1996-97*	*1997-98*	*1998-99*	*1999-00*	*2000-01*	*2001-02*	*2002-03*
1. Coal, coke & briquett (18.8)	1.Organic chemicals (17.1)	1. Organic chemicals (17.9)	1. Coal, coke & briquettes (16.6)	1. Organic chemicals (14.9)	1. Organic chemicals (13.9)	1. Coal, coke & briquettes (17.5)	1. Coal, coke & briquettes (18.9)	1. Electronic goods (27.8)
2. Organic chemicals (7.8)	2. Coal, coke & briquettes (15.2)	2.Coal, coke & briquettes (12.5)	1. Organic chemicals (15.8)	2. Electronic goods (14.7)	2. Electronic goods (13.8)	2. Electronic goods (16.4)	2. Electronic goods (12.9)	2. Organic chemical (10.9)
3. Textile yarn fab. madeup artls (5.1)	1. Medicinal & pharm products (9.1)	3. Medicinal & pharm products (7.8)	3. Electronic goods (9.7)	3. Coal, coke & briquettes (9.9)	3. Coal, coke & briquettes (11.3)	3. Organic chemicals (12.1)	3. Organic chemicals (11.9)	3.Coal, coke & briquett (6.0)
4. Artificial resins & plastic (3.3)	4. Silk raw (7.7)	4. Electroni goods (6.9)	4. In-organic chemicals (6.3)	4. Medicinal & pharm products (6.5)	4. Silk raw (6.8)	4. Silk raw (6.4)	4. Silk raw (6.0)	4. Medicinal & pharm products (5.2)
5. Pulses (3.3)	5. Electronic goods (6.3)	5. Non-ferrous metals (6.3)	5. Medicina & pharm prod. (5.9)	5. Inorganic chemicals (5.7)	5. Medicinal & pharm prod. (5.7)	5.Medicinal & pharm prod. (4.7)	5. Medicinal & pharm prod. (5.2)	5. Silver (4.3)

Source: CMIE (1996 & 2003), *Foreign Trade and Balance of Payments*, Mumbai.
Note: Figures in brackets indicate the percentage share in total.

Table 11
Top Five Products in India's Exports to China

1990-91	*1995-96*	*1996-97*	*1997-98*	*1998-99*	*1999-00*	*2000-01*	*2001-02*	*2002-03*
1.Processed minerals (28.7)	1.Iron ore (20.9)	1. Marine products (12.0)	1.Marine products (16.0)	1.Iron ore (20.6)	1.Marine products (16.3)	1.Iron ore (15.7)	1.Iron ore (21.7)	1. Prim & semi-fin.iron & steel (24.8)
2.I ron ore (6.4)	2.Cotton yarn fab. Madeups (6.3)	2.Other ores & minerals (11.6)	2.Iron ore (13.6)	2.Marine products (12.1)	2. Other ores & minerals (12.1)	2. Marine products (14.0)	2. Plastic & lino-leum products (14.9)	2.Iron ore (20.4)
3.Oil meals (1.5)	3.Inorg/org/ agr. chemical (4.6)	3.Iron ore (10.7)	3. Cotton yarn fab. Madeups etc. (7.7)	3.Cotton yarn fab. Madeups etc. (10.2)	3.Cotton yarn fab. Madeups etc. (10.4)	3. Plastic & linoleum products (12.4)	3. Other ores & minerals (11.9)	3.Plastic & linoleum products (8.4)
4. Drugs, pharmace (1.4)	4.Marine products (4.4)	4.Cotton yarn fab. Madeups etc. (7.4)	4. Other cres & minerals (6.2)	4.Drugs, pharm & fine chemical (10.0)	4. Drugs, pharm & fine chemical (8.5)	4.Other ores & minerals (8.8)	4.Marine products (8.9)	4.Other ores & minerals (6.3)
5. Cashew (1.1)	5. Plastic & linoleum products (4.1)	5.Prim & semi-fin. iron & steel (6.5)	5. Drugs, pharm & fine chemical (5.2)	5. Other ores & minerals (9.3)	5.Inorg/org/ agro chemical (7.3)	5. Cotton yarn fab. Madeups etc. (8.6)	5. Drugs, pharm & fine chemicals (8.4)	5. Marine products (5.4)

Source & Note: Same as above.

in the mid-1990s to $ 7.5 billion last year and is expected to cross $ 10 billion this year–has provided a stabilizing element (Raja Mohan, C 2004), notwithstanding many structural limitations. This seems that economics has begun to drive the relationship between the two and the deeper engagement with China is both necessary and inevitable for India in the event of its way to becoming the world's second largest economy.

It is a known fact that the economic and trade interactions between the two countries are not commensurate with their economic strengths and populations. For instance, the bilateral trade in 2001-2002, though registered an increase of 37.5 per cent over the previous year constituted to just 0.79 and 5.0 percents in Chinese and Indian foreign trade (Padmanabhan S. 2004). Thus there still has a room for expansion in trade between the two, in view of the complementarities and division of labour in the consumer goods industries. The economic cooperation between the two countries, though prevented by political sensitivities, has an ample scope for opportunities for expanding trade and investment flows in trans-regional energy and other economic projects. Border trade and transit trade are also feasible, in view of improving the living standards of the people across the Sino-Indian border.

Section 4: Competition from China in the WTO

In the event of package of economic reforms, the external sector of the SAARC countries has been liberalised to a considerable extent with the hope of getting increased access to the international market. The dismantling of trade restrictions resulted in the integration of these economies with the world market more or less significantly. Consequently, the region is more open in the recent years, notwithstanding the other anomalies. The external shocks, particularly the East Asian crisis of 1997 and the slowing down of the world economy from the past three to four years, which resulted in the compression of import and export demands had no strong bearing on the growth performance of the SAARC countries, like China. The steady expansion of global trend in general is a major factor in raising the global income and reducing poverty. In this light, the slowing down of the global trade over the past decade causes concern. Moreover, the heavy subsidies given by the developed countries reduced the market access for the developing countries. The impact of making the farm prices depressed all over the world and distorting the international grain market caused adverse terms of trade to the farmers of the developing world.

The SAARC countries altogether maintained a common position regarding the WTO content from the time of 3rd Ministerial Conference, attributing the absence at the first two Meets to the Indo-Pakistan hostility in the wake of nuclear positions in 1998. Their common stand-to oppose the overload of WTO agenda with the new issues; to seek the deepening and broadening of the existing agreements like S and D concessions to the LDCs and the other developing countries; to desire the need for greater access to industrial markets and a more meaningful integration of the textiles and clothing sector in WTO–reflected their view point (Mukherjee 2003). This stand has been extended to the next two Ministerial Conferences with slight modifications. And due to the division in the regional members as developing countries and the LDCs, there was a diversion in the prioritization of issues between these two groups in the region, which further aggravated by the political mistrust.

In contrast to the poor chances of SAARC countries in the WTO, the membership in the WTO appears to fetch some gains to China. Though imports of China will continue to grow faster than its exports with the accession of WTO and causing gradual decline in the trade and current account surplus, the significant foreign investment flows to the country are likely to offset a part of this decline. The further opening up of the Chinese economy is expected to raise the FDI flows also. By forcing the economy to reallocate resources, in line with the comparative advantage from capital to labour-intensive sectors, the WTO membership of China should also generate more employment for a given rate of growth of the economy, besides increasing the export prospects. China has only 3.1 per cent unemployment rate as against 7.3, 7.8 and 8.2 percents in India, Pakistan and Sri Lanka respectively in 1999-2001 (Asian Development Bank). The WTO membership involves significant opportunities, besides challenges for the Chinese economy. Over the long-term, China's accession and its commitment to cut tariffs, liberalized trade and investment and open up domestic sector to foreign participation should lead to significant efficiency gains. Many studies estimate that the long term gain from China's WTO membership will be equal to about 1-2 per cent of GDP per year (Asian Development Bank). However the positive effects will take time to make them realized. In the meantime the country's commitments could pose adjustment challenges especially in protected sectors, such as agriculture, automobiles, banking, insurance, and telecommunications. To face the challenges, the government is making efforts to speed up economic reforms and create more business environment.

The negative side of China's accession into WTO is that South Asia and China compete in the global market for a number of labour-intensive and matured technology goods such as textiles and garments, leather goods, light engineering goods, chemicals, pharmaceuticals among others. China has already offered tough competition to the South Asian exports in many commodities in the industrial markets. Moreover, China's entry into the WTO strengthens its competitiveness and hence may affect exports of the SAARC countries adversely (RIS 2001-02). However, the exact impact of the accession of China to the WTO on the export prospects of the region cannot be easily determined, as it will depend upon the future balancing of these two affects. Till recently, the South Asian countries like India and Pakistan are able to increase their market share to the US and EU owing to the decreases in barriers, though China is having relative advantage in textiles and clothing exporting industries. Now, China's gains from joining the WTO will be magnified due to the improved efficiency of the economy, especially in labour-intensive sectors and may cause some loss to South Asia along with Indonesia due to increased competition (Elena Ianchovichina & Will Martin 2003).

However, it appears that there will be an immediate difficulty for Indian industries for certain sectors, such as textiles and leather products as China is concentrating its resources and skills on these sectors, in view of the better positioning in the international markets. The another possibility of threat coming from China to India in future is in software and allied sectors where India has been enjoying some advantage in the recent years. Keeping in view of all these possibilities, India should make a breakthrough in foreign exchange earning sectors/products by all means and face the challenge of competition from China in the industrial markets.

Section 5: Conclusion

Politicization of global trading system becomes a major impediment to the common position of SAARC countries in line with the other

Third World countries, as the developed countries' market access was linked to political benefits. Most of the SAARC countries that depend heavily on garments' exports entered into some bilateral treaties with the US, in view of the likely end of Multi Fibre Agreement in 2004. India remains isolated in such initiatives and hence follows protective steps to counter the pressure of developed countries through appropriate measures.

From the recent conclusion of the WTO's Fifth Ministerial Conference at Cancun, the developing world had learnt the art of negotiations by joining hands with some of the middle-income countries to build alliances on some key issues. India showed some maturity and flexibility by undertaking modest liberalisation in industrial goods and also agreeing to negotiate on two of the four Singapore issues, viz., transparency in government procurement and trade facilitation. India's joining the larger group of developing countries, i.e., the G-21 that included Brazil and China has an important influence on the perception of the developed countries towards trade liberalization. Its ability to adjust the domestic policy to the demands of a multilateral global trade system is the key to the success of its negotiations.

The desired level of agricultural liberalization, sought from the developed countries, particularly the US and the EU cannot be fulfilled, unless India displaying a matured thinking and gets China's cooperation. India has to initiate steps taking the other South Asian countries into confidence for trade and investment cooperation with China even in a limited way to begin with. To face the challenges from the developed countries, the developing countries would take a lead and reap the benefits from the acceleration of trade among themselves by lowering their own trade barriers, through appropriate initiatives. In other words, south-south cooperation appears to be the ultimate solution now. In this context, India with an export trade of 40 per cent with the developing world and China, could make significant impact, if cooperate with each other. By taking a pragmatic view of the emerging situation in the world trading system and to settle issues amicably with the fastest growing economy of China, India should follow cautious steps to overcome the present problems. The present global trade scenario underscores the need for some economic understanding between these two fast growing developing economies. The positive political steps to boost bilateral relations between India and China would hopefully contribute to bilateral economic cooperation that would ultimately protect the cause of developing countries.

References

Asian Development Bank (2002), *Asian Development Outlook*, New York: Oxford University Press, pp. 26-29.

Ibid., table A.12.

Ibid., tables A. 7 & 8.

Elena Ianchovichina & Will Martin (2003), "Trade Policy Reform and China's WTO Accession" in Deborah Z. Cass, Brett G. Williams and George Barker (eds.), *China and the World Trading System: Entering the New Millennium*, Cambridge: Cambridge University Press, p. 114.

Graeme Thomson (2003), "China's Accession to the WTO: Improving Market Access and Australia's Role and Interests" in Deborah Z. Cass, et. al, *Ibid.*, p. 69.

Ibid., p. 76.

Ian Dickson (2003), "China's Interest in the WTO's Deregulation of International Textiles Trade" in Deborah Z. Cass, et. al, *Ibid.*, p. 201.

IMF (2002), *International Financial Statistics Year Book*, Washington, D.C., World and Area tables, p. 164.

Jeffrey L. Gertler, (2003), "China's WTO Accession–The Final Countdown" in Deborah Z. Cass, et. al, *op.cit.*, p. 59.

Michael Finger, J., (2002) "The Doha Agenda and Development: A View from the Uruguay Round", ERD Working Paper Series, No. 21, *Asian Development Bank*, September, p. 1.

Mukherjee, I.N. & Saman Kalegama (2003), "WTO and South Asia: From Doha to Cancun", *Economic and Political Weekly*, Mumbai, September 13-19, pp. 3864-66.

Niti Sury (2004), *Foreign Direct Investment: Global and Indian Aspects*, Delhi: New Century Publications, pp. 99-121.

Padmanabhan S. (2004), *Business Line*, April 6.

Raja Mohan C. (2004), *The Hindu*, July 29.

RIS (2004), *South Asia Development & Cooperation Report*, pp. 21-22.

Ibid., p. 41.

Ibid., (2001-02), pp. 10-12.

World Bank (2003), *World Development Report*, New York: Oxford University Press, table 4.

Ibid., (various years).

14

Nepal and World Trade Organisation: Challenges and Opportunities

Mahendra P. Lama

Section 1: Introduction

The World Trade Organisation (WTO) membership is critical to Nepal's development and integration into the world trading and economic system. It was a long wait for Nepal since 1989 to enter as the 148th member into the mainstream multilateral trading regime represented by the WTO. There are widespread apprehensions and skepticism about the role of WTO in promoting the case of developing countries in an objective manner (Benjamin & Hayduk 2003). Though it is widely believed that the negotiations are structurally tilted towards developed countries, this forum ensures continuation of policy in a much more "transparent" and predictable manner and provides the member country to move ahead in trade related affairs in a much more stable manner. Dependence on one or two countries will be also reduced as there will be multiplicity of actors and institutions. This brings Nepal's trade liberalization efforts of last one decade upfront and in a much more pronounced manner. In fact the impact of all these measures could already be witnessed in various investment ventures both foreign and domestic including in the energy sector and financial sector particularly banking and insurance.

"It is our conviction that joining this organization would not only enhance effectiveness and efficiency in trading capacity but would also result in the expansion of trade capacity, leading to a higher level of growth and enhancement of quality of life of our people." Besides very specific and special gains and provisions that Nepal can enjoy as a least developed country under this rule-based trading regime, by joining WTO, it can now fully enjoy the rights that all members have under the WTO agreements. These can be broadly summarized as:

(i) Non-discrimination by other WTO members

(ii) Expansion of trading opportunities because of low tariffs and elimination of non-tariff barriers in member states and gain competitive strength.

(iii) Enhancement of effectiveness and efficiency in trading capacity thereby leading to expansion of trade and higher level of growth.

(iv) Raise level of productivity and quality of life of our people.

(v) Ability to use the WTO dispute settlement procedure as it contains neutral procedure for resolving the differences based on an agreed legal foundation.

Section 2: Nepal and Bilateral Trade Arrangements

The WTO agreement, known as Differential and Special Treatment, specifically recognizes trade, financial and development needs of the LDCs. The provisions, also referred to as positive discrimination, recognize the economic and trade interests of LDCs, allow them to assume fewer obligations to be met and provide a longer time frame for the implementation of certain obligations (UNCTAD 2000).

However, a frequently debated issue is whether SAARC's and within it Nepal's quest for regional integration through both regional and bilateral route/forum will be inconsistent with and contradictory to the multilateral trade liberalization (Till & Kennedy 1993). Except Bhutan all the other six constituent states of SAARC are members of World Trade Organisation (SAARC Chamber of Commerce and Industry 2000). So by becoming a member of regional trading arrangement (RTA) like SAARC, do these countries or Nepal depart from the guiding principles of non-discrimination i.e. most favoured nation treatment (MFN) defined, *inter alia*, in Article I of GATT and Article II of GATS? Though SAARC is yet to evolve into a full-fledged RTA, the debate has crystallised into the acceptance of the fact that WTO members are permitted to enter into such agreements like RTA under specific conditions (Richard & Henderson 1993). These conditions emanate from three sets of rules viz. (WTO).

(i) Paragraphs 4 to 10 of Article XXIV of GATT (as clarified in the Understanding on the Interpretation of Article XXIV of the GATT 1994) provide for the formation and operation of customs unions and free-trade areas;

(ii) The Enabling Clause (i.e., the 1979 Decision on Differential and More Favourable Treatment, Reciprocity and Fuller Participation of Developing Countries) refers to preferential trade arrangements between developing country Members; and

(iii) Article V of GATS governs the conclusion of RTAs in the area of trade in services.

Though there are divergent views on the interpretation of certain elements of the above-cited WTO rules governing RTAs, nearly all of the WTO's 140 plus Members have concluded RTAs with other countries. In the period 1948-1994 alone, GATT contracting parties notified 118 RTAs relating to trade in goods, of which 38 in the five years ending in 1994. Since the creation of the WTO (1995), 80 additional RTAs covering trade in goods and services have been notified.

Trade Sector Reforms

The sweeping reforms in the foreign trade regime in Nepal include delicensing of exports and imports of all goods, full convertibility of the Nepalese Rupee on current accounts transactions and unprecedented relief to the imports of machin-ery, raw materials and consumer goods. Arrangements have also been made to allow import of specified commodities from India at payment of foreign exchange. With effect from July 1993 import license requirements were eliminated for all industrial raw materials that were previously under the foreign exchange auction system. They were put under the Open General Licensing (OGL) System. These moves were bold both in terms of the fact that it meant a loss of substantial auction revenue to the Government and secondly, with current account convertibil-ity, imports of consumer items were also freed up from quantita-tive restrictions.

Given the rigid history of tariff regime, the rationalisation of its structure in the last few years has been both relatively faster and substantive. Peak tariff rates fell from 245 per cent in 1991-92 to 110 per cent in July 1994 and further to 40 per cent 2000. The tariff rate structure has been considerably simplified with the reduced number of slabs (categories) from 100 in the 1980s to 6 in 1994-95. However, even when the highest slab was 110 per cent in 1994, there were hardly five items in the peak group whereas the largest number of import items comes within the custom duty of 20-30 per cent.

These economic measures are aimed at: (i) doing away with the inconsis-tencies and imbalance surfacing in the financial sector in the past, (ii) enhancing the competing capacity of the Nepalese indus-tries, (iii) simplifying supply system and ensuring regularity in the supplies of imported and indigenously produced commodities and (iv) introducing more open import system with a view to making import more dynamic and transparent (Institute of Trade and Development 1993).

Trade Direction and Composition

Among the top ten destinations for Nepal's exports market, India has again emerged as the most important destination constituting around 60 per cent of Nepal's exports to the world. It is followed by USA (19.4 per cent) and Germany (8.4 per cent) in 2001-02. Table 1 clearly reveals that these selected top major destination constituted over 95 per cent of Nepal's total world exports.

It can be seen from the table 2 that India is also again the main country of origin for Nepal's import (among the top selected sources of import). It constitutes over 43 per cent of the Nepal's imports from the world followed by USA, (9 per cent); Malaysia (4.57 per cent); Saudi Arabia (4.33 per cent) and China (3.9 per cent) in 2001-02.

Aspects of Obligations

The unilateral economic liberalization implemented by the Nepalese Government over the last decade or so are triggered mainly by the conviction that economic reform and trade liberalization would attract investments, promote development and, contribute to generate productive employment and alleviate poverty, in a general framework of equity, participation and market-based efficiency.

Table 1
Nepal's' Exports to the Major Trading Partners 1990-91 to 2001-02

(Million Rs.)

Sl. No.	*Country*	*1990-91*	*1994-95*	*1998-99*	*2001-02*
1.	India	1552.20	3369.10	12530.70	28865.20
2.	USA	1400.50	5141.60	9520.30	9377.80
3.	Germany	2728.80	6549.60	7820.70	4043.20
4.	U.K	169.00	330.50	521.80	808.70
5.	Italy	146.20	358.70	385.00	566.56
6.	Japan	29.10	75.40	230.80	492.80
7.	France	59.10	140.90	479.20	473.47
8.	Switzerland	49.71	46.44	281.50	382.82
9.	Canada	51.40	158.00	156.10	305.97
10.	Belgium	174.50	270.10	283.30	295.10
	Total 10 :	6360.51	16440.34	32209.40	45611.62
	Total 10 :	87.28	91.85	91.32	94.44

Table 2
Nepal's Imports from the Major Trading Partners 1990-91 to 2001-02

(Million Rs)

Sl. No.	*Country*	*1990-91*	*1994-95*	*1998-99*	*2001-02*
1.	India	7323.10	20791.20	32119.70	45364.30
2.	USA	3377.10	1089.00	9679.00	7846.30
3.	Germany	228.40	494.70	1779.80	4818.30
4.	Japan	17.60	462.10	1431.00	4572.80
5.	U.K.	1102.40	2295.90	5252.10	4315.80
6.	Italy	317.03	143.40	7545.20	4205.70
7.	France	206.90	637.00	1565.90	3278.16
8.	Switzerland	91.29	323.02	1157.70	2877.65
9.	Belgium	153.00	825.00	1639.50	2795.30
10.	Canada	162.70	428.10	1317.90	2525.60
	Total 10 :	12979.52	27489.42	63487.80	82599.91

As per the broad commitments given to WTO by Nepal, it has to:

(i) Accept an average tariff binding of 42 per cent in agricultural products and around 24 per cent in industrial goods. Within these also a majority of the import items fall in the customs duty range of 10-20 per cent. Items like cars will have maximum tariff rate of 130 per cent and daily consumption will have as low as five per cent.

(ii) It has agreed to amend or enact 38 various acts and regulations to become compatible with WTO provisions. This includes legislation on valuation of imports for customs and taxation purposes. It will now have to have its technical and financial capabilities to increase competitiveness.

(iii) It has conditional commitment to open up sectors like legal service, engineering, architecture, R&D, advertising, market research, courier, telecom, musical products, higher education, financial service, hotels, restaurants.

Major Challenges

Despite some specific safeguard measures like other developing countries, Nepal will be exposed to fierce global competition which if not tackled in an institutionalized and sustainable manner may prove to be quite costly and painful to both its society and economy. Options and alternatives are all related to compliance with the regimes first and then strategizing the entire approach to cope up with the provision and get maximum mileage out of them.

The priority issues would be the likely impact of WTO agreements on livelihoods of the poor particularly food security and employment, eco-labeling as a strategy of export promotion, trade related intellectual property rights issues particularly related to safeguarding traditional knowledge and conservation of biodiversity, indigenous seeds production the social environmental clauses and the movement of people.

Some of the major challenges that Nepal is likely to confront are primarily in the arena of: (i) Primary Commodities; (ii) Anti-Dumping; (iii) Social Clause; (iv) Movement of Natural Persons; (v) Reforms and IPRs; (vi) Agriculture Subsidies; (vii) MFA Phasing out; (viii) Access to dispute settlement board; (ix) Competition Policy.

(i) Primary Commodities

The average share of primary commodities in Nepal's exports to the world in 1974-79 was at the peak level of 83.17 per cent which steadily declined and reached the lowest ever 14.77 per cent during 1989-94. On the other hand, there was more or less a *pari-passu* increase in the exports of manufactured products during the same period. However, in Nepal's imports from the world the share of manufactured products have always remained at a very high level. (Figures 1 & 2).

Figure 1: Nepal's Global Exports Classified by Primary and Manufactured Commodities Groups (SITC 0 to 9): 1974-75 to 2000-01

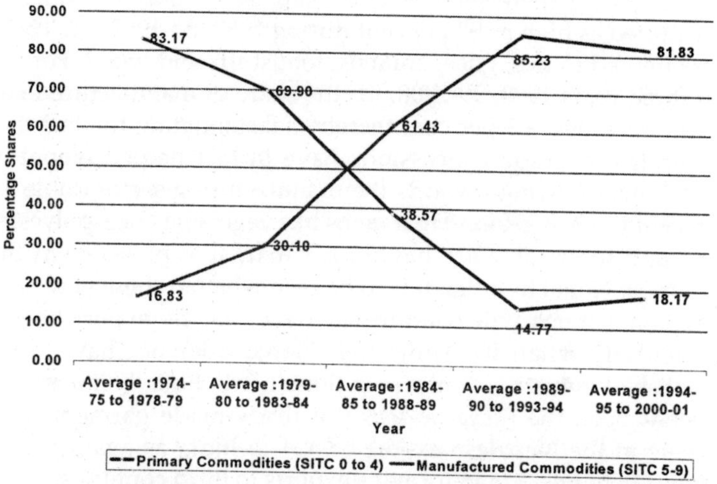

Figure 2: Nepal's Global Imports Classified by Primary and Manufactured Commodities Groups (SITC 0 to 9): 1974-75 to 2000-01

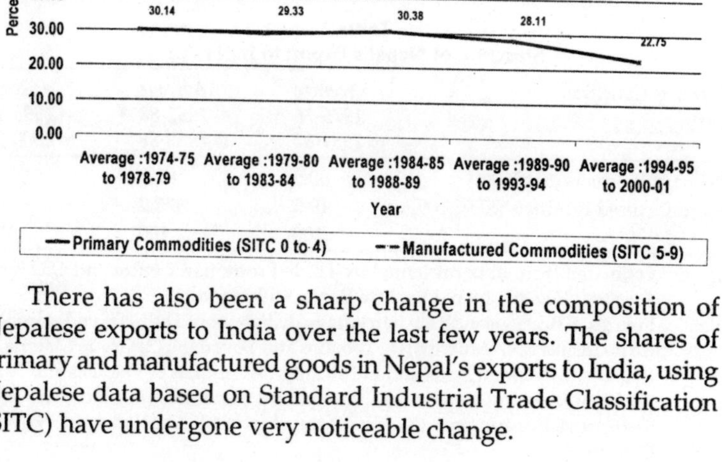

There has also been a sharp change in the composition of Nepalese exports to India over the last few years. The shares of primary and manufactured goods in Nepal's exports to India, using Nepalese data based on Standard Industrial Trade Classification (SITC) have undergone very noticeable change.

For decades together primary products constituted an overwhelming share (SITC 0-4) of Nepalese exports to India. It constituted as high as 93 per cent during 1982/83-1987/88. These were limited to rice, ghee, animals, foodstuffs and wood. For the last three years 1998/99-2000/01, the share of manufactured has in fact been over 63 per cent thereby substantiating the fact that the unilateral trade concessions have in fact helped Nepal in increasingly moving towards the manufacturing sector (table 3). In recent years, it is found that items like vegetable ghee, polyester yarn and toothpaste are having a remarkable presence in the exports of Nepal to India. It is to be seen whether these new non-traditional items will continue to figure in the export basket particularly when we know that Nepal does not have well-established industrial ventures in these items. Equally interesting fact has been the literal absence of ready-made garments and carpets in the Nepalese export basket to India as against their omnipresent position in former's exports to third countries.

However, the strict adherence to the provisions of WTO including the phasing out of multi-fibre arrangement and to the social clauses may bring the Nepalese primary commodities to the forefront again. And if a commodity like tea again enters into the export basket in a much more pronounced manner, it could bring about a semblance of vulnerability in the export performance mainly because of the long prevailing instability in the prices of primary commodities in the international market.

Table 3
Structure of Nepal's Export to India (%)

Products Classified	*Average 1975-76 to 1981-82*	*Average 1982-83 to 1987-88*	*Average 1998-99 to 2000-01*
Primary Products (SITC 0-4)	80.5	92.7	36.42
Manufactured Products (SITC 5-9)	19.5	25.2	63.58
SITC 0-9	100	100	100

Source: Estimated from data presented by Trade Promotion Centre and *Quarterly Economic Bulletin*, Nepal Rashtra Bank, Kathmandu.

Note: Figures in Brackets indicate percentage distribution. The SITC codes imply: (0) Food and Live Animals; (1) Tobacco and Beverage; (2) Crude Materials; Inedible (3) Mineral Fuels and Lubricants; (4) Animals & Veg.Oils and Fats; (5) Chemicals and Drugs; (6) Classified by Materials; (7) Machinery and Transport Equipment; (8) Misc Manufactured Articles; and (9) Not Classified.

This is where Nepal needs to integrate the trading activities with the investment activities from both within and outside. Trade-investment linkage in Nepal is rather critical on very strong grounds like (i) poor industrial base, (ii) very narrow export base and (iii) serious structural weaknesses. One of the reasons attributed to its serious balance of trade deficit problems vis-à-vis a relatively more industrialized member country like India, has been the limited number of exportable items.

The effect of the SAFTA, WTO regimes and other tariff reductions will also vary widely according to the level of industrialization in Nepal. This has been the case in many other countries and regional groupings. For example, in many regional blocs, the countries which have an advanced industrial structure have gained more from the preferences, whereas the industrially less developed countries' share in total intra-community trade and extra regional trade has not under gone any significant change. This has led to some discontent among the latter countries The resulting tendency has been for these countries to impose a number of quantitative restrictions on their imports of industrial products from other member countries (UNCTAD 1996). Therefore, the issues related to FDI will be increasingly very critical. This needs to be looked into as extensively as possible keeping natural resource management, technology, domestic participation, labour market and internal resources and trade composition in mind.

(ii) Anti-Dumping Measures

Nepal will have to introduce legislation on anti-dumping, countervailing duties and other safeguard measures within one year from the date of accession, in order to safeguard Nepali industries against unfair trading practices such as dumping and subsidies by exporting countries. These measures are used in reaction to the alleged dumping of goods in foreign market.[3] Anti-dumping investigations could lead to three different situations viz., definitive measures, termination or price undertaking.

It is quite interesting to note that in the global anti-dumping trends US, the EC, Australia, India and Canada are the largest users of anti-dumping measures. New users have gradually emerged which consist of India, Argentina, Mexico, and Brazil. India has primarily used such measures against the exports from China and the EC. Of the 35 measures imposed against the EC between 1995 and 2002, 22 were from the Indian investigating authority. Similarly Indian goods (anti-biotics, polyethylene terephthalate (PET) film, stainless steel bars and wires and hot rolled steel coils are subjected to vigorous anti-dumping measures in the EC (Krista & Bansali 2003a). Almost 80 per cent of he anti-dumping measures are within 5 sectors viz., base metals (35 %), chemicals (17 per cent), machinery and electrical goods (11%) plastics (9 per cent and textiles (7 per cent) (Krista & Bansali 2003b). Therefore, the level of vulnerability of a country to anti-dumping measures could be indicated by the percentage of its total exports that fall within the five sectors that are most hit by anti-dumping measures. Due to the increasing weight of these exports in their total exports, LDCs and developing countries have become more vulnerable to anti-dumping measures over the 1990s. Philippines, Mexico, Hungary, Malaysia and Thailand are the most vulnerable countries.

Nepal's ongoing tussle with India on certain export items and the subsequent imposition of countervailing duties and quantitative restrictions are also considered to be measures towards the same direction. Though this has been done on the basis of the violation of rules of origin criteria under the free trade agreement between these two countries, the exercise of this measure is vehemently protested. The Government of India has thus imposed quota ceilings on the following manufactured items from Nepal as per the Trade Treaty of 2002. (table 4).

Table 4
Quota Ceilings on Nepalese Manufactured Items

Nepalese Article	*Quantity in Metric tones per year*
Vegetable Ghee (fats)	100,000
Acrylic yarn	10,000
Copper products under Chapters 74 & Heading 85.44 of the HS code	7,500
Zinc oxide	2,500

Further, the certificate of origin has also been made more complex. As against the simple format of the certificate of origin provided under the 1996 Treaty, the latest 2002 Treaty puts certain new features in the certificate of origin to be submitted by the Nepalese Government. For instance, in the new Treaty the name of the producer of the article and location of the factory are also to be mentioned. When the simplification is the bane of liberalization, these provisions would only put the clock back.

(iii) Social Clause

After the prolonged imposition and institutionalized operationalisation of traditional discriminatory rules of trade including tariff and non-tariff barriers, the developed countries gradually shifted to newer areas of trade including that of services. For this they devised and increasingly adopted non-traditional and newer rules of trade game. This is how the social and environmental clauses have come into the trade discourse. Demand to append the social clause to the WTO agreement includes elimination of child labour, amongst other labour standards. This is a non-trade issue. In the past if not direct trade sanctions, a range of restrictive measures have been put on trade on the basis of non-compliances with the core labour standards by developing countries. Examples from the South Asian countries include garments from Bangladesh, hand woven carpets from Nepal and football from Pakistan. This is because they have justified both on pure social grounds and on moral standing of using child labour as a means of production. In India, even tea industry is likely to be subjected to these clauses.

Among the number of triggering factors the developed countries have resorted to such action partly because of the employment crunch in the developed countries where the lower labour standard erode the comparative advantage of the developed countries. Even if the labour standard clauses are aimed at improving the working conditions, living standards and social progress and establishing rules and norms to guarantee basic worker's rights, the elimination process of child labour should definitely consider both the socio-economic conditions and traditional practices. This can be only done away with in the long run by comprehensively helping and supporting the developing countries to consolidate in the development process.

Are the developed countries willing to do this? In fact this was the core content of entire discourse between the North and the South led by G-77, Non-aligned Movement and the UNCTAD in the whole of 1960s to 1980s. The Pearson Commission Report (1969) and Brandt Commission Report (1980) did make substantive recommendations towards this direction. The developed countries paid only lip service to this and kept their ears and eyes closed when it came to the question of implementation of some of this policy recommendation at the global level.

(iv) Movement of Natural Persons

For a country like Nepal, remittances from abroad are very crucial in its balance of payment and foreign exchange management. More than this, the real integration with the world economy of a LDC and landlocked Nepal will only be possible if there are free flow of goods, services, capital and the people to other countries. Therefore, at least the demand in general by the developing countries about Temporary Movement of Natural Persons (TMNP-Mode 4)[4] is vital in the ongoing trade negotiation process (GATS). As of today, the TMNP accounts for less that 2 per cent of global services trade. Reponses by the developed countries to this demand of the developing countries have been marred by a large number of questions and resistance (UNDP 2003). This includes:

(i) Extreme political sensitivity to the very question of TMNP as reflected in various laws and other legal regimes including the immigration provisions.
(ii) Consciously equating the temporary mobility with larger issue of migration both legal and illegal and forced and voluntary.
(iii) Advocacy by some sections about the cost of social commitment, economic burden and displacement of indigenous workers and
(iv) Linking even the limited movement of natural persons under TMNP (mode 4) with the extension of provisions like that of national treatment of the foreign investors in the developing countries.

This is in sharp contrast to the market demand situation since the developed countries where demand for skilled work forces have increased as against the backdrop of fast ageing population. The existing skilled workers in the developed countries cater mostly to the upper echelons of job market thereby leaving a major supply gap in the lower echelons of job market.

The developed countries would like to have restricted or regional arrangements for recruiting specific service providers. They fear that labour mobility under the General Agreement on Trade in Services (GATS) could serve as a tool to establish permanent residence and thus conflict with immigration policies is increasingly used by the developed countries to restrict access to even the skilled and qualified people from the developing countries.

The other side of the story is that despite no commitments under the GATS, the health workers from Asia have been going to the European countries. But Mode 4 of the GATS makes an argument that such commitments would benefit the sending countries by providing a more predictable and transparent framework that is based on non-discrimination. This will encourage the flow. Secondly, this makes the inflow more secure and employers will have both continuity and certainty and could provide better adjustment in the direction towards comparative advantage. The mode 4 could also be used as tool to overcome the bias in favour of highly qualified labour.

(v) Reforms and IPRs

Economic reforms have posed significant challenges to Nepal particularly the people living in the hills and the mountains. Traditionally, the hills and the mountains remain largely far off from the mainstream business centers. But the reforms and globalization process may change the entire existing paradigm in the mountain areas. For instance, in the mountain region, there has been very marginal integration of money, factor, product and labour markets. Pace of integration itself has been very slow and differential. The existing system cannot do much about it whereas the forces of globalisation would like this integration process to be both quicker and substantive. In the newly emerging paradigm, the multinational corporations (MNCs) and other private entrepreneurs are going to the hills and the mountain areas to harness the natural resources, tourism and other hitherto restricted sectors. Their dictum of strategic alliances, and mergers and acquisitions will largely eliminate the traditional small and medium entrepreneurs in the hills and the mountains. The likely impact on mountain areas is in aspects of market, natural resources, land, poverty and the traditional niches.

There are strong possibilities that the patents and intellectual property rights will be monopolized. For example, in the case of medicinal plants which are considered to be prime properties of the mountain areas, the losses could be encountered on four counts i.e., (i) these plants have been over exploited, (ii) there has been severe loss of intellectual property rights, iii) there has been a big loss to the state exchequer as this trade is done informally and iv) traditional communities do not gain anything out of the commercial exploitation. For instance, a major question has been: what do the companies actually offer and provide to the communities who once owned these plants?

This has raised very many questions that emanate from the inclusion of Trade Related Aspects of Intellectual Property Rights (TRIPs) Agreement in the WTO. Nepal will find it very tough to comply with the provisions of the TRIPs both because of the institutional weaknesses and burdensome process of negotiations that actually facilitates the use of 'limited monopolies'. Almost 70 members of WTO were not able to comply with the requirements of TRIPs within the prescribed deadline (December 31, 1999). When Nepal fails to protect the intellectual property right relating to geographical indication and biodiversity, it will lose patenting. "This agreement in its present form is extremely deleterious to the interests of the Nepalese farmers, indigenous communities, consumers, biodiversity and traditional skills, knowledge and technologies. Thus to prevent an open assault of the TRIPs Agreement on Nepal's livelihood, legislation aimed and protecting biodiversity, farmer rights and rights of the indigenous communities need to be enacted and effectively enforced" remarks Ratnakar Adhkari (2001). Though Nepal is said to be preparing new Industrial Property (Protection) Act, which will incorporate all the substantive provisions of the TRIPS agreement, the government needs to move rather fast in the legislative actions and in initiating the process for their documentation and/or registration. As a member of World Intellectual Property Organization (WIPO), Nepal should now try to become a party to Berne and Paris Conventions so as to protect its intellectual property even in foreign countries.

(vi) Agriculture Subsidies

The talks in the last WTO Ministerial meeting in Cancun collapsed mainly on the issues of agriculture subsidies and the inclusion of new issues including investment and competition policy. The new negotiating alliance of 21 mid level developing countries wanted the agriculture subsidies that are inherent in the agriculture policies and products of developed countries to be a key discussion issue

(Margalit 2003). This leads to glut in production and fall in prices of their products in the international market thereby making the prices of agricultural commodities from developing countries uncompetitive. Further, these developed countries do use other protective weapons including duties like "Tariff peaks" and "Tariff escalation" on processed goods like coffee bans, tea bags."

For Nepal it is crucial because it still has over 40 per cent of its GDP and over 80 per cent of the population dependent on agriculture. It's a question of livelihood. Lifting of restriction on the import food produce and allied products under the World Trade Organisation and fixing of import tariff at the minimum level possible will largely affect the farmers and their dependence in both on and off farm activities in Nepal (Lama 2002). If such import openings are not responded to or preceded by a drastic phase out / reduction in the subsidies in the agricultural, dairy and poultry in the developed countries, the farmers in Nepal will be knocked out from whatever comparative edge they have today. Food security experts are more concerned on the imports of both raw and processed imports. A noted Indian Scientist Swaminathan remarked (Swaminathan 2000). "Imports of raw foodgrains, pulses, fish and milk will badly hit farmers, fishermen. The cost of producing food in India, despite low labour costs, is rising steadily. In the West, automation is pushing costs down. We produce 75,000 million tonnes of milk- it forms the livelihood for 80 million women owning just one buffalo and two cows. For the same output, the West deploys 100,000 people. Our fishermen don't own cold storage chains; they have to sell their catch the same day. Processed food imports will ruin micro enterprises.... India should learn to deploy the West's vocabulary more creatively. Under the WTO, any nation can now impose non-tariff barriers on two grounds-environmental securities and livelihood security. We must link food security to livelihood security". So more seriously its a question of livelihood security for the Nepalese farmers. The apprehension that a completely free trade in food grains may be highly disastrous to the question of food security has also gathered momentum.

(vii) MFA Phasing out

The phasing out of the quota premium in the textile and clothing thereby ending the multi-fibre arrangement (MFA) by January 2005 could bring about dislocation in some of vital nerves of the

Nepalese economy. Ready-made garment sector constituting over 42 per cent of Nepal's total exports (table 5) and a major portion of employment is likely to become a vulnerable sector, as main driver of the Nepalese exports in this sector –has been MFA quota for market penetration. An overwhelmingly significant proportion of export of garments of Nepal is directed to quota countries including USA, UK, Germany and France. The textile and garment sectors have not been able to attract much of foreign investment in Nepal.

Table 5
Percentage Share of Readymade Garments in Total Exports

(Rs. Million)

Countries	*1980-81*		*2001-02*	
	Total Export	*%*	*Total Export*	*%*
Nepal	604	2.2	7752	42.1

Source: Economic Sur-vey, 1997-98, Ministry of Finance, His Majesty's Government, Kathmandu; Nepal Overseas Trade Statistics 2001-02, Trade Promotion centre, Kathmandu, 2003.

Though there are views that a de-restricted market may enhance Nepal's market access, a majority of the exporters in Nepal opine that post-MFA situation could be disastrous for Nepal as competition from new entrants such as China and Vietnam and also from the preference-enjoying entrants such as Mexico and the Caribbean countries may be very stiff. But the government does not seem to have any programme in hand at this stage to be prepared to tackle this inevitable crisis. A tentative idea about the likely impact of the MFA phasing out on Nepal is given in the following table 6.

Table 6
Nepal : Post MFA Scenario

Countries	*Current Policies*	*Future Scenario*
Nepal	GSP benefit, Quota free Status to EU	• May lose because of changes in the rules of the origin of GSP.

There are urgent need for the designing and the operationalisation of strategies by Nepal at the domestic level and in collaboration with other exporting countries in South Asia. All these have to cope with other challenges like shortening of lead time, shift in consumer demand from the lower end to the middle of the demand curve, commerce and the imposition of increasing responsibilities on the enterprises by the buyers (Mustafizur 2003).

(viii) Access to Dispute Settlement Board

The WTO as an acceptable court of law not only settles trade disputes but also authorizes sanctions on offenders. However, even to access and make effective use of the dispute settlement board (DSB), a country requires relevant expertise and institutional and financial arrangements. Private sector cannot access DSB and hence this requires a strong partnership between the government and private sector.

(ix) Competition Policy

Competition law and policy per se are an instrument to achieve efficient allocations of resources, technical progress, consumer welfare and to regulate concentration of economic power detriment to competition particularly in the context of constantly changing market conditions. It discourages anti-competitive behaviour and provides freedom of trade, freedom of choice, access to markets and achievement of economic efficiency to maximize consumer welfare. For consumers such policies could lead to lower prices and improved services. Domestic competition law could also put a check on international anti-competitive practices like cartels etc. However, the very designing and successful implementation of such laws would need consistent and strong political will, expertise, efficiency and resources. There is no common understanding, let alone agreement, among countries on what the competition concept and issue means in the WTO context, especially in terms of its 'interaction' with trade and its relationship with development. The whole set of issues relating to competition, competition law and competition policy and their relation to trade and to development is extremely complex.

There are arguments that common theme of three of the issues (investment, competition, government procurement) are advocated to maximize the rights of foreign enterprises to have market access to developing countries through their products and investment. This is further aimed at reducing to a minimum the rights of the host government to regulate foreign investors; and to prohibit government from measures that support or encourage local enterprises. Therefore, there are a lot of skepticisms in the promotion of competition policy and law (brought to the WTO forum by the European Union in Doha in 2001). Developing countries view it as another subtle instrument of freely penetrating in their markets by the TNCs backed by their rich home countries. These TNCs have inherent advantages in terms of their scale and a scope of their operations, and dominations over domestic firms. In many cases they tend to enter into the domestic market via the route of artificially low prices just to capture the market share from the domestic firms. Once they drive the local firms out of the market by literally wiping them out, they tend to raise the prices to achieve a monopolistic position. At the same time in order to prevent the use of this very instrument of predatory pricing, a competition law is required that can regulate the behaviour of such firms (Bhattacharjea 2003).

Any competition policy and the law should therefore have in it consumer welfare as the core intent in them. This also requires adequate resources, creation of a strong independent authority, coordination among the governmental departments and strong drive towards consumer awareness. There are examples that how some of the monopolistic companies have stifled various domestic policies in South Asia. The pesticides residues found in the Pepsi and Coco Cola, higher tea prices maintained by Lever brothers (Brookbond and Lipton) in Pakistan (Lama 2001) and sole distributorship rights given to the Tashi Group of Companies by the Hindustan Lever Limited (HLL) in Bhutan.

Nepal will have to start discourses and sensitization on these issues.

Section 3: What Preparations are Required?

The post-WTO membership opportunities and challenges have to be carefully tackled and utilized. It requires adequate preparation and massive restructuring of the exiting institutions. The national level policies in many cases may not exactly represent intricate matrices of geographical compulsions, socio-cultural practices and economic dimensions that prevail in very many contrasting regions and locations in the country. Nepal has to take cognizance of these matrices also. Nepal's experience in dealing and coping with the multilateral trading regime has just begun. There are various shreds of opinion about the Nepalese government approach to dealing with the WTO regimes.

Since the WTO rules are rather new and many of them are yet to be brought into practice in Nepal, the crying necessity of acquiring requisite expertise, capacity and knowledge on the WTO rules is increasingly felt. Nepal is gradually appreciating the criticality of enhancing the capability of its policy makers, private sector, non-governmental organization and the civil society at large to understand these highly technical rules and accordingly evolve and frame our negotiating position. In other words, the multilateral rules and standards need to be comprehended very thoroughly before Nepal really implements them. Nepal needs to have a fairly advanced level of preparedness in order to take full advantage of the opportunities created by the new trading norms and other reform measures.

It is also essential to build technical capacities for deft management of international negotiation and match this with domestic policies and human, institutional capacities to tackle the challenges of globalization. This requires a much wider and institutionalized consultation by the government with the private sector, non-governmental organization and other segments of the civil society to solicit as diverse and wider views that feed into policy making at domestic and international levels.

At the same time the need to sensitize the international organizations like the WTO towards devising, amending and implementing the norms of international trading that are friendly to the majority of the primary stakeholders will always be one of Nepal's primary activities. This process of sensitization among the international law makers is very complicated, complex and an intricate task. Though Nepalese authorities have shown "openness and inclusiveness" that are pre-requisites in grappling with the newly emerging trends and contexts, it requires substantive and sustainable interventions in the following areas:

(i) Sensitization and awareness generation among the policy makers and across the board stakeholders. This requires a very well designed and protracted sensitization effort in order to render a sense of preparedness among the people concerned. This can be done only by educating the people at large in a much more scientific and practical manner.

(ii) Restructuring of the exiting institutions and creation of new institutions.

(iii) Reorientation and rewriting of a chain of legal framework.

(iv) Building capacity of the implementing agencies and also other stakeholders by creating Center of Excellence on areas of WTO regimes. This has to be done in the line of what UNCTAD is doing in India along with the Ministry of Industry and Commerce.

The WTO Centre of Excellence will support the Government Ministries in particular and the policy makers in general through preparation of various well researched and discussed submissions which will be based on highly technical research. This will also work towards creating and disseminating a huge database to mobilize an informed view and present a persuasive case before the negotiations. This research will be done on region and sector specific issues so that the proposed Centre of Excellence can provide inputs to the government on a continuous basis.

It will: (a) enhance capacity to develop appropriate position in international trade negotiations, (b) encourage and conduct high quality research, (c) increase awareness of trade related impact with improved capacities to advocate constructive policy positions and (d) develop institutional and human capacities.

This process would also help in designing such policy interventions that will incorporate the needs and aspirations of marginalized and poor people and will enable the country's negotiator to put forth their cases and views in a much more convincing and forthright manner. Further, this will also help in removing the fears and suspicions of the people particularly among the rural mass about the globalisation process, the role of WTO and other matters of reforms and liberalisation.

(v) Making a substantive international coalition of the LDCs to get newer and better provisions for making them stand firmly under the WTO system. Nepal should increasingly play an upfront role from among the 49 least developed countries, which constitute 10. 7 per cent of the global population with hardly 0.5 per cent shares in the global gross national product.

The Doha Ministerial level meeting (November 2001) declared that "we commit ourselves to the objective of duty free, quota free market access for products originating from LDCs. Inthis regard, we welcome the significant market access improvements by the WTO members in advance of the Third UN Conference on LDCs (LDC III) in Brussels, May 2001. We further commit ourselves to consider additional measures for progressive improvements in market access for LDCs" (Mehta 2002). This process has to be taken to the logical end.

(vi) Get maximum variety and concentrated doses of technical assistance from the WTO and other international agencies in as many spheres of concerns.

Notes

1. Statement made by the Head of the Nepali delegation and the Minister of Industry and Commerce and Supplies in the accession ceremony of Nepal's entry into WTO in September 2003.
2. WTO Members (as, previously, GATT contracting parties) are bound to notify the RTAs in which they participate. Out of the total of 198 RTAs notified to the GATT/WTO, 119 are presently in force. All notified customs unions and free-trade areas, as well as some of the RTAs in the services area and of the preferential arrangements concluded among developing countries, undergo in-depth review by WTO Members. A Committee on Regional Trade Agreements (CRTA) was set up in 1996 by the WTO General Council to centralise in a single body the effort of the various working parties devoted to examining individual RTAs, and to provide a forum to discuss the systemic implications of RTAs for the multilateral trading system and the relationship between them.
3. An exporting country is said to be dumping when it sells its goods abroad for a price lower than it sells domestically or if it sells these goods abroad at a price lower than its unit cost.
4. Mode 1 : cross border supply of services (mode1)

   Mode 2 : consumption abroad.

   Mode 3 : establishment of a commercial presence.

   Mode 4 : movement of persons providing the service.

References

Adhikari, Ratnakar (2001), "Nepal and WTO: How Prepared We Are", Spotlight, Kathmandu, Vol. 20: No. 39, Apr. 13-Apr. 19.

Bhattacharjea, Aditya (2003), " Trade, Investment and Competition Policy: An Indian Perspective", in Aaditya Mattoo and Robert M. Stern (Ed.), *India and the WTO,* Oxford, 2003 and CUTS, *Putting our Fears on the Table: Analysis of the Proposals on Investment and Competition Agreements at the WTO,* Jaipur.

Blackhurst, Richard & David Henderson (1993), "Regional Integration Agreements, World Integration and the GATT" in Anderson, Kym & Richard Blackhurst, *Regional Integration and the Global Trading System,* St. Martin's Press, New York; Macmillan, John, "Does Regional Integration Foster Open Trade? Economic Theory and GATT's Article XXIV" in Anderson, Kym & Richard Blackhurst, Ibid; Torre, Augusto dela & Margaret R. Kelly, *Regional Trade Arrangements,* International Monetary Fund, Washington DC, March 1992; United Nations, *Handbook of Economic Integration and Cooperation Groupings of Developing Countries,* Vol. I, UNCTAD, Geneva, 1996.

Edelman, Margalit (2003), "Nepal joins the WTO in Cancun but is it worth it?", *The Boss,* Kathmandu, 15 Ocotber-14 November.

Geiger, Till & Dennis Kennedy (Ed., 1993), Regional Trade Blocs, Multilateralism, and the GATT: Complementary Paths to Free Trade, Pinter, A. Cassell Imprint, London, 1996; Anderson, Kym & Richard Blackhurst, Regional Integration and the Global Trading System, New York, St Martin's Press, Lawrence, Robert Z., Regionalism, Multilateralism, and Deeper Integration, The Brookings Institution, Washington DC, 1996 and Regionalism and its Place in the Multilateral Trading System, OECD Documents, Paris, 1996.

Institute of Trade and Development (1993), *Full Convertibility and other recent Economic Measures: Effects on the Nepalese Economy,* Occasional Paper, Kathmandu.

Lama, Mahendra P. (2001), "Integrating the Tea Sector in South Asia: New Opportunities in the Global Market". *South Asian Survey,* Delhi, January-June.

Lama, Mahendra P. (2002), "Globalisation and South Asia: Capturing Primary Concerns and Vulnerabilities", International *Studies,* Sage, April-June, 2001. Also read Joseph Stiglitz, *Globalization and its Discontents,* Penguin Books, New Delhi.

Lucenti, Krista and Sharad Bhansali (2003), "The Use and reform of Anti-dumping Measures" in Winters L Asian and Pradeep S Mehta (eds), *Bridging the Differences: Analysis of Five Issuès of the WTP Agenda,* Cuts, University of Sussex and European Institute for Asian studies, 2003.

Ibid.,

The General Agreement on Trade in Services (GATS) covers four different modes of supply.

Rahman, Mustafizur (2003), "Phase-out of MFA: Concerns and Interest of South Asia", *Liberal Times,* Volume XI, No. 1.

SAARC Chamber of Commerce & Industry (2000), SAARC *Means Business: Opportunities for Partnership,* Federation of Indian Chambers of Commerce and Industry, New Delhi, 2000.

Shepard, Benjamin and Ronald Hayduk, From Act up to the WTO : Urban Protest and Community Building in the Era of Globalisation, Verso, London, 2003.

Swaminathan, M.S. (2000), *Outlook*, Delhi, February 21.

UNCTAD (1996), p. 32.

UNCTAD (2000), The Least Developed Countries 2000 Report, Geneva.

World Trade Organisation Website www.wto.org in Internet.

UNDP (2003), Making Global Trade Work for People, New York.

Mehta, Pradeep S. (2002), *WTO and India: An agenda for Action in Post Doha Scenario*, Consumer Unity & Trust Society (CUTS), Jaipur.

15

Current Status, Challenges and Opportunities of Trade for India Under the WTO and Proposed SAFTA Regimes

D. Krishnamoorthy

Section 1: Introduction

Foreign trade often plays a paramount, if not a benign, role in the economic development of a country. Foreign trade is the treasure house of static and dynamic gains. It provides resources to world beside markets. It is the major source of foreign exchange to many countries. In smaller Non-oil Exporting Countries foreign trade brings 25 to 100 per cent of monetary GNP and in oil exporting Gulf countries, foreign trade accounts for as high as 70 per cent of National Income. Foreign trade provides access to scarce resources needed to promote economic growth viz., raw materials, machinery, capital goods, and intermediary producer goods that are indispensable for economic growth. It is supposed to be an indirect transmitter of capital often through MNCs. It improves the allocative efficiency of nations through international specialization in the production of goods and services. Foreign trade is expected to promote an atmosphere of healthy competition among trading nations by checking Monopolies and Restrictive Trade Practices. It is considered to be the perennial source of technical know-how, managerial talents and entrepreneurial capabilities. Foreign trade widens the horizons of consumption possibility frontiers of countries far in excess of domestic production constraints. The choice of the consumers increases greatly as different varieties of the same good (differentiated products) are available in an open economy. Foreign trade is supposed to bring growth oriented structural changes in the economy by changing the composition of GNP, employment and consumption. Foreign trade is considered to be a better alternative to foreign aid, foreign direct and portfolio investments as the latter are politically vulnerable. Apart from the above benefits accruing to individual countries, world as a whole also benefits from international trade. The world production of every commodity is maximized, through international allocation of resources. More over, there will be greater international equality in real incomes, factor prices and consumption levels and consequently in welfare levels across countries of the world. The relative wage levels would increase in a labour abundant country and fall in a capital abundant country, there by equalising real wages of labour in all the trading nations (Todaro 1993). In view of these reasons, the classical and neo-classical economists considered free trade as the first best policy to promote growth. In fact, Robertson termed trade as an 'Engine of Growth'. According to him, foreign trade accelerates the economic growth of a country by bringing new ideas, new technologies, and new tastes, which in turn stimulate innovation. (Robertson 1949). The unemployed natural resources and unutilized manpower are put to better use. The economic history of present day developed countries like U.K, USA, Germany and Japan clearly shows that an increase in the volume of foreign trade helps the acceleration of economic growth.

This optimistic role of foreign trade in economic development perpetuated until Gunnar Myrdal (1956), Hans Singer and Raul Prebisch (1959) challenged it. These economists argued that foreign trade widened the economic disparities that exist between the rich and the poor countries. According to them, unfavourable effects of unrestricted exports of primary commodities by developing countries far outweighed any gains occurred to these countries through efficient allocation of resources. They contended that low income and price elasticity of demand for primary products altered terms of trade to go against the developing countries. The dissenters of traditional trade theory support a policy of deliberate import substituting industrialization to further the economic development in developing countries. This phase of export pessimism based on the 'Secular Deterioration Thesis' held sway in Development Economics until 1966-67. Since then, there has been a hectic discussion in the literature about the relationship between exports and economic growth and the phase of export optimism began (Attri 1996).

Recognizing the need for free international trade in promoting the national cake of countries, several measures were taken at the global level under the auspicious of General Agreement on Trade and Tariffs (GATT) and its successor World Trade Organisation (WTO). GATT that was established in 1947 successfully completed eight rounds of talks with a view to bringing down tariff and non-tariff barriers and to liberalise the world trade. Over the period of 47 years of its existence of GATT till 1994, it has done yeoman service to widen the coverage of commodities and services as well as countries within its purview. Nevertheless, GATT was not recognized by the Parliaments of countries and its rules were not binding on the countries. Accordingly, at the end of VIII round of Uruguay negotiations, WTO, an institution approved by the Parliaments of countries replaced GATT.

Section 2: Implications of WTO Agreements for India

The WTO came into existence on 1st January 1995 consequent upon the Marrakesh Agreement of 1994. The fundamental aim of WTO is to provide the contracting parties the maximum opportunity for expanding the production and trade in goods and services, and to ensure the optimal use of the world's resources in accordance with the objective of sustainable development. The WTO seeks to enforce fair and rule based trade among the member countries. It provides a forum for implementing various agreements and commitments, and a wide array of policy instruments affecting the trade in goods and services and intellectual property rights. It also provides a unique and advanced mechanism for a fair and objective resolution of trade disputes that arise among the member countries. (Hegde, 2002, p. 48). WTO strictly enforces the most favoured nation (MFN) clause, national treatment principle and prohibition of quantitative restrictions (QRs). All these are necessary to get access to other member countries' markets. WTO seeks to promote better market access opportunities through two methods. The first method is through tarification of non-tariff barriers (NTBs) and reduction of existing levels of tariff protection. The second method is through the implementation of minimum market access rule for imports. Reduction in the levels of subsides and anti-dumping methods also add to the arsenal list of WTO (Damodaran 2002).

The plethora of agreements reached under WTO is not an unmixed blessing to India. These include agreements like phasing out of Multi-fiber Arrangements (MFAs), Agreements on Agriculture, General Agreement on Trade in Services (GATs), Trade Related Intellectual property rights (TRIPS) and Trade Related Investment Measures (TRIMs). The latter three agreements are particularly useful for India to reap national comparative advantage in computer software industries to build and promote indigenous patented software. The TRIPS, however, has great implications for Indian medical and pharmaceutical industries as it requires the extending of product patent to medicinal products in contrast to process patent that the industry used to extend up to now (Sivasankar and Krishnamoorthy, p.185). India needs to pay one million dollars as royalty to US alone when the product patent comes to effect from 2005. The removing of quantitative restrictions (QRs) and minimum market access agreement has, on other hand, greatly affected Indian industries particularly the small-scale industries.

Section 3: WTO and the Regionalism

The WTO aims at global free trade whereas the regional trading blocks like European Union and ASEAN aim at free trade at regional level. The relationship between regionalism and globalisation is an important issue of contemporary interest. Regional trade Agreements can be 'trade creating' or 'trade diverting' as pointed out by Jacob Viner and they can lead to welfare improvement or welfare deterioration. Some observers feel that the proliferation of regional arrangements in recent years undermines the multilateral system while others view that regional trade agreements provide a necessary spur to global liberalisation in the present era. This is because WTO envisages the principle of non-discrimination in trade among the member countries by incorporating the clauses like national treatment and most favoured nation clause. But in reality many countries including the industrialized countries, associate themselves with some regional trade organizations. It is estimated that more than two-fifth of world trade is carried out through the preferential trading organizations. The tariff rates within these blocks are much lower than that envisaged by WTO. (Gautam 2004). EU in the West and ASEAN in the East have been highly successful in fostering cooperation among the member countries. As a result countries outside the block found very difficult to push up their trade relations. The severity of the problem could be understood from the fact that even the American President, George Bush was forced to launch the Enterprise for ASEAN Initiative (EAI) during the APEC summit in 2002. India also seized of the grim situation and signed BIMSTEC (Bangladesh-India-Myanmar-Sri Lanka-Thailand Economic Cooperation) agreement with the objective of initiating joint ventures in sectors of trade, technology, tourism, investment and industry. Recently it also signed the SAFTA among the members of SAARC in January 2004.

Evolution of SAFTA

Realizing the potential benefits of regional cooperation specially in alleviating the poverty, malnutrition and illiteracy in the region, the seven countries of South Asia viz., India, Pakistan, Bangladesh, Nepal, Bhutan, Sri Lanka and Maldives formed the South Asian Regional Cooperation (SARC) in 1983. It was transformed into South Asian Association for Regional Cooperation (SAARC) in 1985. Nevertheless, during the two decades of its existence, the SAARC countries have not set aside their petty political differences, and could not rise above the narrow concepts of nationalism and parochialism. No effort was made to establish and widen their mutual trade relations. It was only at the 12th SAARC summit held in Islamabad on January 4, 2004, that a schedule for framework treaty was reached to float the South Asian Free Trade Association (SAFTA) from the 1st January 2006. Modalities were also framed for developed and the least developed countries of the region to phase out their tariff levels gradually and to integrate their trade with SAFTA. As per the treaty, the tariff levels will be brought down to 20 per cent in non least-developed (LDCs) and to 30 per cent in the least developed SAARC countries. The tariffs will be further brought down to 0.5 per cent in non-LDCs of SAARC in Subsequent five years and in LDCs of SAARC, it will be brought down to that level within the next eight years (Narayan 2004).

Current Status of India's Trade with the SAARC Region

India embarked upon large-scale economic liberalisation particularly on external sector from July 1991. Import trade was liberalised greatly by brining down the tariff levels. Foreign investments were allowed in areas hitherto restricted to domestic sector. Quantitative restrictions were dismantled for over 4000 commodity lines. What are the effects of trade liberalisation on India's exports and imports? Unfortunately, the benefits and costs of trade liberalization are difficult to quantify. There are several methodological and practical problems in estimating such gains. However, the benefits of trade liberalisation undertaken during 1990s are evident in the higher average annual growth rates of exports and imports realised during 1990s as compared to 1980s. A eleven year period on either side of 1991, the year in which large scale liberalization measures were initiated, have been taken for the analysis of the present study. As could be seen from table 1, India's exports in rupee terms have grown on an average by 16.14

Table 1
India's Exports to SAARC Region and World during the Pre and Post-Liberalisation Periods
(Rs. in crores)

Pre-liberalisation Period				*Post-liberalisation Period*			
Years	*India's Exports to SAARC*	*India's total Exports*	*%*	*Years*	*India's Exports to SAARC*	*Indiu's total Exports*	*%*
1980-81	236.26	6711.0	3.52	1991-92	1532	44041.8	3.48
1981-82	200.50	7803.0	2.57	1992-93	2133	53688.3	3.97
1982-83	236.58	8803.0	2.69	1993-94	2817	69751.4	4.04
1983-84	251.72	9771.0	2.58	1994-95	3815	82674.1	4.61
1984-85	354.42	11744.0	3.02	1995-96	5755	106353.3	5.41
1985-86	328.17	10895.0	3.01	1996-97	6041	118817.1	5.08
1986-87	371.25	12452.0	2.98	1997-98	5987	130100.6	4.60
1987-88	406.01	15674.0	2.59	1998-99	7064.6	139753.1	5.06
1988-89	562.45	20232	2.77	1999-00	6043.3	159561.4	3.79
1989-90	696.00	27658.4	2.52	2000-01	8810.4	203571.0	4.33
1990-91	957.00	32557.6	2.93	2001-02	N.A.	209018.0	4.60
CGR %	15.21	16.14	-	*CGR %*	19.24	16.56	-
r^2	0.91	0.94	-	r^2	0.87	0.97	-
t-value	9.44	12.00	-	t-value	7.36	17.74	-

Source: Reserve Bank of India (2001), *Handbook of Statistics on Indian Economy*, Mumbai: RBI., pp. 190-192.

Note: N.A. = Not Available.

per cent during the pre-liberalisation period and there was a marginal surge in the rate of growth of exports at 16.56 per cent during the post-liberalisation period. However, there has been spurt in the growth of exports to SAARC region. India's exports to SAARC region went up by 15.21 per cent during the pre-liberalisation period, whereas that during the post-liberalisation period soared at a higher rate of 19.24 per cent. Thus a momentum towards increased trade relations with the SAARC countries is clearly discernible during the post-liberalisation period. Nevertheless, India's exports to SAARC region have been highly insignificant ranging from 2.57 per cent to 3.52 per cent in various years of the pre-liberalisation period. In view of the constructive efforts taken to boost India's trade with her neighboring countries, the share of India's exports to SAARC region has been gradually increasing in the post-liberalisation period. It touched the all time high level of 5.46 per cent during 1995-96. The volatile nature of the shares of India's exports to SAARC countries clearly indicates that SAARC region is not the dependable destination for India's exports. All the growth rates were statistically significant as could be observed from the high values of 't'. The r^2 values were also more than 0.9 for all the variables during the period under study.

On the import front, the SAARC region presents a still grim picture. India's imports from the SAARC region in rupee terms grew by paltry 6.22 per cent per annum during the pre-liberalisation period of from 1980-81 to 1990-91 (table 2). In contrast to this, India's imports from the world rebounded by 12.40 per cent during the same period. The r^2 and t-values were also very high at 0.94 and 12.05 for the imports from the world as against only 0.34 and 2.16 in the case of the imports from the SAARC region. These clearly indicate that the India's imports from the SAARC region are highly insignificant. In spite of the existence of the advantage of low transport cost, India's imports from the SAARC countries are highly disappointing. During the pre-liberalisation period under study, India's imports from the SAARC region formed highly insignificant proportion ranging from 0.29 per cent to 0.67 per cent of India's total imports. During the post-liberalisation period, the situation seemed to have greatly improved on the import front also. India's imports from the SAARC region increased at a higher rate than that from the world. Again by referring to the table, it is observed that India's imports from the SAARC region skyrocketed by whopping 23.8 per cent as against only by 17.97 per cent from the world. Again due to higher relative growth of India's imports from the SAARC region as compared to that from the world, the proportion of India's imports from the SAARC region in relation to her total imports improved substantially from a low of 0.49 per cent in 1993-94 to a high of 1.1 per cent in 1998-99 and again in 2001-02. The findings of an unpublished thesis on India's foreign trade carried out in the Department (Subba Reddy 2004) clearly indicated that during the post-liberalisation period the shares of India's trade with developing world particularly with the SAARC countries have been growing at a higher rate than that with the European Union and North America even though in absolute terms these regions still account for a lion's share in India's foreign trade. With the formation of SAFTA to be effective from January 2006, new trust and a new impetus are expected to India's trade with individual SAARC countries.

Table 2
India's Import from SAARC Region and World during the Pre and Post-Liberalisation Periods
(Rs. in crores)

Pre-liberalisation Period				*Post-liberalisation Period*			
Years	*India's Imports from SAARC*	*India's total Imports*	*%*	*Years*	*India's Imports from SAARC*	*India's total Imports*	*%*
1980-81	236.26	6711.0	3.52	1991-92	1532	44041.8	3.48
1980-81	60.70	12549.0	0.58	1991-92	326	47850.8	0.68
1981-82	127.56	13671.0	0.89	1992-93	513	63374.5	0.81
1982-83	97.37	14293.0	0.62	1993-94	357	73101.0	0.49
1983-84	102.12	15831.0	0.60	1994-95	555	89970.7	0.62
1984-85	133.22	17134.0	0.67	1995-96	858	122678.1	0.70
1985-86	86.65	19658.0	0.43	1996-97	858	138919.7	0.62
1986-87	105.66	20096.0	0.48	1997-98	871	154176.3	0.56
1987-88	92.72	22244.0	0.39	1998-99	1958.6	178331.8	1.10
1988-89	141.50	28235.2	0.53	1999-00	1723.1	215236.5	0.80
1989-90	103.24	35328.4	0.29	2000-01	2127.9	230872.7	0.92
1990-91	235.81	43192.9	0.54	2001-02	N. A.	245199.0	1.10
CGR %	6.22	12.40	-	CGR %	23.8	17.97	-
r^2	0.34	0.94	-	r^2	0.9	18.06	-
t-value	2.16	12.05	-	t-value	8.9	0.97	-

Source: 1. Reserve Bank of India (2001), *Handbook of Statistics on Indian Economy*, Mumbai: RBI., pp.190-192.

Note: 1. N.A. = Not Available.

India's Exports to Individual SAARC Countries

What are the major trading partners of India within the SAARC region? One would expect that Pakistan would be the obvious answer in view of her stronger economic position relative to other countries in the region. Unfortunately this is not the case for many reasons. Firstly, there are no cordial political and economic relations between India and Pakistan. The relations are characterized by mutual suspicion and occasional tensions culminating in near war like situation between the two countries. Consequently both the countries have to divert and earmark their precious resources from the development activities to defence. Social and economic problems like, poverty, illiteracy, ignorance, malnutrition, lack of infrastructure facilities still continue to be omnipresent in both the countries. It is only for the last six months both countries seemed to have realised the need for fostering the connectivity in all the areas of interest concerning the two countries. The new trend is reflected in the opening up of rail and road transport, airways, civil aviation, relaxation of visa system, sending Indian cricket team to Pakistan and above all in the establishment of SAFTA.

Table 3
Percentage shares of Individual SAARC Countries in India's total Exports to the SAARC Region during the Pre-liberalisation Period

(Rs. in Crores)

Year	*Paki-stan*	*Bangla-desh*	*Nepal*	*Bhutan*	*Sri Lanka*	*Mal-dives*	*Total %*	*Total Exports to SAARC*
1980-81	0.42	31.67	33.01	—	48.68	0.81	100.00	236.26
1981-82	2.46	32.38	38.65	—	32.93	0.98	100.00	200.50
1982-83	3.00	18.54	42.85	—	13.44	0.79	100.00	236.58
1983-84	4.90	24.25	29.89	—	30.76	0.60	100.00	251.72
1984-85	3.65	30.12	30.04	—	7.09	0.61	100.00	354.42
1985-86	4.46	39.23	30.99	—	9.32	0.78	100.00	328.17
1986-87	4.16	44.18	27.70	—	9.69	0.66	100.00	371.25
1987-88	4.71	45.98	23.23	—	25.62	0.73	100.00	406.61
1988-89	6.43	46.28	20.14	—	38.23	1.12	100.00	562.46

Source: Venkatasubbulu (1996), *India's Trade with SAARC Countries*, New Delhi: Discovery Publishing House, pp. 155-157.

During the pre-liberalisation period under study, as could be seen from table 3, in the year 1980-81, out of the total exports of Rs.

236.23 crores to the SAARC region, Sri Lanka accounted for about 49 per cent, Nepal about 33.01 per cent and Bangladesh about 31.67 per cent. The share of Pakistan in India's total exports to the region was paltry 0.42 per cent. Over the pre-liberalisation period, the share of India's exports to Pakistan has risen to 6.43 per cent and that to Bangladesh to 46.28 per cent in the year 1988-89. Correspondingly, the shares of Nepal and Sri Lanka in India's total exports to the region fell to 20.14 per cent and 38.23 per cent respectively in the same year.

In the post-liberalisation period, (table 4), Bangladesh and Sri Lanka emerged as the dominant trade partners of India within the SAARC region. Particularly, Bangladesh's relative position at times touched the peak level of 62.18 per cent in 1994-95. This might be due to the formation of free trade agreement BIMSTEC with Bangladesh and Sri Lanka along with other South and South East Asian Counties. Pakistan, Maldives and Bhutan also improved their relative shares in India's total exports to the region.

Table 4
Percentage shares of Individual SAARC Countries in India's total Exports to the SAARC Region during the Post-liberalisation Period

(Million US $)

Year	*Paki-stan*	*Bangla-desh*	*Nepal*	*Bhutan*	*Sri Lanka*	*Mal-dives*	*Total %*	*Total Exports to SAARC*
1990-91	6.42	52.17	12.36	0.16	28.09	0.80	100.00	623
1991-92	7.23	49.10	10.15	0.28	32.13	1.11	100.00	719
1992-93	7.06	52.38	9.14	0.61	30.09	0.73	100.00	821
1993-94	5.77	50.98	8.32	0.68	32.68	1.57	100.00	1022
1994-95	4.53	62.18	6.93	0.78	24.81	0.78	100.00	1544
1995-96	8.54	50.45	9.55	0.61	27.78	3.07	100.00	1650.3
1996-97	12.69	44.19	10.06	0.59	32.02	0.46	100.00	1463.3
1997-98	6.74	51.16	15.94	0.58	24.06	1.52	100.00	2029.5
1998-99	6.39	48.77	17.92	0.66	24.37	1.89	100.00	1908.3
1999-00	8.15	42.57	19.48	0.71	27.03	2.06	100.00	2018.8
2000-01	9.34	46.31	18.44	0.68	23.30	1.95	100.00	2347

Source: 1. Reserve Bank of India (2001), *Handbook of Statistics on Indian Economy*, Mumbai, pp.190-192.
2. United Nations Organisation, Foreign Trade Statistics of Asia and Pacific. (Various Issues) for data in Dollars.

Note: 1. N.A. = Not Available.

India's Imports from Individual SAARC Countries

With regard to import trade, as noted already, India's imports from the SAARC region was very low ranging from Rs. 60.7 crores to 141.5 crores during the various years of the pre-liberalisation period. In the total imports from the SAARC region, Nepal and Sri Lanka accounted for a lion's share. Only in the later years of the pre-liberalisation period, India's imports from Pakistan have been growing in relative terms to reach the all time high level of 36.61 per cent in 1988-89 (table 5). Sri Lanka continued to be the India's major import trade partner during this period.

Table 5
Percentage shares of Individual SAARC Countries in India's total Imports from the SAARC Region during the Pre-liberalisation Period

(Rs. in Crores)

Year	*Paki-stan*	*Bangla-desh*	*Nepal*	*Bhutan*	*Sri Lanka*	*Mal-dives*	*Total %*	*Total Imports to SAARC*
1980-81	7.52	4.89	38.90	—	48.68	0.01	100.00	60.70
1981-82	19.13	7.95	39.99	—	32.93	0.01	100.00	127.56
1982-83	19.03	5.86	41.66	—	13.44	0.01	100.00	97.37
1983-84	27.47	6.04	35.72	—	30.76	0.01	100.00	102.12
1984-85	11.84	34.16	46.85	—	7.09	0.06	100.00	133.22
1985-86	30.69	4.91	55.04	—	9.32	0.04	100.00	86.65
1986-87	17.95	15.58	56.76	—	9.69	0.02	100.00	105.66
1987-88	20.94	13.32	40.11	—	25.62	0.01	100.00	92.72
1988-89	36.61	6.83	18.33	—	38.23	—	100.00	141.50
1989-90	—	—	—	—	—	—	100.00	—

Source: Venkatasubbulu (1996), India's Trade With SAARC Countries, New Delhi: Discovery Publishing House, pp.155-157.

During the post-liberalisation period (table 6), there were wide fluctuations in India's imports from the SAARC region varying from a low of $95 million to a high of 483.7 million. The share of Pakistan reached the peak level of 75.26 per cent in the year 1991-92 and then plummeted steeply to reach the floor level of 11.48 per cent in 1996-97. Correspondingly, Nepal and Bangladesh could improve their share in India's imports from the region.

Table 6
Percentage shares of Individual SAARC Countries in India's total Imports from the SAARC Region during the Post-liberalisation Period

(Million US $)

Year	*Paki-stan*	*Bangla-desh*	*Nepal*	*Bhutan*	*Sri Lanka*	*Mal-dives*	*Total %*	*Total Imports to SAARC*
1990-91	61.05	6.32	20.00	0.01	12.63	0.00	100.00	95
1991-92	75.26	5.15	11.86	0.52	7.22	0.00	100.00	194
1992-93	47.47	13.13	19.19	3.03	17.17	0.00	100.00	99
1993-94	36.43	26.36	10.85	2.33	24.03	0.00	100.00	129
1994-95	18.78	39.59	13.71	8.12	19.80	0.00	100.00	197
1995-96	19.55	29.38	25.03	8.36	17.68	0.00	100.00	197.4
1996-97	11.48	21.12	38.66	5.85	22.90	0.00	100.00	184.7
1997-98	44.88	13.40	30.43	3.08	8.21	0.00	100.00	483.7
1998-99	25.55	14.54	41.50	4.19	14.22	0.00	100.00	374.9
1999-00	17.13	14.45	46.93	4.75	16.74	0.00	100.00	381.2
2000-01	16.69	15.33	45.27	4.56	18.15	0.00	100.00	436.3

Source: Computed for the data obtained from Reserve Bank of India (2001), *Handbook of Statistics on Indian Economy,* Mumbai, pp.190-192.

Section 4: Trade Intensity Indices

In order to understand the bilateral trade orientation of India's trade with each of the SAARC countries, an attempt was made to compute and use the Trade Intensity Indices for both exports and Imports. J. Brown developed the trade intensity indices and K. Kojima further refined it. The Export Intensity Index of ith county with the jth country (x_{ij}) is defined as

$$x_{ij} = \frac{X_{ij} / X_i}{M_j / M_w - M_{-I}} \times 100$$

Where X_{ij} = Exports of ith country to partner county j.

X_i = Total exports of county i.

M_j = Total imports of country j

M_w = Total World imports

M_{-I} = Total imports of country i.

Similarly, the Import Intensity Index of ith county with the jth country (M_{ij}) is defined as

$$x_{ij} = \frac{M_{ij} / M_i}{X_j / X_w - X_{-I}} \times 100$$

Where M_j = Imports of ith country to partner county j.

M_i = Total imports of ith country to county i.

X_j = Total exports of country j

X_w = Total World imports

X_{-I} = Total exports of country i.

The minimum value of the index is 0 and the ideal value is 100. The value zero implies that there is no trade relationship between the two countries. An export intensity index of more (or less) than 100 indicates that country is exporting more (or less) to the ith country than might be expected from that country's share in total world trade. The same argument holds true in the case of import intensity index. Export intensity indices were calculated for India's trade with each of the SAARC countries for the post liberalization period and that for the pre-liberalization period were taken from a study made by T. Venkatasubbulu. The data published in Direction of Trade Statistics (DOTS) by IMF are taken for the computation of export and import intensity indices.

India's export intensity indices for each of the SAARC country were very low (less than 100 except for Nepal in the year 1981) during the pre-liberalization period (table 7) under the consideration. India's export intensity indices to Pakistan varied between a low of 15.79 and a high of 84.03 during the pre-liberalization period indicating that Pakistan was exporting to less to India as compared to her share in World trade. A similar fluctuating trend could also be observed from India's exports to Nepal, Bangladesh and Sri Lanka. The export intensity indices of India vis a vis Bangladesh and Nepal were very low when compared to that of Pakistan and Nepal during the pre-liberalization period.

However, during the post-liberalization period (table 8), the situation has dramatically changed particularly in the case of Bangladesh and Sri Lanka, which had very low export intensity ratios earlier. India now has very high export intensity ratios with these countries. Except for Pakistan, the export intensity indices were more than one thousand implying that Indian's export intensity with each of these SAARC countries improved dramatically during the post-liberalization period.

Table 7
Intensity Indices of India's Export Trade with Various SAARC Countries during the Pre-liberalisation Period

(Values in terms of %)

Year	*Pakistan*	*Bangladesh*	*Nepal*	*Sri Lanka*
1980	15.79	9.20	98.42	11.28
1981	17.36	5.13	102.72	9.46
1982	18.55	2.94	54.38	6.78
1983	31.45	2.59	51.50	10.21
1984	57.25	3.51	56.34	9.40
1985	84.03	4.27	53.57	6.79
1986	66.34	3.94	55.50	7.61
1987	48.59	4.78	39.33	6.79
1988	70.51	4.83	52.36	6.51
1989		5.67	54.91	11.40

Source: Venkatasubbulu, T. (1996), India's Trade With SAARC Countries, New Delhi: Discovery Publishing House, p. 165.

Table 8
Intensity Indices of India's Export Trade with Various SAARC Countries During the Post-liberalisation Period

(Values in terms of %)

Year	*Pakistan*	*Bangladesh*	*Nepal*	*Bhutan*	*Sri Lanka*	*Maldives*
1991	88.89	2051.51	3368.09	NA	1216.83	557.83
1992	123.56	2209.62	3636.63	NA	1507.95	966.28
1993	121.40	2638.33	3165.61	NA	1459.80	604.77
1994	123.75	2544.03	2931.36	NA	1553.03	1209.60
1995	122.01	3063.50	3059.49	2080.17	1511.36	763.87
1996	206.39	2377.40	4553.03	1331.28	1750.95	2337.14
1997	217.95	1349.64	2779.75	802.54	1115.79	250.46
1998	230.89	2304.23	4922.43	1281.92	1317.80	1303.84
1999	206.50	2247.37	5257.36	1104.36	1327.64	1201.80
2000	236.95	1752.73	4443.70	1203.97	1166.51	1432.47
2001	276.85	1814.80	4118.97	1238.59	1294.03	1610.04

Source: Computed for the data obtained from

1. IMF, Direction of Trade Statistics Yearbooks, and 1997 and 2001, p.4.
2. Reserve Bank of India (2001), Handbook of Statistics on Indian Economy, Mumbai, pp.190-192.

A similar but less pronounced increase was observed in the case of India's import intensity indices with the SAARC countries between the pre and post-liberalization period. It could be observed that during the pre-liberalization period the import intensity indices were less than 10 for Pakistan, Bangladesh and Sri Lanka but the same varied between 30 and 60 in the case of Nepal that had relatively more imports from India (table 9). During the post-liberalization period the index soared to more than one thousand in the case of Nepal and a definite rising trend could be discernible in the case of imports from other SAARC countries (table 10). For example, in the case of India's import intensity from Sri Lanka, the index varied between a low of 106 to a high of 230 between the beginning and end of the post-liberalisation period. Similarly, in the case of Bangladesh, the index varied between 61 and 382 during the period under study. These data are clearly indicative of the fact that India's import intensity from the SAARC countries is much lower than that of its export intensity as the raw data revealed.

Table 9
Intensity Indices of India's Import Trade with Various SAARC Countries During the Pre-liberalisation Period

(Values in terms of %)

Year	*Pakistan*	*Bangladesh*	*Nepal*	*Sri Lanka*
1980	3.66	0.64	41.86	3.88
1981	3.36	2.22	59.69	6.88
1982	2.26	2.92	60.83	2.03
1983	1.05	1.16	52.24	3.08
1984	1.09	3.32	49.10	0.97
1985	1.51	3.32	33.46	0.56
1986	0.70	0.93	33.93	1.16
1987	0.65	1.25	35.83	0.83
1988	1.34	0.85	29.82	1.56
1989	2.23	1.59	30.43	4.72

Source: Venkatasubbulu (1996), India's Trade With SAARC Countries, New Delhi: Discovery Publishing House, p. 67.

Section 5: Opportunities and Challenges for India

There are many commodities and commodity groups that India is exporting to the rest of the world. SAARC countries import many of these commodities from the rest of the world. If appropriate measures are taken to identify these commodities and divert the import trade of SAARC countries in these commodities from the rest of the world towards India, India and SAARC countries can richly benefit from the new trade creation. India would find new markets in her vicinity and SAARC countries also benefit from

Table 10
Intensity Indices of India's Import Trade with Various SAARC Countries During the Post-liberalisation Period

(Values in terms of %)

Year	*Pakistan*	*Bangladesh*	*Nepal*	*Bhutan*	*Sri Lanka*	*Maldives*
1991	132.24	60.88	1333.26	NA	106.01	NA
1992	410.23	87.92	1278.33	NA	119.97	NA
1993	126.85	98.83	955.18	NA	125.52	NA
1994	121.08	205.21	704.68	NA	183.04	NA
1995	76.74	381.16	1472.48	NA	202.83	NA
1996	60.65	233.99	2193.31	NA	149.75	NA
1997	35.75	103.87	2103.27	NA	125.04	NA
1998	332.89	185.25	4277.14	NA	125.09	NA
1999	153.12	170.49	4491.88	NA	188.32	NA
2000	87.95	128.90	3734.22	NA	167.95	NA
2001	90.49	189.20	3767.77	NA	230.54	NA

Source: Computed for the data obtained from

1. IMF, *Direction of Trade Statistics Yearbooks-* 1997 and 2001, p. 4.
2. Reserve Bank of India (2001), *Handbook of Statistics on Indian Economy*, Mumbai, pp. 90-192.

lower transport charges. Similarly, there are many commodities that India is currently importing from the rest of the world and SAARC countries are also exporting the same to the rest of the world. These commodities should be identified and India should divert her imports from the rest of the world to SAARC countries so that India can benefit from lower transport charges and lower risks. SAARC countries would also find profitable markets for her exports in their vicinity. This will be more profitable under the proposed SAFTA where the tariffs and other non-tariff barriers would be completely abolished and there will be free trade in commodities. Venkata Subbulu made such an exercise in her study at SITC-3 level and she identified many potential export commodities that India can export to SAARC Countries. In SITC–0 group, the potential export commodities include wheat to Pakistan, Bangladesh and Sri Lanka, oil seeds, nuts, kernels to Bangladesh, Pakistan and Nepal, vegetables fresh and processed to Sri Lanka, sugar and honey to Bangladesh and Sri Lanka and tea and mate to Pakistan. Similarly, from SITC-3 group, the potential export items from India to Bangladesh and Sri Lanka are identified to be petroleum products, from SITC-4 group, fixed vegetable oil, from SITC-5 group, organic and inorganic chemicals to Bangladesh and Pakistan. Other potential items of India's exports to SAARC countries will be essential oil perfumes, woven textile products, iron steel pipes and tubes, agricultural machinery, office machines, electrical power machinery and switch gears, domestic electrical appliances, railway wagons and engines, and other manufactured goods (Venkatasubbulu).

The potential items of India's imports from the SAARC countries include, fish fresh and preserved particularly from Bangladesh, vegetables and spices from Nepal, rubber and synthetic from Sri Lanka, textile yarn and thread from Bangladesh and Pakistan, pearls, precious and semi-precious stones from Sri Lanka and clothing not of fur and other manufactured goods from Pakistan. Several subsequent studies also identified many potential items of India's exports to and imports from the SAARC region. Based on SITC-3 digit level data obtained from International Trade Statistics Year Book 1995 published by IMF, (Shobha 2001) computed Index of Trade Advantage in Bilateral Trade between India and SAARC-ASEAN countries. An index of value greater than 0.4 indicates a higher degree of complementarity and vice versa. The study revealed that except Pakistan and Sri Lanka in the case of manufactured goods classified by material, no other SAARC country had an index value of more than 0.4 in any of the 10 commodity groups that were studied. Indo-Pak trade comprises a mere 8 per cent of actively tradable items followed by Bangladesh (4 per cent) and Sri Lanka (3 per cent) Shobha. In view of these low index values, she concluded that the scope for furthering Indo-SAARC trade is very less and hence India has to concentrate on the more developed countries in the ASEAN region. However, the SAFTA agreement has given a ray of New Hope and optimism to the business community in the region and their expectation are very high now. (Sharma 2004). India has emerged as an important player in the global information technology industry. Indian Software industry has been growing at an average annual growth rate of 50-60 per cent since 1991. It has provided about 4 lakh direct jobs and it is expected to touch the level of 22 lakhs by 2008. A recent study revealed that United States continues to absorb the largest chunk of India's software exports followed by Europe. ((Asheref Illiyam 2001). In view of importance of IT sector in today's information technology world for the every SAARC country, India can direct her software exports to these countries. In the context of proposed SAFTA and globalisation being pushed forwarded by the international institutions particularly the WTO, Swamy suggested that India can profitably export cereals, processed fruits and vegetables, dairy products, cut flowers, eggs, broiler chicken, processed fish and prawn in a big way (Swamy 2002). When the agricultural exports to the region pick up momentum, the farmers need not depend on the government for water, electricity, and fertilizer subsidy or for fixing domestic support prices for their production of rice, wheat, sugarcane etc. The increased export earnings can be ploughed back in the provision of infrastructure facilities in agriculture so that the productivity of agricultural sector can be increased on par with that achieved in other developed countries. Similarly, market promoting infrastructure facilities such as Internet connections, fax machines, marker information centers abroad, cold storage facilities, low cost air flight services have to be established. The phasing out of multi-fiber arrangement may result in the surge of textile exports not only to the developed countries but also to SAFTA countries. This again requires the immediate modernization of our textile industry within next one or two years when the quota system will be phased out. Other potential items of exports from India include auto components, transport equipment, leather manufactures, electronic and communication equipment, metal and metal products, plastic products, metallurgy, chemicals, rubber products, processed foods, pharmaceuticals, etc (Gautam 2004) Another potential area of trade is tourism and tourism related activities. All these will generate huge employment opportunities for the youth, who are now distracted towards anti-social activities like theft, cheating, terrorism etc. There is a high degree of concentration in India's exports to and imports from SAARC countries. Particularly the import items have concentrated on the top 10 or 20 items. Hence efforts are to be made to diversify the export as well as the import baskets of India with regard tot the proposed SAFTA countries.

Role of India in Regional Investments and Joint Ventures

If SAARC is to progress towards stronger economic integration, there is every need to broaden its frame work of activities identified in the Integrated Programme of Action (IPA) to include investment, industry and finance within its purview. Long back the member countries have shown interest to bring about the core areas within the sphere of activities. Bangladesh suggested the setting ûp of a multi-sectoral investment institution. At Katmandu Summit, held in 1987, a close attention was paid to this concept suggested by Bangladesh. A decision was taken to identify regional projects that could exploit the existing regional complementarities in skilled manpower and financial resources as well as technology. The Secretary General of SAARC commissioned studies to explore the possibilities of joint ventures in agriculture, industry and energy, and to analyze the benefits from the expansion of intra-regional trade including the transit problems of the land-locked countries.

Even prior to the establishment of SAARC, Investment cooperation among the South Asian nations had been taking place on a bilateral basis. According to the Indian Investment Center, New Delhi, Indian enterprises had set up 186 joint ventures (JVs) in 37 countries by March 1987. Out of them, 152 were already in operation and 34 were in different stages of implementation. The countries in the SAARC region had hosted 29 joint ventures of which 23 were in operation and 6 were in implementation. These bilaterally agreed joint ventures were concentrated in the two SAARC countries only viz., Sri Lanka (16 JVs) and Nepal (12 JVs). The one joint venture on Sponge iron project was hosted by Bangladesh. However, in order to have mutually beneficial economic cooperation among the SAARC countries in the long run, the investment cooperation ought to be conceived within the framework of regional investment plan. Since South Asia now possesses a formal identity as a regional group with necessary institutional framework, the creation of infrastructure needed for an effective programme of investment cooperation would not pose serious problems. Assuming that the needed infrastructure is provided, the following areas of investment cooperation in industry and service sectors could be established (Schokman 1990).

(i) Joint ventures in resource base industries such as rubber paper, cement, fertilizers, and agro-based industries such as forest products, processed food, fruits and vegetables;

(ii) Joint ventures in intermediary goods like chemicals, petrochemicals, transport equipment and components, agricultural machinery and hand tools.

(iii) Consume goods like textiles and garments, consumer electronics etc.;

(iv) Power generation and distribution;

(v) Shipping services linking major ports in south Asia;

(vi) Telecommunication and Railways;

(vii) Banking and Insurance.

In the light of vast accumulated experience of Indian enterprise in setting up and managing successfully a wide range of industrial projects, the study undertaken by RIS suggested the following categories of units to be established in the SAARC region with the Indian Assistance (Wadhwa 1987) These include:

(i) Local market oriented units such as food processing units agro-based units, textile and leather, metal and metal products, transport equipment, electrical equipment, electronic and communication equipment, chemical and mineral based industries;

(ii) Export oriented ventures such as garment industry, sericulture, Fishing and Deep-sea fishing, coffee and gems;

(iii) Regional market oriented units such as news print, wood pulp, gas based fertilizer units, phosphoric fertilizers and rubber products.

The ICRIER study suggested the establishment of joint ventures between India and Bangladesh for the production of spare parts for the jute and textile mills in Bangladesh and between India and Sri Lanka for the production of automobile parts and coir based units.

The Investment cooperation among the SAARC countries should be viewed in a long-term perspective. A holistic and integrated approach needs to be adopted to over come the institutional and physical constraints that impede the process of investment cooperation among the SAARC countries. In order to encourage the setting up of JVs in identified products, member countries should further relax the policy measures to attract investments for such ventures. Appropriate networking of existing financial institutions of the member countries needs to be encouraged and the facilities for the identification and funding of regional projects should be strengthened. India as a major power in the region should assume a proactive role in the promotion of regional investments and intra-regional trade in the SAARC region.

It is argued that the economic cooperation among the SAARC countries should be further strengthened to move towards common market for the factors of production including labour, capital and entrepreneurship. There should be free movement of people from one country to others in the region. Not all the countries in the SAARC region suffer from the problems of high density of population, mass unemployment and rampant poverty. While Nepal and Bhutan have low density of population, Bangladesh, Pakistan and India have very high density of population and high incidence of poverty and unemployment. Sri Lanka is relatively better in the case of poverty, health and human development. The level of techno economic development is also not uniform in all the SAARC countries. While India and Pakistan are relatively advanced countries, others are backward in science and technology. Under such circumstances, the question of freer mobility of people across the SAARC region has to be examined carefully and its pros and cons should be weighed thoroughly.

India, the Natural Leader of the Region

Given the large size and clout in SAARC region, India has to play a major and diplomatic role in fostering the economic cooperation among the countries of the SAARC region. India's economic advances in recent years make its supremacy in the region inevitable. It would be realistic for the countries in India's neighborhood, to rely on India's economic strength for their own progress rather than seeking help from outside. But the countries of the SAARC region often do not take kindly to the economic supremacy of India over the rest and would rather seek assistance from western advanced countries. This has been the major reason for the tardy progress made by SAARC in promotion economic cooperation among the member countries. India in turn should also realize its responsibility as a benevolent big brother in the region. India would also benefit richly from its participation in the regional economic cooperation in SAARC since it would be able to avail of the markets of other SAARC countries in its vicinity. India can play a major roe in the region in eradicating poverty and under development and also to fight against the evil designs on the region by the powers outside the region. United States, in particular, attempts to destroy the smooth and gradually improving relations between India and Pakistan by designating the latter as "US's major non-NATO alloy". All the countries in the region should collectively fight out the divide and rule policies of the super power. India, with the help of other countries in the region has to take this to appropriate international forums and fight it out tooth and nail. The potential for economic cooperation among the SAARC countries is very high. The momentum, as noted in the analysis of trade flows in the post-liberalization period, has already started and this needs to sustained and strengthened. SAARC by building appropriate structures and establishing the necessary institutional infrastructure will hopefully strengthen this momentum. The peace and development in the region will provide invaluable contribution towards promoting global peace and development. India has to play a decisive role in all these activities.

Section 6: Concluding Remarks

The process of liberalisation and globalisation is unstoppable or irreversible. There will be further integration of markets for commodities, services and financial assets. The regional groupings like EU, ASEAN and SAFTA will become the building blocks towards building a global architecture. They are bound to play a catalytic role in the process of globalisation and hence they cannot be isolated from the process of globalisation. SAFTA particularly India will have to play a major role in the global economy in the next 10 to 20 years to come. Regional level connectivity in South Asia is sine quo non-for world-class connectivity. However, there are many daunting challenges on us. First, the current momentum of improved bilateral relations between India and Pakistan, the two major players in the region, is to be maintained. The easing of tensions between India will save enormous amount of resources that are currently diverted to defence budgets in both countries, which can profitably be diverted to provide the massive economic infrastructure facilities that are badly needed in both the countries and to alleviate the poverty and illiteracy. Secondly, the political and economic insecurity concerns of the small and the least developed countries of the region will have to be addressed in a right manner by both India and Pakistan. There is a need to announce further unilateral Tariff reductions by India and Pakistan on imports originating from the least developed countries of the SAARC region. Thirdly, in India, transport, communication, and other infrastructure facilities on the border areas need to be further improved to increase the connectivity between the neighboring countries and to handle the expected amount of voluminous trade among the members of the region. India needs to identify potentially tradable commodities among the SAFTA countries and provide required boost to these commodities. The signing of the SAFTA is indeed a great leap forward for the South Asian countries and the expectations generated among the business community must be transformed in to the reality by taking appropriate measurers at all the levels. This is indeed the testing time for the members of the SAARC to set aside their petty political differences, rise above the narrow concepts of nationalism and parochialism and collectively work for the development of the SAARC region to fight out poverty, unemployment, illiteracy, ignorance and abysmally low levels of human development in the region. We hope that the new Congress led Progressive Democratic Alliance government in India with its experienced foreign minister; Mr. Natwar Singh would continue the unfinished tasks of his predecessor.

References

1. Asheref Illiyan (2001), 'Software Export: An Analysis of Indian Potential, Performance and Problems', *Foreign Trade Review,* Vol. XXXV, No. 1&2, April-September, pp.18-33.
2. Attri, V.N. (1996), 'Export-led Growth in Developing Countries-1960-1980', *The Indian Economic Journal,* Vol. 43, No. 3, Jan.-March, p. 19.
3. Bawa, R. S. (2001-02), 'Challenges and Opportunities of Globalization-Implications for India', *The Indian Economic Journal,* Jan.-March, Vol. 49, No. 3., pp.1-8.
4. Chennaiah, M. (1997), India's Foreign Trade a Study of its Growth and Instability, (unpublished M. Phil. Thesis), Kavali: Department of Economics, S.V. University Post-graduate Centre.
5. Damodaran, A. (2002), 'TRQ and the WTO: Policy Options for India', *Foreign Trade Review,* Vol. XXXV, No. 1&2, April-September, pp.53-68.
6. Gautam Purkayastha (2004),'Regional Cooperation among China, India, Myanmar and Bangladesh', *Yojana,* Feb.2004, pp. 19-21.
7. Ishwar V. Hedge (2002), 'WTO and Indian Software Industry: Some Strategic Options', *Foreign Trade Review,* Vol. XXXV, No. 1 & 2, April-September, pp. 53-68.
8. Kojima, K. (1964), 'The Pattern of International Trade among the Developed Countries', *Hitosubashi Journal of Economics,* Vol. 5. No. 1. June.

9. Myrdal, G. (1956), *'An International Economy'*, London: Harber and Brothers.
10. Narayan, V. Mohan (2004), 'Breakthrough at SAARC Summit", *Yojana*, Feb. 2004, pp. 7-10.
11. Prebisch, R. (1959), 'Commercial Policies in the Under developed Countries', American *Economic Review, Papers and proceedings*, Vol., 49, No. 2, May, p. 251. F.F.Singer, H.W. (1950), 'The Distribution of Gains Between Investing and Borrowing Countries', *American Economic Review*, Vol. 40, May, p. 439.
12. Robertson. D. H. (1949), 'The Future of International Trade', *Readings in the Theory of International Trade*, Blankiston: AEA & Co., p. 507.
13. Sharma, G.K. (2004), 'Regional Economic Cooperation: Signing of SAFTA' *Yojana*, Feb. 2004, pp. 11-12.
14. Shobha Ahuja (2001), 'Potential for Augmenting Trade and Commercial Ties between India and SAARC-ASEAN Region', *Foreign Trade Review*, Vol. XXXV, No. 1 & 2, April-September, pp. 53-68.
15. Sivasankar, P.R. and D. Krishnamoorthy (1994), 'Implications of TRIPS for Indian Industry and Agriculture', in G.S. Batra and Narinder Kaur (eds.), *GATT: Implications of Dunkel Proposals*, New Delhi: Anmol Publications Pvt. Ltd.
16. Subba Reddy, V. V. (2004), "Growth and Instability of India's Foreign Trade: A Study of Pre- and Post-liberalisation Periods", (unpublished Ph. D. Thesis), Kavali: Department of Economics, S.V. University Post-Graduate Centre.
17. Subramanian Swamy (2001-02), 'WTO Challenges and Opportunities', *The Indian Economic Journal, Jan.-March*, Vol. 49, No. 3, pp. 1-8.
18. Todaro, Michael P. (1993), *'Economic Development in the Third World'*, Hyderabad: Orient Longman, p. 365.
19. Venkatasubbulu, T. (1996), *India's Trade with SAARC Countries*, New Delhi: Discovery Publishing House.
20. Schokman,Y. (1990), 'Prospects for Investment Cooperation in South Asia', *South Asia Journal*, Vol. 3, No. 4, April-June, pp. 360-367.
21. Panchamukhi, V.R. et al. (1990), *Economic Cooperation in the SAARC Region" Political Constraints and Policies*, New Delhi: Interest Publications, pp. 172-184.
22. Wadhwa (1987), *Regional Economic Cooperation in Asia*, ICRIER, New Delhi.

16

The Impact of the WTO on South Asia

Hailay Gebretinsae Beyene

Section 1: Introduction

During the last two decades major changes occurred in global markets that have important implications for South Asian countries exports and growth prospects. During these times, South Asian countries have undergone substantial reforms, which have involved trade liberalization to enhance their integration with the world trading system. The Uruguay Round that led to the establishment of WTO (World Trade Organization) attempted to alter the conditions under which international trade is conducted. Among the Round's major concerns were the reduction of tariff and non tariff barriers to trade with the aim of promoting free-trade in the world that leads to eradication of world poverty, and ensuring growth, development and prosperity.

The major issues of the WTO undoubtedly have significant impact on the welfare and trade pattern of South Asian countries. Hence, the study has made its focus on the analysis of the impact of WTO and the prevailing trading circumstances on South Asia. The WTO agreements have had significant effects on and implications for developing countries, of which countries in South Asia are part of it. As many other developing countries, South Asian countries are facing serious bottlenecks arising from the implementation of the Uruguay Round agreements. The issues, which could lessen the confidence of the South Asian countries over the WTO's performance and its strength in achieving its aims are highlighted as described below.

Lack of Anticipated Benefits for South Asian Countries

At the conclusion of the Uruguay Round, developing countries in general fully expected that in return for agreeing to expand the mandate of the GATT system to areas such as intellectual property rights and services, they would benefit significantly from increased access to developed country's markets, especially in agriculture, textiles and clothing. However, since the WTO came into being, these benefits have mostly not been forthcoming, while traditional problems such as low commodity prices and declining terms of trade continue to plague developing countries trade performance. These bulwark set up of the developed countries, against developing countries directly affect the South Asian countries as their major export destination is on the developed countries' markets.

Some of these impediments that negatively affect the trade performance of South Asian countries are:

Continued Protection in sectors of most interest to South Asia Countries

One of the most disappointing aspects of the trading system to South Asian countries is that the developed countries have continued to keep their markets protected in sectors that are of most interest to South Asian countries. As B.L. Das points out (2000a) "In agriculture and textiles and clothing ... it is clear developing countries have received little or no benefits, but have had to take on iniquitous obligations. In fact in agriculture, as in textiles and clothing, a fraud has been perpetrated on developing countries in terms of liberalization of trade and improving market access to their exports. In the agriculture sector the major developed countries have technically fulfilled their obligation of reducing domestic subsidies when in reality, by a very clever use of the provisions of the Agreement on Agriculture, they in fact have increased the quantum of subsidy. It shows that the pronouncements of the industrialized countries in the WTO about liberalization and reduction of subsidies in agriculture are not backed by political will" (UNDP 2001).

Section 2: Textiles and Clothing

The frustrations of developing countries are most keenly felt in the case of textiles. The 10-year phase-out of this special treatment under the Agreement on Textiles and Clothing was supposed to be the Uruguay Round's greatest benefit to the South. However, over the past decade of the implementation period, liberalization has not really occurred, due to the developed countries choice to 'end load' implementation. Most products chosen for 'liberalization' so far were not actually restrained in the past.

The agreement requires the developed countries to liberalize 16 per cent, 33 per cent and 51 per cent of their imports by volume (of 1990), respectively on 1, January 1995, 1, January 1998 and 1, January 2002. The major developed countries have technically fulfilled their obligation until 1, January 1998 while in fact removing the import restrictions negligibly. In the first stage, starting on 1, January 1995, while Canada liberalized only 0.27 per cent of restricted products, the United States and the E.C. liberalized none of them. In the second stage, starting on 1 January 1998, liberalization of the restricted products by the United States, the European Union (E.U.) and Canada was only 1.30 per cent, 3.15 per cent and 0.70 per cent, respectively (Das, 2001b).

The impact of the failure of fulfilling obligations by the developed countries as per the requirements of the WTO to South Asian countries will be enormous. Because, the SAARC countries exports majorly goes to the industrial countries. As K.C. Reddy pointed out "the pattern of direction of export of SAARC countries showed a tendency of concentration towards industrial countries. In the developed countries, the United States and the European Union (E.U.) are the significant export destinations of SAARC countries and the share ranged from more than half to nearly three fourths of their total exports; country-wise 78 per cent in Bangladesh, 52 per cent in India, 72 per cent in Nepal, 57 per cent in Pakistan and 72 per cent in Sri Lanka in 1997. He added that, among them, EU has emerged as a major market for the exports of SAARC countries during the period 1985-97 ..."(Reddy & Devi 2002). "The 1990s saw a redirection of the region's exports away from Eastern Europe and developing countries, and an increasing concentration towards developed countries, which absorbed nearly 50 per cent or more of total exports (table 1). The United States and European Union have become especially important markets for Bangladesh, Pakistan and Sri Lanka, and East Asian Countries markets for India. The growing concentration of exports to industrial countries has been particularly acute in Bangladesh and Sri Lanka, where they make up more than three-quarter of total exports"(Haq 2000) in the 1990s, the South Asian countries' export market concentration on the industrialized countries has increased, with the exception of Nepal which showed a decreasing trend in contrast to others (table 2).

Table 1
Direction of Exports as a % of Total Exports in 1998

	EU	*USA*	*Japan*	*Industrial Countries*	*SAARC*
Bangladesh	46	36	2	87	2.7
Bhutan	-	-	-	-	-
India	27	21	5	57	5.6
Maldives	24	34	9	68	18.4
Nepal	33	26	1	61	36.5
Pakistan	31	22	3	60	5
Sri Lanka	29	38	5	76	2.6
SAARC	29	24	5	42	5.3

Source: IMF (1999), Direction of Trade Statistics.

The impact of failure to liberalize by the developed countries on SAARC countries can be further elaborated by having a look at the prevailing export diversification and structure conditions. Over the past two decades, South Asian exports have followed the trend being pursued by the East Asian Countries, gradually shifting away from primary commodities, such as, unprocessed cotton, jute and tea, towards processed manufactured goods. "The share of manufactured goods in the region's total merchandise exports grew from 53.8 per cent in 1997, comparable to the world (79.6 per cent) and East Asian ratios (82.4 per cent) (Table 3). The ratio in 1998 ranged from 91 per cent in Bangladesh to 73 per cent in Sri Lanka" (Haq). The more the countries exports and markets are diversified, the lesser the risk becomes from market protection and price fluctuations. Hence, dependence on a few export items and export markets increases significantly the risks associated with market and price fluctuations. With the exception of Bhutan and Maldives which still had primary commodities more than 50 per cent of total exports during the 1990s (ESCAP 1997b), most South Asian

Table 2
Direction of Exports of South Asian Countries (in per cent)

	Industrial Countries	of which USA	EU	Japan	Developing Countries	of which Africa	Asia Asia	South Asia & China	East Europe	East East	Middle America Others	Latin	Others
Bangladesh													
1991	75.8	26.6	41.3	3.1	23.6	1.8	10.5	4.7	5.6	4.4	5.9	0.9	0.9
1995	82.7	31.9	44.3	3.3	16.9	1.8	9.0	2.7	6.0	2.2	3.2	0.5	0.9
1999	75.6	31.2	40.0	1.6	9.3	0.9	5.1	1.9	3.0	1.0	1.9	0.3	16.3
India													
1991	57.7	16.3	28.3	9.3	39.7	2.6	15.4	3.5	11.7	11.3	9.7	0.4	3.1
1995	54.7	17.4	27.0	7.0	41.2	4.4	21.9	5.1	16.4	4.9	8.9	0.8	5.0
1999	56.6	22.2	25.1	5.2	40.5	4.6	20.6	5.1	14.1	3.8	9.0	1.4	9.2
Maldives													
1991	63.0	22.2	37.0	3.7	37.0	0.0	37.0	18.5	18.5	0.0	0.0	0.0	0.0
1995	64.0	20.0	38.0	6.0	36.0	0.0	36.0	22.0	12.0	0.0	0.0	0.0	2.0
1999	76.5	17.0	36.6	1.3	23.5	13.4	9.8	5.2	3.9	0.0	0.0	0.0	0.0
Nepal													
1991	88.3	23.7	58.0	0.8	11.7	0.0	11.7	8.2	2.7	0.9	3.3	0.0	0.0
1995	88.9	30.6	49.9	0.6	10.8	0.0	10.2	9.3	0.0	0.0	1.3	0.3	0.3
1999	59.8	30.8	24.6	0.9	38.7	0.0	31.6	29.5	1.9	0.4	0.0	6.7	1.7
Pakistan													
1991	56.0	11.4	32.4	8.0	44.0	4.3	22.7	3.4	15.8	4.2	12.2	0.2	4.0
1995	56.2	15.1	30.4	6.8	43.4	3.7	23.1	3.2	16.5	3.4	11.6	1.1	4.4
1999	60.3	22.9	29.2	3.6	39.7	4.4	20.3	3.6	12.2	1.4	10.7	1.1	6.4
Sri Lanka													
1991	65.5	28.1	28.4	5.1	30.2	0.7	10.8	3.1	7.6	1.5	16.0	1.2	4.5
1995	75.5	35.5	31.6	5.2	22.6	0.9	9.2	2.7	6.5	4.1	7.1	0.9	2.4
1999	76.4	39.9	29.3	3.6	20.8	1.1	8.0	2.8	5.0	2.7	7.8	1.3	5.6

Source: RIS based on IMF data.

Table 3
Structure of Merchandise Exports

	Food (% total)		*Agricultural Raw Materials* (% total)		*Fuels* (% total)		*Ores and Metals* (% total)		*Manufactures* (% total)	
	1980	*1998*	*1980*	*1998*	*1980*	*1998*	*1980*	*1998*	*1980*	*1998*
East Asia & Pacific	18.2	6.4	12.3	1.8	16.4	5.4	6.8	2.1	44.8	82.4
Latin America & Caribbean	32.3	25.4	4.3	2.9	31.1	12.8	12.3	9.1	19.7	49.2
Middle East & North Africa	3.2	4.1[e]	1.2	0.6[c]	87.4	76.0[e]	3.0	2.3[e]	6.1	16.9[e]
South Asia	28.0	15.5[f]	10.0	2.2[f]	2.8	1.0[f]	5.1	2.1[f]	53.8	77.6[f]
Bangladesh	12.0	7.0	19.0	2.0	0.0	0.0.	0.0	0	68.0	91.0
Bhutan	92.0	23[d]	1.0	8.0[d]	n.a.	26.0[d]	0[a]	3[d]	4.0	40.0[d]
India	28.0	18[f]	5.0	2[f]	0.0	1.0[f]	7.0	3[f]	59.0	74.0[f]
Maldives	84.0	n.a.	5.0	n.a.	1.0	n.a.	2.0	n.a.	9.0	n.a.
Nepal	21.0	10[f]	48.0	1.0[f]	n.a.	n.a.	0.0	0[f]	30.0	77.0[f]
Pakistan	24.0	14.0	20.0	2.0	7.0	0.0	0.0.	0	48.0	84.0
Sri Lanka	47.0	21[d]	18.0	4.0[d]	15.0	0[d]	1.0	1[d]	19.0	73[d]
Sub-Saharan Africa	22.3	n.a.	6.2	n.a.	26.5	n.a.	8.6	n.a.	12.3	20.1[c]
Low income	16.3[b]	9.2	n.a.	1.9	32.5[b]	6.2	2.8[b]	2.5	39.0[b]	76.7
World	12.5	8.1	4.4	1.9	10.9	4.4	4.8	3.0	65.9	79.6

Source: World Bank (2000), *World Development Indicators*, CD ROM.
a: 1981; b: 1984; c: 1991; d: 1994; e: 1996; f: 1997

economies have decreased their vulnerability to events in commodity markets.

The export basket of all South Asian countries is dominated by manufactures (table 3). In fact, the share of manufactures has shown an increase over the 1990s with a corresponding decline in the share of primary commodities. However, primary commodities still do account for a significant proportion of South Asian countries' exports. These include jute in the case of Bangladesh, tea for Sri Lanka and India, rice for India and Pakistan, iron ore for India, etc. (see in Appendix table). Among manufactured exports, 'textile and manufacturing thereof' are found to predominate the export basket. While three quarters of exports consist of textiles in Bangladesh, Nepal and Pakistan, the proportion of such products in total export is lower for Sri Lanka and India at 45 per cent and 33 per cent respectively. As a result, the export commodity structure is more diversified for India and Sri Lanka than that for the other South Asian countries (RIS 2001-02).

Export vulnerability, however, can also result from dependence on a limited number of export products. A high dependence on a few exports can render countries vulnerable to variations in export earnings and economic performance, independent of whether exports are primary commodities or manufactured goods. Although most South Asian countries have shifted away from primary commodities their export structures remain relatively concentrated into a limited number of exports (table 4 & Appendix table). The percentage of total exports accounted for by the three most important products in 1994-95 was above 60 per cent in the Maldives and Nepal, and 40 per cent or more in Bangladesh and Pakistan. Only India had a ratio of less than 30 per cent, comparable to that found in high-exporting countries of East Asia. Nepal, Maldives and Pakistan's concentration indices all rose during the 1990s, suggesting increasing exposure to export risk. The major source of the region's export concentration has been as already mentioned, the textile and clothing industries, which in some countries accounted for more than 75 per cent of export revenue (table 5). A further insight into the nature of the export basket of South Asian countries is apparent from the importance of the top ten commodities (at the three digit level) in their total exports. The evidence in Appendix Table shows that the top ten commodities comprise mostly of textile and garment items, although their proportions vary across countries. While these top ten commodities account for over 82 per cent of total exports of Bangladesh, the Maldives and Nepal, 74 per cent for Pakistan and 66 per cent for Sri Lanka, in India's case their share is only about 42 per cent (RIS). The concentration of exports on cotton fiber, fabric and garments leaves countries not only vulnerable to savings in cotton prices, but also to production failures, for instance, from drought, disease and pests. In Nepal, the situation has been precarious with just one product, carpets, accounting for more than half of all merchandise earnings (UNCTAD 1999b).

Table 4
Percentage of Total Exports Accounted for by Top Three Products

	1983-84	*1994-95*
Bangladesh	56.4	46.3
India	30.7	24.5
Maldives	n.a.	64.0
Nepal	36.7	80.9
Pakistan	35.0	41.4
Sri Lanka	69.0	38.1
Korea	36.10	25.0
Malaysia	48.7	28.8
Singapore	41.1	37.8

Source: UNCTAD (1999b).

Table 5
Share of Textiles in Exports of South Asian Countries in 1990s

Country	*1991*	*1995*	*1998*
Bangladesh	75.3	76.8	86.3
Bhutan	0.0	0.0[a]	n.a
India	33.9	31.1	31.3[b]
Nepal	77.1	80.7	72.4
Pakistan	73.7	77.6	76.6
Sri Lanka	43.7	52.6[a]	n.a

Source: RIS based UNCTAD data.
Note: [a]1994, [b]1997

The need for export diversification has been acknowledged for many decades, but success has been slow in coming and how the traditional export sectors are also facing the new rules of the game. That is, as per the Uruguay Round, Southern nations have reduced tariffs only to find an aggregate reduction mechanism employed by the North, which enables them to selectively keep tariffs high on items of interest to the South. The high tariffs on such items are being felt by South Asia's clothing and textiles sector, due to which exports to the US have not risen. If South Asia improves its competitive efficiency, the Multi Fiber Arrangement abolition may bring benefits in terms of increased exports but will also leave the once protected quotas exposed to free market competition. Value-added goods need to be a part of the strategy to benefit export interests, for example, the products of raw cotton, textiles, new leather, leather goods and agricultural products (cotton, wheat and rice). The backward linkages between this sector and the poor elevate its socio-economic importance to South Asian policy makers interested in policy eradication. Tariff escalation, a traditional tactic of the North also needs to be dismantled so that the processed products may be exported from the South with greater ease and may encourage the demand for skilled labor. For example, EU and US tariff behavior places a lower tariff on raw leather than it does on leather goods. This practice does not encourage export of South Asia's value-added products (Haq). So far, market liberalization has been one sided. While developing economies have been forced to drastically reduce their tariff rates, their northern counterparts have not delivered the promised tariff reductions on goods of key interest to poor countries (Haq).

Despite efforts to liberalize trade, success into the world economy is far from universal. The continued anti-export biases created by the border trade policies and the 'behind the border policies' adopted by countries are deterring the realization of potential gains from trade. 'Behind the border' barriers to trade integration – for example, lack of access to finance, high cost and low-quantity distribution and transport services, absent supporting health and education services that expand human capital will make the long-term dynamic gains of trade liberalization limited. 'Border barriers' are tariffs, which could be less important than the behind-border barriers, if their shortage is a major obstacle.

When it is seen the overall barriers (border and behind border), border barriers remain important in many low-income countries, even though significant liberalization has occurred in developing countries. "However, traditional trade policies continue to imply significant anti-export biases in South Asia and the Middle East. Average (unweighted) tariffs in these regions are in the 20 per cent range or higher, and still have far to fall in order to attain the 10 per cent average found in many nations in East Asia, Latin America and Europe and Central Asia (table 6). Tariff revenue remains important for many low-income countries. Pursuing further reform of the level and structure of the tariff requires development of alternative domestic tax bases and efforts to ensure that a reliance on revenue tariffs does not needlessly distort resource allocation incentives – e.g., move towards uniformity (Tarr, 2002). In the small number of countries where non-tariff barriers continue to be tariffication will generally generate revenue. In considering further trade liberalization, determining the incidence of the tariff structure and the implications of this incidence – especially for the poor – is important in designing and mobilizing support for reform".

Table 6
Average Unweighted Tariff Rates by Region

Region	*1978-80*	*1981-85*	*1986-90*	*1991-95*	*1996-99*
Africa	38.2	29.3	26.9	22.3	17.8
East Asia	23.5	26.9	20.7	14.6	10.4
Latin America	28.1	26.4	24.1	13.9	11.1
MENA (ex-OPEC)	29.6	24.6	24.1	22.9	19.3
Europe/Central Asia	12.0	21.6	14.9	8.1	10.1
South Asia	n.a.	71.9	69.8	38.9	30.7
Industrial Economies	11.9	8.9	8.2	6.8	6.1

Source: World Bank.

"The 'border agenda' in many low-income countries is more institutional than the trade policy related. Although non-tariff barriers have come down substantially in most developing countries (with the exception of South Asia) a major achievement (table 7) inefficiencies in public administration are often an impediment to trade. Customs clearance and logistics related transactions costs can be a major disincentive for investment in tradable sectors, especially in activities that are time sensitive or where it is important to be integrated into global production networks that operate on the basis of just-in-time supply chain management. Exporters must have access to imported intermediate inputs at world market prices in order to be competitive. In countries where tariffs continue to be needed for revenue mobilization, this requires well-functioning customs regimes that refund taxed paid on imported inputs, or, preferably, allow exporters to import inputs duty free (so-called temporary admission or green channel treatment). Many low-income countries do not have well-functioning drawback regimes, creating anti-export bias" (Hackman 2002).

Table 7
Frequency of Core NTBs in Developing Countries 1989-98

Country	1989-94 %	1995-98 %
East Asia and the Pacific (7)	30.1	16.3
Latin America and the Caribbean (13)	18.3	8.0
Middle East and North Africa (4)	43.8	16.6
South Asia (4)	57.0	58.3
Sub-Saharan Africa (12)	26.0	10.4

Source: World Bank.
Note: Parenthesis indicates the number of countries per region for which data are available.

From the above tables, it can be understood that South Asia has undergone a significant change particularly in liberalizing tariff, albeit the average unweighted tariff rate is the highest of all. Moreover, the higher tariff rate implies the potential for further integration into the world trade, "A great deal of research has documented that there is still a large market access related agenda. Further liberalization will significantly increase real incomes and reduce poverty in developing countries (Hackman). It is worth to note that, even-though the average tariff of the most favored nation (MFN) of the Quad (Canada, the EU, Japan and the US) have fallen to about 5 per cent, and the industrial economies in general (Table – 3), tariffs for some commodities are over 100 per cent. Such tariff peaks of these developed countries are often concentrated in products that are of export interest to developing countries. Among these, they include major agricultural staple food products, such as sugar, cereals and fish; tobacco and certain alcoholic beverages; fruits and vegetables; food industry products with a high sugar content, clothing and foot wear. In addition the Uruguay Round has actually raised the tariff dispersion, due to the tariffication of products who were under the non-tariff type of protection. This resulted in to the imposition of high tariff on those agricultural products which previously been quota constrained. As a result, it is not uncommon tariffs, which are more than three times the average MFN duty in the Quad. Over 30 per cent of LDC exports and 15 per cent of all developing country exports are potentially affected by a tariff above 15 per cent in the Quad (Hoekman Ng and Olarreaga, 2002).

Tariff peaks are also common in developing country tariff schedules, adversely affecting South-South trade. Bangladesh, India, Pakistan, Costa-Rica, Egypt, Mexico, Morocco, Poland, Ukraine and Zimbabwe (among others) have tariffs above 200 per cent for some products. However, on average, tariff peaks (relative to average levels of protection) are higher in OECD nations – where the highest tariffs are on average 40 times the average tariff, whereas among the developing countries, the ratio is 12. For the Quad, the ratio is 55. On the other end of the spectrum are Sub-Saharan African countries for which this ratio is only around 5 – indicating a much more uniform structure of protection (Hackman).

Section 3: Agriculture

One of the major disappointments is that developed countries have made little progress in reducing protection and subsidies in the agriculture sector, which is an area of high potential export growth for many developing countries. Several years after the Uruguay Round agreement came into force, however, the reality is that: *High tariffs on selected items of potential interest to the South have had to be reduced only slightly.* In the first year of the agreement, there were tariff peaks at very high rates in the United States (sugar 244%, peanuts 174%); the EC (beef 213%, wheat 168%); Japan (wheat 353%), and Canada (butter 360%, eggs 236%) Das 1998a: 59). According to the agreement, developed countries had to reduce their tariff by only 36 per cent on average by the end of 2000, and thus the rates for some products remain prohibitively high (Das, 1998a).

Domestic support has increased rather than decreased. Although the agreement was supposed to result in decrease in domestic support in agriculture, in fact, the overall value of such support has increased. The agreement obliged developed countries to reduce the Aggregate Measurement of Support (AMS), which is a measure of domestic support, by 20 per cent during 1995-2000 from the average annual level of the base period of 1986-88. However, two categories of subsidies are exempted, and while the major developed countries did reduce their AMS, they also increased their exempted subsidies significantly, thereby offsetting the AMS reduction, which resulted in an increase in total domestic support. According to OELD data, the Producer Subsidy Equivalent (PSE) for all developed countries rose from US $ 247 billion in the base period to US $ 274 billion in 1998. In the E.C. it rose from US $ 99.6 billion in the base period to US $ 129.8 billion in 1998, and in the United States from US $ 41.4 billion to US $ 46.9 billion over the same period (Das 2000a: 2-3). A more comprehensive coverage of domestic support in agriculture calculated by the OECD is the Total Support Estimate (TSE), which for the 24 OECD countries rose from US $ 276 billion (annual average for base period 1986-88) to US $ 326 billion in 1999 (OECD 2000).

What is more ironic is that most developing countries, by contrast, had previously little or no domestic or export subsidies. They are now bared by the Agriculture agreement from having them or raising them in the future (Das 1998a: 62). There is clearly a major imbalance in a situation in which developed countries with very high domestic support are able to maintain a large part of their subsidies (and, due to loopholes in the agreement, to raise their level) while developing countries with low or no subsidies are prohibited from using their level beyond the diminimis amounts. The largest level of subsidy is provided by the European Union (EU). The average annual value of subsidies is approximately 60 per cent of total world trade in agriculture and about double the value of exports from developing countries (World Bank 2000).

Export Subsidies are still high.

Regarding export subsidies, the agreement also committed developed countries to reduce the budget outlay by 36 per cent and the total quantity of exports covered by the subsidies by 21 per cent. The base level was the average annual level for 1986-90 and the reduction is to be done over the period 1995-2000. Thus, even in the year 2000 the level of export subsidies is allowed to be as high as 64 per cent of the base level (Das 2000a: 3).

As it has been discussed earlier, for South Asia as a whole, the EU and the USA are very important as an export market. Both EU and USA absorb the bulk of the export items of SAARC countries. The agricultural products such as coffee, tea, jute, tobacco etc., exported by SAARC countries had not been away from adverse impacts of the tariff rises and subsidies, support being made by the developed countries. According to John S. Wilson (2002) in South Asia, when we see the trade in the period 1996 to 1998, South

Asia is a net agricultural exporter throughout this period. Actually, the trade flows from India and Sri Lanka; both net agricultural exporters exceeded that of the other South Asian countries, which are net agricultural importers. He added that 'the South Asia Region exhibits a higher importance of agriculture, though not as much as Latin America and Caribbean". In other words, the most fundamental problem in agricultural trade lies with the domestic policies of developed countries. "Agriculture in most developed countries is sheltered behind high tariff, walls, farm subsidies, loan guarantees and non tariff barriers that place those developing countries that are heavily dependent on agricultural exports at a great disadvantage. Agricultural trade is not being liberalized as fast as trade in manufactured goods. In developed countries, tariff on agricultural products have remained at 40-50 per cent range; Japan had a tariff of 1000 per cent on rice last year, 2000" (Haq).

This is one of the most important reasons for developing countries lack of trust in the workings of the WTO. While South Asian countries are reducing tariffs and domestic support on a whole range of products, the United States, European Union (EU) and Japan continue to subsidize and enable their farmers and multinational corporations to sell agricultural products at lower prices, while maintaining higher costs. The farm subsidies in developed countries hurt developing countries on three counts: first, it keeps the world prices low; secondly, it excludes developing countries from the food markets of rich countries; and finally, developing country food producers suffer due to dumping of cheap food imports from developed countries (UNDP 1997). The labor-intensive southern farmers are at a disadvantage in terms of the economies of scale realized by the capital-intensive northern farmers. Few measures have so far been taken to protect the subsistence farmers and fishermen in the new Agreement on Agriculture (Haq). South Asian agriculture needs to be treated differently in view of the dependence of most people on agriculture as well as the wide spread rural poverty in South Asia. 'India's most recent proposal to the WTO recommends that any support aimed at alleviating poverty, rural development or the diversification of agricultural products be exempted from WTO – sponsored commitments to reduce domestic support'. (The Economist 2001).

Industrial Tariffs

In the case of industrial tariffs, the developed countries reduced their trade–weighted average tariff for industrial products from 6.3 to 3.8 per cent as a result of the Uruguay Round. However, they have continued to maintain tariff peaks and tariff escalation in some industrial products that are of export interest to developing countries. This has also been a barrier to the developing countries efforts to export industrial products and to produce and export-processed raw materials or to climb up the value-added chain for their basic commodities (UNDP, 2001). A Study for UNCTAD (Supper 2000) found significant numbers of tariff peaks among the Quad countries (Canada, EU, Japan and United States) in the industrial sector, especially for food industry products; textiles and clothing, footwear, leather and travel goods; automotive products and consumer electronics and watches. Tariff escalation is particularly pronounced precisely in those sectors that offer a realistic chance for developing countries to enter into industrial exports (e.g. food, textiles, clothing and shoe industries, wood industry products (Erich 2000).

This indicates that the tariff structure of developed countries shows significant tariff escalation, so that market access for more processed products (embodying greater value added) is more restricted. For example, fully-processed manufacturing food products face tariffs twice as large as products in the first stage of processing in the EU and Japan, with final goods confronting an average MFN tariff of 24 and 65 per cent, respectively. In Canada the ratio is even higher: tariffs on fully processed food products are 12 times higher than for 1st stage processed products i.e., the MFN tariff on fully processed is 42 per cent (Hackman). As these are the major interests of South Asian countries, they had been affected negatively inhibiting the move towards industrialization.

Uses of Non-Tariff Barriers (NTB)

Even as a meaningful increase in market access has not materialized, developed countries have continued their use of some non-tariff protectionist measures to block products of developing countries. A significant part of these have been applied to textile and clothing products (UNDP). Among the measures reported by the International Textiles and Clothing Board (ITCB) are:

(i) A large number of unjustified safeguard actions for new restrictions;

(ii) Change in rules of origin;

(iii) Unduly cumbersome customs and administrative procedures; and

(iv) Ant-dumping actions, particularly targeting products that were already under quota restrictions (Hongkong, China 2000).

An UNCTAD study on the impact of anti-dumping and countervailing duty actions found that these are now the most frequently used remedies. Developed countries are the main users of anti-dumping measurers, while developing countries have also increased their use. In the first five years of operation of the WTO agreements (1995-99) there were 1,229 anti-dumping initiations of which 651 (or 53%) were initiated by developed countries and 578 (or 47%) by developing countries and economies in transition. However, developing countries continued to be the main targets of anti-dumping measures, accounting for 818 (66.6%) of the 1,229 cases. 'This has the effect of creating instability and uncertainty for their exports, which has resulted in reductions in trade volumes and market shares for their goods'. (UNCTAD 2000b:1).

Meanwhile, nearly 20 per cent of the EC's anti-dumping measures in the first five years of the WTO's operation were related to textiles, aimed primarily at exports from developing countries. These exports had already been subject to quota restrictions. There was repeated recourse to anti-dumping action against several products from a number of developing countries. For example, the EC repeatedly initiated investigations from 1994 to 1997 over grey cotton fabrics originating from six countries (China, Egypt, India, Indonesia, turkey and Pakistan), causing concern to textile-exporting countries. According to the International Clothing and Textiles Bureau (ITCB), EC import volume of cotton fabrics from the six-targeted countries fell from 121,891 tons in 1994 to 88,306 tons in 1997 and their market share fell from 59 per cent in 1993 to 41 per cent in 1997. The case was ultimately dropped with no anti-dumping duties imposed (UNCTAD 2000b:8). Anti-dumping measures that are used against developing countries can have immediate impact on trade flows and prompt importers to seek alternative sources of supply. Even if duties are not imposed finally, the initiation of investigations itself creates a huge burden for developing countries, which feel they have been 'harassed' (UNDP).

When the general trend of the South Asian countries manufactured goods is seen, its share has shown a progressive increase over the past two decades. 'Within manufactures, labor intensive goods, such as garments and textiles, gems and jewellery and leather products, dominated manufactured trade (see, eg. World Bank 1997a). Fibers, textiles and clothing, in particular, have become extremely important to South Asia's exports. Their share increased in all countries for which data is available, comprising nearly three-quarters of all exports by the mid–1990s in Bangladesh, Nepal and Pakistan, and nearly half in Sri Lanka (Haq).

Given the importance of textiles and clothing in exports, the gradual phasing out of the Multi-Fiber Arrangement (MFA) by 2005 holds important consequences for South Asia's world shares in these sectors. The potential effects of removing the imposed quotas on exports of garments to developed countries depends on a number of factors, but the gains to South Asian countries from phasing out of the MFA are expected to be large because they are severely constrained by quotas and are among the lowest cost producers (see, e.g., ESCAP, 1998b). The largest gain will most likely be in India, which has the most constrained apparel sector in South Asia. Other South Asian countries will also benefit from abolition of quotas, but less so, as they are typically less-restricted suppliers (Haq).

While these labor-intensive industries, are a source of growth in employment and exports, and historically have been important for the industrialization in other countries (e.g., the UK and Japan), what is particularly important in the age of rapid globalization is the extent to which countries are moving from traditional exports to producing goods of higher value-added, particularly technologically advanced products. There has been growing concern that labor–intensive, low-technology manufactures are beginning to acquire the features of primary commodities in world markets, facing a secular downward trend (UNCTAD 1999a). In South Asia, the share of high technology exports has been marginal, rising slightly from 2.1 per cent of total manufactured exports in 1991 to 3.85 per cent in 1997 (table 8). In contrast, high-tech exports rose rapidly in East Asia and Latin America during the 1990s, accounting for nearly one-quarter and one-tenth of total exports, respectively. India is the country with the fastest growing share of high-technology exports (Haq).

Table 8
Share of High Technology Exports in Manufactured Exports

	1991	*1992*	*1993*	*1994*	*1995*	*1996*	*1997*
Bangladesh	0.05	0.06	0.02	0.07	0.03	0.06	0.01
India	3.07	2.32	2.63	3.20	4.52	5:38	5.09
Pakistan	0.03	0.04	0.07	0.04	0.05	0.05	0.10
Sri Lanka	0.67	1.05	1.12	1.27	n.a.	n.a.	n.a.
South Asia	2.08	1.56	1.82	2.30	3.36	3.99	3.85
Memo Items							
East Asia & Pacific	20.64	16.93	19.12	20.52	23.40	25.02	26.60
Latin America & Caribbean	5.63	6.79	6.64	7.45	8.87	9.04	9.55

Source: World Bank (2000), World Development Indicators, CD-ROM.

Section 4: Strengthening the Competitiveness of South Asian Exports: Future Challenges

In the increasingly globalizing world economy and the emerging WTO regime, there is a strong emphasis on international competitiveness all around. In the earlier era, comparative advantage based on natural resources largely determined the countries' competitiveness (RIS). In the modern world, countries build their competitive advantage with conscious strategic interventions (Poster 1990). Against this backdrop, some of the challenges facing the South Asian countries are discussed as given below.

Upgrading the technology Profile of South Asian Exports

It has been shown that South Asian exports structures continue to be dominated by relatively simple technology and labour intensive goods. The South Asian exports are widely perceived to lack dynamism not only in terms of growth but more importantly in terms of their skill and technological content. Studies have analysed the South Asian export structure in an international comparative perspective, viz., Mayer and Wood (2000), and Lall (2000). From their studies one can understand that textile, clothing, leather manufacture and foot wear, and wood products as labour intensive manufactures. The studies indicated that South Asia has a large pool of labour, relative to its supply of both important resources skill and land, and so its exports are concentrated on type of goods, which use large inputs of labour and small inputs of both the skill and land.

South Asia export structure is significantly reliant on low technology products. South Asia shows modest gains in share in the low technology manufactures, but with little diversification over time for textiles and other products. In fact, the lack of diversification from clothing is an important trend even for successful clothing exporters like Sri Lanka, Bangladesh, Pakistan and others (RIS). The South Asian countries have not been able to upgrade their export profile in favour of the relatively more skill and technology intensive goods unlike the South East Asian countries such as Malaysia and China. The low skill and technology intensive goods are not only low value adding compared to knowledge intensive goods but also slow moving because of increasing price competition. Therefore, the inability of these countries to diversify their export structure in favour of modern products has cost them dearly in terms of slower export growth and lower value realization. A part of the explanation lies in the relative neglect of science and technology and R&D activity by these countries (RIS 1999) that the key to international competitiveness in knowledge intensive industries. All South Asian countries presently spend much less than one per cent of their national income on R&D.

Increasing Value Addition in Traditional Export Commodities

As is typical of poor countries, a number of traditional export commodities of the South Asian countries are exported in bulk. Owing to lack of marketing power and other constraints, it has not been possible to increase the value added realization over time.

Preparing the Textiles and Clothing Industry to face the Post–MFA scenario

For South Asian countries the biggest challenge is to prepare their textile and garment industry for the post- MFA regime. Under the Agreement on Textiles and Clothing, the MFA quotas will be phased out by AD 2005. The South Asian countries will then be competing with China, the South East Asian countries, in the textiles and clothing market. The accession of China to the WTO and the consequent MFN status it gains from the WTO members could have some implications on South Asia's export competitiveness. This is because both the South Asia and China compete in the international market in those products which are of labour intensive such as textiles and garments, leather goods, etc. it is viewed that the accession of China could make the competition more stiff which could bring adverse repercussion to South Asian countries' exports.

Textiles and garment have emerged as one of the most important items of exports for all the South Asian countries. Paradoxically, protectionism in the form of MFA quotas has helped some of the South Asian countries such as Bangladesh, Nepal and Sri Lanka to develop their export oriented garment industries by insulating them from direct competition from established producers. Bangladesh, for instance, now derives some 60 per cent of its export earnings from garment exports. Therefore, the challenge is to improve the competitiveness of the South Asian garment industry by increasing vertical integration, capturing economies of scale and specialization incorporating innovative design, and taking a stake in the global marketing networks.

A Co-ordinated Approach to WTO Negotiations

The WTO process has an increasingly important role in shaping the patterns of trade. Hence, South Asian coordination is important for securing their common interests. Owing to the consensual approach adopted in WTO negotiations, a coordinated response by the South Asian countries would be more effective in realizing their objectives. The South Asian countries have already begun extensive consultations on WTO issues under the SAARC umbrella. The SAARC Common Ministers have been meeting regularly to prepare for the WTO Ministerial Meetings.

Realizing the Potential of Regional Economic Cooperation in South Asia

As observed earlier, one characteristic of the South Asian countries' exports to outside the region is the low realization of value added. The bulk of the products are exported at a rather early stage of processing. Much of the value addition in garments, for instance, takes place at the stage of promotional marketing such as branding. The South Asian countries should consider setting up South Asian level mega- companies–South Asian Multinationals to foster an integrated South Asian textiles sector. This approach could avoid the intense competition that prevails today causing mutual disadvantage.

Section 5: Conclusion

South Asian countries have undergone some positive moves as desired by the agreements of the Uruguay Round. South Asian countries have liberalized their trade by making substantial tariff reductions during the past two decades. South Asian countries, with the exception of Bhutan and Maldives, have exhibited a shift trend from primary commodity to processed manufactured products export, albeit highly concentrated on few export products and markets. The rising concentration indices imply increasing export vulnerability to export risk. Most of the South Asian exports are concentrated on textiles and clothing and others whose basic input materials come from the agricultural field where by the incidence of production failures of such inputs due to some natural calamities worsens the export risks. Even though shift towards the export of processed industrial products is encouraging, the developed countries continued to maintain tariff peaks and subsidies at some products that are of interest to developing countries. This act of the developed countries deters the efforts of South Asian countries efforts to climb-up the value-added chain for their basic commodities that offer a realistic chance to enter into industrial exports.

South Asian countries need to be cautious in their transformation strategies aimed at exports as there 'is a growing concern that a labor intensive, low technology manufactures are beginning to acquire the features of primary commodities in world market. From South Asian countries, India is assuming a status of becoming one of the fastest growing shares of high tech exports. The rest have been marginalized in the last decade. While developing countries had little or no domestic or export subsidies, in contrast to the WTO agreements, there had been an increase in domestic support by developed countries, which had adverse impact on South Asia's trade. The agricultural exports had not been liberalized as fast as the manufacturing products whereby in the developed countries the tariff rates on agriculture remained at 40 – 50 per cent range. Moreover, while the South Asian countries continued reducing impediments to trade on the whole range of products, the major export destinations of South Asian countries, viz., US, EU, and Japan continued to subsidize their agricultural products which constrained exports of the South Asian countries.

The gradual phasing out of multi fibre arrangement (MFA) by 2005 are expected to bring gains to South Asian countries as they are severely constrained by quotas. The prevailing tariff rates of South Asian countries is one of the highest, though substantial subsequent reductions have been made in the last two decades. There are some tariff peaks common in developing countries that adversely affect South–South trade, but that of OECD's are much higher. To strengthen the competitiveness of South Asian exports with respect to the future challenges they are supposed to encounter, the South Asian countries need to build their competitive advantages through conscious strategic interventions such as by upgrading the technology profile of their textile and clothing and other exports; increasing the value addition in the traditional export commodities; prepare the textiles and clothing industries with sound marketing to withstand the would be free global intense competition after 2005 provided that the developed countries will reduce their trade impediments as per the rules of WTO; strengthen the already going on cooperation and coordination of South Asian countries in their common interests to WTO negotiations; and expand their scope of integration that promotes their comparative advantage and tackle the intense competition that is to prevail in the world by setting up South Asian multinationals.

APPENDIX

Share of Top Ten Commodities in Exports of South Asian Countries in 1997-1998

(in per cent)

	of country's total	*of developing countries*	*of world*
Bangladesh			
All commodities	100.00	0.32	0.09
Men's outwear not knit	22.08	5.60	3.19
Under garments not knit	18.20	9.47	6.19
Women's outwear	11.89	2.43	1.32
Outer garments knit non elastic	9.74	1.94	1.10
Under garments knitted	9.32	2.61	1.48
Shell fish fresh, frozen	5.67	2.40	1.66
Textile articles nes	3.45	1.92	1.09
Leather	2.55	1.86	0.83
Jute, and other textile fibers	2.04	91.13	86.32
Other woven textile fabric	1.73	3.57	0.84
Remainder	13.34		
India			
All commodities	100.00	2.39	0.65
Pearl, prec-, semi-p stone	12.90	55.88	12.08
Textile yarn	5.74	13.17	5.69
Women's outwear not knit	4.86	7.40	4.02
Cotton fabrics, woven	2.80	9.51	4.69
Medicinal, pharm products	2.73	13.48	1.05
Feeding stuff for animals	2.72	11.11	4.05
Shell fish fresh, frozen	2.62	8.27	5.72
RiceUnder garments not knit	2.61	16.06	11.26
Textile articles nes	2.43	10.13	5.75
Remainder	58.11		
Maldives			
All commodities	100.00	0.01	0.00
Fish, fresh, chilled, frozen	30.58	0.31	0.11
Fish, etc. prepd, prsvd nes	24.67	0.33	0.19
Under garments knitted	14.10	0.06	0.04
Men's outerwear not knit	8.58	0.04	0.02
Fish salted, dried, smoked	7.62	1.12	0.22
Women's outerwear non knit	6.12	0.02	0.01
Outer garments knit non elastic	3.69	0.01	0.01
Feeding stuff for animals	0.99	0.01	0.00
Shell fish fresh, frozen	0.86	0.01	0.00
Under garments not knit	0.31	0.00	0.00
Remainder	2.48		

	of country's total	of developing countries	of world
Nepal			
All commodities	100.00	0.02	0.01
Floor coverings, etc.	42.00	4.39	1.41
Men's outerwear not knit	16.52	0.32	0.18
Special transactions	8.80	0.16	0.02
Women's outerwear non knit	4.53	0.07	0.04
Veg. etc. fresh, simply prsrvd	4.45	0.21	0.07
Leather	1.96	0.11	0.05
Under garments knitted	1.41	0.03	0.02
Base metal hhs. Equipment	1.21	0.11	0.04
Spl. text. fabrics, products	1.07	0.06	0.02
Seeds for other fixed oils	1.05	1.18	0.37
Remainder	17.00		
Pakistan			
All commodities	100.00	0.60	0.16
Textile yarn	15.09	8.72	3.77
Cotton fabrics, woven	14.55	12.41	6.12
Textile articles nes	11.97	12.55	7.12
Woven man made fib fabric	6.59	3.68	1.87
Rice	6.20	9.60	6.73
Headgear, non textl clothing	5.08	5.58	3.66
Under garments knitted	4.84	2.55	1.45
Men's outerwear not knit	3.90	1.86	1.06
Toys, sporting goods, etc.	3.13	1.75	0.79
Outer garments knit non elastic	2.66	1.00	0.57
Remainder	26.00		
Sri Lanka			
All commodities	100.00	0.33	0.09
Women outwear non knit	18.07	3.81	2.07
Tea and mate	9.25	19.28	15.64
Men's outwear not knit	8.69	2.28	1.29
Outerwear knit non elastic	8.13	1.67	0.95
Under garments knitted	6.27	1.81	1.03
Under garments not knit	5.18	2.78	1.82
Pearl, prec-, non textile clothing	4.12	2.46	0.53
Headgear, non textile clothing	2.60	1.57	1.03
Travel goods, hand bags, etc.	2.54	1.99	1.12
Rubber tyres, tubes, etc.	2.37	2.05	0.45
Remainder	32.78		

Source: RIS based UNCTAD, 2000c, data.

References

Bernard Hoekman (2002a), "Economic Development and the World Trade Organization After Doha", *Policy Research* Working Paper No. 2851, June, pp. 4-5.

Bernard Hoekman (2002b), *Ibid.*

Ibid., p. 9.

Ibid.,

Das, Bhagirath Lal (2001a), "Negotiations on Agriculture and Services in the WTO: Suggestions for Modalities/Guidelines", *Trade and* Development, Series No.10. Penang, Malaysia: Third World Network.

Das Bhagirath Lal (2001b).

Hong Kong, China (2000), "Statement by Hong Kong, China at special session of the WTO General Council on 22 June 2000 on behalf of International Textiles and Clothing Bureau, WT/GC/W/405.

John S. Wilson (2002), "Liberalizing Trade in Agriculture, Developing Countries in Asia and the Post-Doha Agenda", *Policy Research* Working Paper No. 2804, The World Bank, March, pp. 4-5.

Lall, S. (2000), " The Technological Structure and Performance of Developing Country Manufactured Exports, 1985-1998." Oxford: University of Oxford International Development Center (mimeographed).

Mahbub Ul Haq Human Development Center (2001), *Human Development in South Asia, Globalization and Human Development*, p. 26.

Ibid., p. 24.

Ibid., p. 128.

Ibid.,

Ibid., p. 129.

Ibid., pp. 129-130.

Ibid., pp. 24-25.

Ibid., p. 25.

Ibid.,

Mayer, J. and A. Wood, (2000), *"South Asia's Export Structure in a Comparative Perspective"*, IDS Working Paper 91. Sussex: Institute of Development Studies.

Porter, M.E, (1990), *The Comparative Advantage of Nations*. New York: The Free Press.

OECD (2000), *Agricultural Policies in OECD Countries: Monitoring and Evaluation*, Paris, OECD Secretariat.

Reddy, K.C. and Nirmala Devi, T. (2002), "Economic Reforms in SAARC Countries: An Assessment of the Strategies and their Impact with Focus on Human Development and Poverty Alleviation", *Regional Cooperation in South Asia: New Dimensions,* pp. 52, 54.

Research and Information System for the Non-Aligned and other Developing Countries (2001/02), *South Asia Development and Cooperation Report,* p. 87.

Ibid., p. 88.

Ibid.,

Ibid., (2000).

See RIS (1999), for a profile of South Asian countries in science and technology.

Supper, Erich (2000), 'The Post Uruguay Round Tariff Environment for Developing Country Exports: Tariff Peaks and Tariff Escalation', *UNCTAD, Positive Agenda and Future Trade Negotiations,* Geneva, pp. 89-123.

Tarr, David (2002), "Arguments For and Against Uniform Tariffs", in B. Hoekman, A. Mattoo and P. English (eds), *Development, Trade and the WTO: A Handbook,* Washington DC : World Bank.

UNCTAD (2000), "Trade Related Investment Measures", *Positive Agenda and Future Trade Negotiations,* Geneva, p. 1.

Ibid., p. 8.

UNDP (2001), "The Multilateral Trading System: A Development Perspective", *Third World Network,* Dec, p. 17.

UNDP, *Ibid.,* (2001).

Ibid.

Index

I-34369
ICB S115
716/-